The Power of Faces
Looking at the Global Refugee Crisis

Daniel Farber Huang + Theresa Menders

The Power of Faces: Looking at the Global Refugee Crisis

Copyright 2024 by Daniel Farber Huang and Theresa Menders

All Rights Reserved.

Published by Princeton Studios

To M.L.M., for all the wisdom you share – Theresa

To D.R.M., for your bright future – Daniel

Table of Contents

Words

Acknowledgements 1
Introduction – Peter Bilderback 2
The Power of Faces – Theresa Menders 4
The Largest Refugee Camp in the World – Daniel Farber Huang 5
Lathakia – Jakeem 6
Basra – Mohammed 8
The Forgotten Souls – Pothiti "Toula" Kitromylidi 10
Labels – Ratha Kaur Lehall 11
Preventing a Lost Generation – Tahmina Akter 12
A Human Rights Perspective – Ute Ritz-Deutch 13
Rohingya Refugees and Their Resilience – Adem Carroll 14
Documenting the Refugee Crisis – Braden Kelner 16
Partners 18

Images

Chios, Greece: Vial and Souda Refugee Camps 20

Cox's Bazar, Bangladesh: Kutupalong-Balukhali Refugee Camps . 46

Tijuana, Mexico: Barretal Refugee Camp 74

Ukraine: Poland-Ukraine Border Crossings 100

Acknowledgements

No single perspective can capture or encapsulate the global refugee crisis. In our efforts to document the plight of displaced individuals and entire populations, we have had the benefit of meeting advocates, activists, and others who work to make a positive difference. We have included essays and perspectives from several people who have contributed to raising awareness, providing on-the-ground relief, and mobilizing resources to help some of the most vulnerable populations around the world.

Peter Bilderback has led the charge to bring The Power of Faces to Brown University's Watson Institute for International and Public Affairs and has graciously provided the introduction to this book.

Jakeem (his name has been changed to protect his identity) has allowed us to share his experience in a Syrian prison after being falsely accused, and eventually fleeing his home country.

Mohammed (his last name is witheld for privacy purposes) has allowed us to share the fatal events that forced him to flee Iraq, seeking (but not necessarily finding) safety in the ensuing years.

Pothiti "Toula" Kitromylidi has shown us what "turning compassion in action" truly means. Since launching the Chios Eastern Shore Response team in 2015, Toula has coordinated providing relief for countless refugees landing on the shores of Chios island in Greece.

Ratha Kaur Lehall was The Power of Faces' first volunteer in Chios in 2017 and instrumental in bringing our initial portrait idea into reality. With Ratha's help, we realized that providing proper portraits to hundreds of people in the harshest of environments was, in fact, possible.

Tahmina Akter provided us with insight and understanding into the complex situation at the sprawling Kutupalong-Balukhali refugee camps in Cox's Bazar, Bangladesh, enabling us to navigate continually-shifting landscapes and ulitmately tell the stories of people who have had their voices taken away.

Ute Ritz-Deutch has energetically helped us raise awareness and add constructively to the conversation regarding refugees and displaced people by sponsoring exhibitions, talks and interviews about what we are seeing on the ground at refugee camps around the world.

Adem Carroll has shown us the complex opportunities and challenges of addressing the root causes of the refugee crisis. Adem has helped us better understand what is required at the policy level to promote lasting justice for the stateless Rohingya population.

Braden Kelner has helped us raise awareness of the plight of people fleeing the Ukraine war, reminding the broader public that displaced people are not merely numbers or statistics, but individuals who deserve safety and dignity.

There are many individuals who have supported our efforts to humanize the refugee crisis, either while in-country or back home in the U.S., and their names are recognized in our list of partners. We appreciate you.

To everyone who has made The Power of Faces reality, Thank You. It is a privilege knowing, collaborating, and working with each of you.

Theresa Menders
Daniel Farber Huang

Introduction

by Peter Bilderback

Peter Bilderback is the communications specialist and writer at the Watson Institute for International and Public Affairs at Brown University. He also serves on the Art at Watson committee and co-coordinator for the exhibition "The Power of Faces: Looking at the Global Refugee Crisis" at the Watson Institute in the fall of 2024.

"The Power of Faces" is aptly named. Faces are powerful. Neuroscientists are still learning how the human brain responds to faces on the cellular and molecular levels, but we already know that faces are among the most potent visual stimuli our brains confront.

Indeed, the human brain is highly attuned to faces. Faces are extraordinarily rich sources of information for our nervous systems. Without realizing it, we process a vast amount of information just by glancing at a face. We can roughly determine a person's age and sex and evaluate their mental state without giving it any conscious thought. We can recognize a friend's face at a glance, even if we haven't seen the person in years, or pick a familiar face out of a crowd without much effort.

Amazingly, our brains process all this information almost instantly. In experiments that measure brain activity, neuroscientists have found it takes only a few hundred milliseconds.

Brain processing speed aside, humans love faces. We love them so much that sometimes we see them where they aren't: on a piece of toast or the moon's surface. Historically, faces have been among the most popular subjects of art. Close your eyes and think of a person, any person. Chances are, what you just "saw" was a mental representation of their face. For those of us who are sighted and neurotypical, faces are central to our experience of the world.

There are undoubtedly evolutionary explanations for why faces are so important to us, but that is not among our concerns here. What matters is that they are. The mental activity that happens when our brains process the information the human face provides us is among our most important social skills. It enables us to form long-lasting bonds with individuals and groups of people. Faces are the primary way we distinguish one person from another; they are how we recognize a person as an individual.

In their exhibition and book, "The Power of Faces: Looking at the Global Refugee Crisis," Daniel Farber Huang and Theresa Menders have harnessed the power of faces through their skillfully executed photographs to remind us of our shared humanity with those displaced by the current international refugee crisis, the worst since the World War II era.

Their documentary photographs show the appalling conditions of refugee camps in Greece, Bangladesh, Mexico and Poland. But just as importantly, their carefully composed, beautifully executed portraits show us the faces of the refugees, taking their subjects outside the context of the refugee camp and revealing them in all their humanity.

Daniel and Teresa have taken hundreds of photographs of refugees across the globe — many of them not seen in this book or their exhibitions — and in each case, they provided their subjects with copies of the photographs to keep for themselves, another way of recognizing their humanity. These photos become cherished mementos for people living in highly challenging conditions, most of whom have lost everything, including the heirlooms, keepsakes and family photographs that bring us comfort during difficult times.

The current refugee crisis is on a scale beyond imagining. According to the United Nations, "At the end of June 2023, 110 million people worldwide were forcibly displaced from their homes due to persecution, conflict, violence, human rights violations and events seriously disturbing public order."

What 110 million looks like is difficult to visualize, but think of it like this: it represents enough people to fill the average NFL stadium over 1,500 times. It's also equivalent to about one-third of the population of the entire United States. Most of these people would like nothing more than to return to their homes, but they don't know when or if that will be possible. Many are trapped in refugee camps that, as you will read in personal accounts in this book, are dirty and crime-ridden but also sites of occasional beauty that demonstrate the resilience of the human spirit even in the darkest of times.

We would be ignoring the elephant in the room if we did not acknowledge that this book is being published during a U.S. presidential campaign in which the candidate of a major political party, himself a former President of the United States, is engaging in rhetoric that demonizes and dehumanizes displaced persons.

Donald Trump regularly refers to immigrants who come to the U.S. as "animals" and "not human." He claims they were released from prisons and asylums to "invade" the United States. Chillingly, he has repeatedly borrowed the rhetoric of Nazi Germany and claims immigrants are "poisoning the blood" of America. Worse still, many Americans share these opinions, and the negative perception of immigrants and refugees is not limited to the U.S. As you will read in the pages that follow, even in once-welcoming nations in the European Union, attitudes toward refugees have soured as the crisis has continued and expanded, leading to a rise in xenophobia and nationalist sentiment across the globe.

"The Power of Faces" is an essential antidote to this toxic rhetoric: a potent reminder that refugees are, in fact, human and that no politician or degrading system can rob them of their humanity regardless of the horrifying conditions to which they are subjected.

When we look into the faces of the people photographed for this book, regardless of our politics, we instantly know that claims that they are "not human" or "animals" are categorically untrue. Our brains tell us this truth almost instantly: these are full-fledged human beings who think, feel and love just as we do. We know that it is only a matter of random circumstances that we are not in their place, and they are not looking at a photograph of us instead. Because we are human, in only a few hundred milliseconds, we instinctively know these things beyond any doubt through unconscious cognitive processes hardwired into our brains through millions of years of evolution. All we have to do is look.

That is the power of faces.

The Power of Faces

by Theresa Menders

We've all heard about the global refugee crisis. Some of you may even know it personally. Between 2015 and 2023, over 117 million people have been forced to flee their homes due to conflict or persecution. At that massive rate of violence and destruction, that equates to one person becoming a refugee every two seconds.

Every. Two. Seconds.

For the last nine years. And counting...

Hearing statistics like this is staggering to us. We have a hard time picturing what numbers that massive even mean. And if we can't picture this crisis, how can we work towards solving it? For us, we start one face at a time.

There can be a tendency for some of the public to confuse a person who happens to be living in a bad, dirty or dangerous situation as being a bad, dirty or dangerous person, and clearly that is not the case. We show people with their inherent courage, beauty, dignity and grace.

The portraits you see here are from our global photo project "The Power of Faces." We intentionally crop out the context of the refugee camps because we want to focus on the individuals, not merely their label as "refugee." For a fuller perspective, however, it is important we show the oftentimes inhumane living conditions that displaced people are forced to endure every day, which we hope will encourage action, provide relief, and mobilize resources to spur immediate action as well as develop long-term solutions to address this humanitarian crisis.

My husband, Daniel Farber Huang, and I are independent documentary photographers and freelance journalists. We have documented the plight of displaced people in refugee camps in Greece, Turkey, Mexico, and Bangladesh as well as at the Poland/Ukraine border. We seek to raise awareness of injustice and inequality around the world through our photography, our words and our actions. We started The Power of Faces portrait project because we realized most refugees have lost all their material possessions, including their treasured family photographs. Rather than just taking from refugees as journalists and advocates – taking their photos, taking their stories – we wanted also to give something back if possible.

Having a physical photo of family or friends to hold in one's hands can be a great comfort in times of need, so we bring photo printers and instant cameras into refugee camps and give people proper portraits for them to keep, which in many cases are the only physical photos they own since fleeing their homes. We have distributed thousands of portraits to people detained in refugee camps.

Having a photo taken by a third party is, in certain ways, validating. It shows that someone else recognizes them as a person, as an individual. We have found it is incredibly powerful to give parents a photo of their children smiling. It is incredibly powerful to give a family what may be the only photo of them together as a family unit, whatever that unit may be.

For those people who give us permission to share their portraits, we use those images to raise awareness, including the images you see here. We believe if a person can look into a stranger's eyes perhaps they will fear that stranger less.

There is one portrait in this book of a Rohingya father with his four children. His 4-year-old daughter was blinded when she was hit in the face by shrapnel. Her father said she also has blood cancer but has no money to pay for her treatment, and the organizations he has reached out to say they have no money to help her case.

Every person in these portraits has their own story to tell. Every person has suffered their own immeasurable pain and loss. We know we cannot encapsulate any person's plight in a single photograph. What we can do, however, is try to add constructively to the broader conversation about refugees, and encourage the public to engage in informed discussion on how to address this crisis.

Our intention is to bring this portrait project to other refugee camps around the world and continue giving proper portraits to displaced individuals. Our goal is to put a human face to the crisis, and remind the world that refugees are not mere numbers or statistics, but individuals each with their own hopes and dreams for a better life in a kinder world.

These individuals matter.

We are not so naïve to think our world will be completely free from conflict, but we seek to shine a light on the innocent and oppressed so they are not ignored, forgotten or erased.

The Largest Refugee Camp in the World

by Daniel Farber Huang

We live in a complicated world.

Before the global refugee crisis unfolded, my wife, Theresa Menders, and I focused our work on women's issues, children's issues and poverty around the world. Whether it was Haiti, Colombia, China, the Republic of Vanuatu, India or elsewhere, the situations we documented were longstanding, institutional issues. Our goal was to raise awareness and support for local NGOs that had been working locally for years.

As far back as 2015, when we started seeing people fleeing on foot by the tens of thousands or crossing the oceans in overcrowded inflatable boats, and seeing men, women and children dying as they sought safety and protection, we got angry.

We got angry that human life was again being dismissed so easily by the thousands, the hundreds of thousands, the millions. History was not only repeating itself, we as human beings were repeating history with a vengeance. Physical weapons of war have only become deadlier and more effective at causing pain or ending human life and, sadly, many people willingly use these to oppress those who are vulnerable. Sadly, the greatest weapons of oppression are not made of metal but rather the unrestricted willingness of oppressors or those fighting for one side versus another to kill and destroy.

We must believe there are more people in this world who want to live in peace than in conflict. We must believe that our human nature is inherently kind, benevolent and caring. We must believe there are more people who want to help one another than hurt one another.

Theresa and I were in Cox's Bazar, Bangladesh in 2019, learning about the Rohingya refugee crisis firsthand in the Balukhali refugee camps. Men, women and children have been fleeing Myanmar for decades, finding relative safety in Bangladesh. 2017 marked the start of the most recent crisis, with the Myanmar government perpetuating what the United Nations calls genocide.

In the camps, we spoke with a young man named Ramzan. Two years earlier, Ramzan and his family of eight walked three days and three nights from his village to reach a safe area in Bangladesh. Ramzan remembers the bodies floating in the river as he fled Myanmar. He remembers the houses being burned down by the army. He remembers the adults and children that were locked inside as the soldiers ignited the fuel.

He remembers everything.

"I am totally disappointed with my life," Ramzan told us.

Ramzan, along with 1.1 million other refugees primarily from Myanmar's Rakhine state, most of whom are Rohingya, are detained in the Kutupalong-Balukhali Refugee Camps north of the Myanmar border. The vast camp region was once a lush forest where elephants roamed. Today is it as dry as a desert, the trees long cleared to make way for housing or burned as firewood.

Several Rohingya people we interviewed said they want to return to Myanmar, but first want the Myanmar government to return their land to them and provide compensation for all they have lost. The possibility that Myanmar will satisfy these demands is unlikely at best, so Ramzan and 1.1 million others are likely to wait for months, years, possibly generations. For many displaced individuals like Ramzan and his family, there is no Plan B. There is nowhere else to go beyond the boundaries of the camps. So he continues to wait. And hope.

Drug trafficking, human trafficking, sexual trafficking and poverty are constant dangers every displaced person faces, similar to many refugees around the world.

We do the work we do because we have been given a gift. And it's the same gift that so many other people have been given and we encourage others to use. We have the gift of having a voice that we can use on behalf of those who have had their voices taken away. We use our resources, energy and time to raise awareness of the global refugee crisis because we don't want anyone to use the excuse "I didn't know" as a reason not to take a stand against injustice.

Lathakia

by Jakeem

Jakeem was placed in the Souda refugee camp on Chios island, Greece, in 2016. In 2019, when he was 24-years-old, Jakeem shared his experience with Daniel Farber Huang and Theresa Menders.

My story started in August 18, 2015, when I was walking to my home at midnight when the police stopped me and asked me about identity. After I gave them my identity papers they saw that I'm from Aleppo and Aleppo is a known city against President Basar Al-Assad. They arrested me just because I'm from Aleppo.

They took me to the political section in Lathakia, a city under the Al-Assad regime control. They started by putting me in an isolated room, alone, with four walls and no one with me. I don't know why I'm inside, they didn't tell me anything. After four months the soldier took me out. His name was Kazzam, he was more than two meters tall and one meter wide.

He started to hit me in my cheeks and he told me: "You're a son of a bitch. What are you doing in Lathakia? Why aren't you in Aleppo?"

I told him I'm studying in college at Tishreen University's English Department. He told me: "This is not right, you're an informer. They send you to give them information about the Syrian army in Lathakia and about the Shia."

I told him: "No, I'm from Aleppo and I run from the terrorists in my city and I came to Lathakia because I don't like them."

He told me: "This is not true, you are gonna to tell me what information did you give to them and when you started to work with them. If you don't remember I will refresh your mind (mocking me)." I told him: "I'm not an informer and I don't know any terrorists."

Then he started to hit my foot with an iron stick, after that he tied my feet together and two soldiers started to hit me with the iron until my feet started bleeding. I didn't say anything, I stayed as my first word, that I don't know any terrorists and I'm not an informer. He told me: "OK, son of a bitch, we will see..."

They asked another soldier to bring handcuffs and a rope. Then, they put the handcuffs on my wrists and tied the handcuffs with the rope up to the roof of the room. They let me stay there — in the air, just the top of my toes touched the ground. I was put like that every day for eight hours for six weeks.

I stayed all these days telling them I'm not a terrorist anytime that I had a choice.

I was six months inside the political section without any reason and any hope to know when I will get out. The soldier spoke with me again: "Do you remember or I do have to refresh your mind more?"

I told him again: "Sir, I'm not an informer, I'm a college student. I don't know why you arrested me."

He told me: "I will refresh your mind." Then he turned to the other soldier and said: "Give me the electric stick." He started to hit me with the electric stick on my legs, hands and neck. In one weakness moment I felt that there's nothing I could lose if I would tell them that I'm an informer just to stop this torture.

I told them: "Sir, I'm an informer. Ok, I remember now, just let me down, just leave me alone, I cannot take more of this suffering."

Then, he let me down and took me again to the isolated room.

This was another way of torturing. A mind torture. I started to believe that there was no sunshine anymore and there are no people walking in the streets anymore. I thought that it was the apocalypse. Every day in the morning, I heard the voices of the people who were being tortured. It was exactly five days of body comfort but my mind was still in torture. The same four walls for 24 hours a day.

They started to ask me again: "Which kind of information did you give to the terrorists? Who is the boss of the terrorist group you worked with? How much information about the military situation in the area did you give to them? Before you became an informer for them, how many people have you killed? How many battles were you in? Which kind of information did you have?"

I answered: "Sir, I'm not an informer either, I just told you this to stop the torture. I'm not a terrorist, I didn't touch a gun in my whole life, I don't even killed an ant in my life."

He told me: "You need to refresh your mind again." He put me in the air again for 14 hours without any stop. I stayed defending my version all this time and I begged him to stop this.

I told him: "It's not my problem the fact that I was born in Aleppo, that doesn't mean that I'm with the terrorists."

He brought the pliers and started with my toes. He took out my big toenail. It started to bleed a lot, all the ground was full of blood, but he didn't care.

After this he told me: "Do you remember or do I have to refresh your mind more?"

I told him the same version from before. Then he took out my other big toenail, and I stayed with the same version: "I'm not a terrorist and I didn't touch a weapon in my whole life." After this, he took three more toenails from one foot. Then another toenail from my other foot.

Then, I told him: "Write everything you want in the report and I will sign it, just let me down, let me alone."

He told me, laughing: "I don't want what I want, I want what you did."

I told him: "I didn't do anything."

He told me: "OK, we will complete refreshing your memory."

I told him: "Stop, I'm an informer, I gave them information about military area in Lathakia. I worked with a group of terrorists named Fallak Alsham." I thought that this was the name of a well-known group of terrorists in Aleppo, but I didn't know them and I never ever worked with them. I lied only for protecting my body against more tortures.

He told me: "This is not enough."

I cried begging him: "Please, I'm a good person, I never worked with them, I just told that to stop this. I'm a college student, do you know what that means? I'm a well-educated person and I know who's wrong and who's right. All people know who's wrong."

He told me: "You are a son of a bitch, because you are from Aleppo and all the women in your family work as whores for them. Do you want me to believe that there's a Sunni Muslim from Aleppo not with them?"

I answered him: "There's a lot of people in Aleppo who stay there because they don't have any place to go, so they are still at their homes. That doesn't mean that all of them are terrorists."

He kept torturing me, and in one moment I felt that I had nothing to lose. I did not want to say what they were demanding. Then I said: "Sir, I want to tell you something."

He said: "What?"

I said: "Come closer, I prefer to whisper it." When he came closer I spit on his face and I told them in a loud voice: "All of you are sons of a bitches! Because you want me to say something that I'm not. You know that I'm weak, and I don't have anyone to protect me. You want to do everything on me just to kiss the asses of your bosses. You want to say that you found a terrorist but I'm not a terrorist. You can do whatever you want and I won't say anything else. You could do whatever, but I will remain in silence."

Then, he became angry and feel red and he told me: "Do you know your prophet? Mohammed? If he came now and kissed my ass to let you out, I won't let you out." At this moment, I knew that I was not going out alive.

All these months, outside of the jail, my father was using his knowledge to request a judgment from the Court to release me. He paid U.S. $6,000 to a judge to release me. This judgment released me from the jail.

My father gave this paper to the political section and then they transferred me to the crime section, which took my registration photos with a case number and date of my case. This was to make them know that I was in jail for a terrorism crime. I stayed there two days and they released me and sent me immediately to military service.

When they sent me to military service, I bought a fake identity and I ran to the revolution area to end this nightmare. This was on July 17, 2016, almost one year later. I walked from Idlib—a Syrian city near the Turkish border—and I smuggled myself to Antakya city in Turkey. I walked 12 hours to reach there, and then to Borsa city, and after to Istanbul. Then I went from Istanbul to Izmir, then Çesme and finally I took a boat to Chios, a Greek island. I stayed in Chios for almost nine months, and three more months in Athens.

After, with a fake ID, I went to Germany and i have been here since September 5, 2017 and still waiting for asylum here after being rejected for being in Greece first. I somehow was supposed to jump from Turkey to Germany?

I decided to write my story here on the advice of my therapist that I am seeing for my PTSD and I want to shed some light about what happening in Al-Assad prisons.

Basra

by Mohammed

Mohammed was placed in the Souda refugee camp on Chios island, Greece, in 2016. He shared his experience with Daniel Farber Huang and Theresa Menders.

My name is Mohammed and I'm an asylum seeker in the UK, my home country is Iraq. My home country isn't safe for me to live in anymore, I left my town of Basra in south Iraq in 2015. I left my mum eight and a half years ago and since the day I left my mum I haven't known real safety.

In Iraq, the instability created at the end of the U.S. and UK-led invasion meant that my country became a dangerous place to be. It was dangerous before 2003 but the power vacuum left by the end of the Iraq War meant that lots of militia groups were grappling for control. One of these groups found out I worked for a foreign company and threatened my life if I continued. That gang believed I was being a traitor to my religion and sent many threats to me. I went to the police who told me that this was just an empty threat so I carried on working to earn money for my family.

One day on my way to work the gang came to kill me, they beat me and shot at me. They weren't successful in killing me, but my mum had sent my brother to work with me to protect me and they killed him. My big brother Farid was my best friend and we did everything together, I will never touch him or laugh with him again. After the gang found out I was still alive they came to my family home while I was in the hospital and they burned down my house. My mum told me to run away and find safety, then the rest of my family moved to a different city. Nearly nine years later I'm glad that the people who tried to kill me can no longer find me here in Europe, the threat of murder is gone but I still don't enjoy true security or stability.

In the 15 months that it took me to get from my home in Basra to Europe I was homeless and poor and I went hungry and I was in unsafe situations most days, so when I arrived in Greece I was relieved and thankful and I felt like the hardest part of my story was over. I didn't really know it then but I was in such a state of trauma and my body was stuck in a fight or flight response constantly for those 15 whole months. I had lost contact with my mum and, even though I was 22, I felt like a little boy again and I didn't

know what to do next or whom I could trust.

My relief upon reaching a Greek island was relatively short lived. I very quickly realised that it wasn't as simple as getting to Europe and telling the authorities what happened to me and then starting a new, safe life. I was moved to a camp near the beach and my asylum claim was started. When my translator heard my story he told me that I would definitely get accepted for asylum so I relaxed about that and I just started to focus on living day-to-day in the shared tent I was allocated.

The camp had some families and some women but it was mostly men from many different countries. I had to quickly learn who was safe to be near and who to avoid. I was told that some of the men there liked to cause trouble and that you had to be friendly but not too friendly because they might want you to get involved in trouble with them too. I quickly made two friends and they helped me stay safe while I prepared for the next few of months of waiting for news about my case. I volunteered at the food distributions in the camp because I wanted to improve my English and I liked to have something to do with my time.

Once I had worked out how to stay safe in the camp, I had to navigate life as an asylum seeker in Greece. Before I arrived, I had heard stories about how the locals would bring food down for refugees each evening and help them build a new life there. But that time had passed, the locals had grown tired of being the first landing point in Europe and I was now part of the "undesirables" that nobody wanted there anymore. There were too many of us for the locals' liking.

When some of the men who looked like me caused trouble in the town then we all became labeled as "trouble." When I would walk about town old ladies would shout at me in Greek. When I went into a shop to buy some fruit the shopkeeper thought I was stealing from them. When I went to the phone shop to top up my internet they made me wait until all the locals were served first. I had to learn my place in this new world and in this world I wasn't seen as an individual, I was just one of thousands of people that nobody wanted. I missed my mum.

I did have some fun though, the volunteers that came from all over the world made me feel like I could laugh and learn from them and be useful. These volunteers would come and go and come and go and I wanted so much to have the freedom they did to leave and work and have a proper life.

Time passed and all of a sudden I had been on the island for nearly a year. I met a volunteer from England who I worked with each day handing out food for breakfast, lunch and dinner. We became friends and then after a few months we started a relationship. I was happy and we talked about having a good life together. Two weeks after we started a relationship I had to go to the main camp on the island to renew my ID. When I was waiting for my new document, they took me into a room and told me that my asylum claim was rejected and put me in handcuffs and took me to jail. A few days later, without warning, they took me to another island and started the process of deporting me.

After all that waiting and wondering what my new life in Greece would be like…in a heartbeat I was back to feeling terrified. My partner was able to find me and pay a lawyer to get me out of the prison camp and allow me to go to Athens and appeal my case. I was just so shocked, I didn't understand what had gone wrong. I was expecting that anytime soon I would get my refugee status and start to find work and ask my partner to live with me and start learning Greek. So we moved to Athens and started to wait for my appeal to be processed. We expected to be waiting a few months so my partner stayed with me and we tried our best to make a life in Athens.

We waited three years. Three years of not being able to work. Three years of not being issued ID documents while I waited for my appeal. Every time I left the apartment I was at risk of being arrested for not having ID papers by the police that lined the streets of the city.

Both of our lives were put on hold waiting for news of my fate in Greece.

One day in 2020, I decided that now, at 25 years old, I couldn't wait anymore and I started to make plans to get us out of Greece. My plan worked, but the stress had taken a toll on my partner's mental health and she still suffers with anxiety today.

I made it to the UK, and again I started the process of making an asylum claim. Again I had that sense of relief of believing I could soon be safe and I was so happy that my wife was back in her hometown. When I started my UK claim they told me they would be in touch within two weeks so I quickly found a lawyer. I was lucky that we now had housing security and I had an ID so if I needed medical treatment it was safe to go to a hospital. We started to heal and dream of our life together.

One year later, after hearing no news about when my asylum interview would be, I automatically became eligible to work in the UK. I quickly found a job and we started saving for a happy future that now seemed possible and not just a dream. We were able to get married and we opened a joint savings account. Even though there were still COVID restrictions in place I was able to meet my wife's friends and family.

After a long time with no contact, I was finally able to get in touch with my mum again. Now I had a job, housing and a loving wife, I was able to start the process of healing from what had happened to me back in 2015. I worked and I waited for my asylum interview.

Nearly three years passed and I hadn't heard from the UK government about my interview date. I was still working as hard as I could and my wife and I have been blessed with a son. My son was born in April 2023 and we desperately want to be able to settle down and feel secure so that we can make a life here in my wife's home country. Last summer we asked the lawyer if there was anything that could be done and she was able to request my interview sooner because now I have a British son that depends on me. Thankfully I was given an interview date and things progressed. My lawyer is not confident that I will get refugee status in the UK, not because my case isn't strong but because I spent some time in Greece before making it here.

Six more months have gone by and my son has a daily video call with my mum. This is my happiest time each day but I still long for the day when she can hold him and kiss him, and I can hug her and kiss her. I'm now 29 and I'm patiently waiting for the day I become a recognised refugee and settled resident of a safe country and able to buy a home for my family and I can finally feel like any other person who didn't have to flee from danger.

The Forgotten Souls

by Pothiti "Toula" Kitromylidi

Toula Kitromylidi is the Field Coordinator and Legal Representative in Greece for Offene Arme ("Open Arms," formerly the Chios Eastern Shore Response Team). Offene Arme is the only remaining NGO on Chios, Greece that is continuously providing non-food Items to asylum seekers and refugees through a Free Shop and distribution efforts both at boat landings and throughout the island.

Nine years have passed and the refugee crisis continues, only it is not visible for the rest of the world. Governments have relentlessly tried to hide the problem, secluding asylum seekers in hostile, unlivable camps exposed to extreme weather conditions and overcrowded facilities that nobody should ever live in. In Chios, almost all the NGOs have shut down their operations. Some have decided to focus their efforts on other battles, others have simply collapsed financially.

Nevertheless, people continue to arrive at the shores of the Greek islands. Even if the media remains silent, even when no images are shown on the news, thousands of people are still undertaking long, dangerous journeys, crossing water and land, and facing all sorts of obstacles, both natural and human, guided simply by the hope of finding a better life across the Aegean Sea. Some of them are single young men, others are families with small children, or single parents, or pregnant women, or older people. If they are lucky enough, they will manage to land on the shores of Chios… cold and soaking wet, only to find themselves running across the fields and into the woods so they will not be pushed back. Some organisations and activist groups continue to document and denounce these violent, illegal push backs on social media, collecting videos, images and testimonies from victims. In doing so, they face the possibility of police persecution, as solidarity continues to be criminalised at the borders of the European Union.

In June 2023, a severely overcrowded boat capsized off the coast of Pylos, resulting in the death of over 600 migrants. EU and national representatives alike have expressed their shock and sadness in the face of such tragedy. However, shock and concern are only emotions, what we need are accountability and an effective response. On the 14th of February, 2024, a hearing was held in the European Parliament to discuss the aftermath of the tragedy and the ongoing reports of violence at the Greek borders. We can only hope that this will lead to a change in the current European approach to migration management and to the establishment of policies that protect human rights otherwise history will inevitably repeat itself.

The incoming flow of migrants has increased dramatically since the Pylos tragedy. Non-profit organisations in the islands continue doing extremely huge efforts to help and meet the needs of displaced peoples, despite the lack of institutional support.

At the same time, the gaps in provision become bigger and bigger, and the conditions at refugee camps keep worsening — although hidden from public view. Since 2020, journalists have been facing restrictions to enter the camps, with the COVID-19 pandemic being used as a pretext. In October 2023, the Ministry of Migration and Asylum made a statement announcing that media access to refugee camps is currently restricted in the Eastern Aegean islands, allegedly to avoid any interference with the tasks of workers in the reception centres.

In Chios, the Vial camp is currently facing severe overcrowding. With a population of more than 1,000 residents — most of them coming from Somalia, Afghanistan, Syria, Palestine, Sudan and elsewhere — over 200 people do not have access to electricity or heating.

At Offene Arme, our team is working under great pressure as we try to fill in all the gaps that the Greek government fails to address. The demand for all our services is high and, since the beginning of January 2024, requests from other NGOs and from individuals residing in the camp have at least doubled. We have been able to start providing ultrasound scans for pregnant women residing in Vial (a service that is no longer available at the public hospital) as well as medication, medical equipment and food for babies and toddlers, in addition to all of our pre-existing projects and services.

At the moment, Offene Arme is running 10 projects and it is still not enough. Similar to many other organisations supporting people on the move in Greece, we are being faced with a lack of support that is threatening our capacity to continue providing our services, while the need for these services becomes more and more pressing. Nonetheless, we stay committed to our purpose and mission, in hopes that someday, our work will no longer be needed.

Labels

by Ratha Kaur Lehall

Ratha Kaur Lehall is an activist and advocate currently working with a UK-based charitable organization providing emotional support for young people. Ratha was an early, on-the-ground volunteer with The Power of Faces in Chios, Greece in 2017.

The first time I visited Chios was in November 2016. I had been living in the city of Izmir, Türkiye (formerly Turkey), and made the decision to visit Chios for a few reasons: it's a holiday destination for Turkish people, I needed to get out of Türkiye for a short while because of the terms of my visa, and I planned to join a volunteer group supporting people who had made the treacherous boat journey from Türkiye.

The irony is not lost on me that I, a privileged British person, was travelling for leisure to Chios, to avoid overstaying my visa in Izmir. While I simply got a bus and then a ferry, traveling for maybe two hours and paying around U.S. $50, others are forced to pay a smuggler extortionate fees of thousands of dollars and travel by inflatable boat in the middle of the night, a dangerous and terrifying journey. In fact, a Syrian friend was making that very same journey by dinghy to Chios on the same day. We had spent the last two months as flatmates in Izmir, eating dinner, drinking beer, watching terrible TV and chatting about our dreams for our futures. We met up the next day on the beach, he was staying in a shared tent, and I was staying in a hotel — a surreal experience.

The next time I visited Chios was around nine months later, by then he had moved on and I had been living in Izmir, on and off, for nearly a year.

Living abroad as a British person is "interesting." I considered myself as much a migrant as my Syrian friends. However, that is not the global perspective, and I was reminded of my privileged freedom of movement every day. In Türkiye, I met so many people from all over the world, desperately doing all they can to travel to Europe, through saving money for smugglers or applying for refugee resettlement programs. In Chios, I met the people who have made the journey and survived, and who are now stuck in a grey area — physically in Europe but on an island having to wait for bureaucracy to do its thing to see if they can travel further. In July 2017, Chios housed hundreds of such people mostly in a large tented camp and in the immigration detention centre, as well as in some hotels or apartments.

Growing up, stories of migration and colonialism were part of my everyday life. My grandparents and parents would recount their lives before moving to the UK, stories of the British Empire, the pain of partition, the beauty of India and Kenya, the loss of identity and culture, and the racism they experienced in the first decades of living in the UK. They struggled so I did not have to.

Around the world, the effects of war, climate change, capitalism, borders, and global inequalities continue to make people unsafe in their home countries, forcing them to seek safety elsewhere.

I was taught, by my family and by my school education, that colonialism ended. My time in Chios showed me that its legacy lives on and continues through immigration laws. Living in 2024, with images and news from all over the world, we can be desensitised to what's going on in the world around us. The words "migrant," "immigrant," "asylum seeker," and "refugee" are more commonly used negatively by the media in the UK. They often use other labels such as "illegal immigrant" and "economic migrant" to spark a debate on whether people should be allowed to move here, as though people's safety are things that should be debated. Within this rhetoric, it can be difficult to remember that these are people we are talking about, not numbers, not labels. Through grouping people together under labels, whether by immigration status, or by nationality, or by race, they become nameless, faceless statistics when, actually, we all know we are not our labels. For those of us whose labels are not barriers to living a freer life — because none of us are truly free — we have the privilege of freedom to express and explore our interests, values, and relationships.

The Power of Faces project was like a sparkling rainbow amongst the chaos of legal advice, and clothes and food distributions in Chios. It invited people to spend a moment not as refugees or migrants but as human beings. As families and friends, having their photo taken at the beach. It sparked conversations about previous beach holidays, about what to wear or how to style their hair for the photos, it gave families an opportunity to stand still and hold each other in the sun and laugh and smile.

Preventing a Lost Generation

by Tahmina Akter

Tahmina Akter is a Commonwealth scholar and humanitarian professional with experience in education in emergencies and crisis contexts, early childhood education, gender based violence and research. She currently works as an Education Manager at the Norwegian Refugee Council in Cox's Bazar, Bangladesh.

I started working in the humanitarian sector in 2018 after Bangladesh was smacked by one of the largest refugee influxes in the world. The Rohingya people have experienced violence over decades and been subjected to many different forms of persecution, including killings, arrests, and tyranny. The persecution consists of rape, physical atrocities such as murder, burning of homes and mosques, forced labor and relocation, property confiscation, and rape leading to recurrent fleeing and asylum seeking to neighboring countries such as Bangladesh, India, Thailand, Sri Lanka, and Malaysia. By denying them official citizenship and omitting them from the list of 135 ethnic communities acknowledged by the constitution, the "Myanmar Citizenship Act 1982" officially ended the Rohingya people's statelessness. Around 800,000 Rohingyas in Rakhine have been branded stateless since the citizenship law deprived them of their citizenship.

Bangladesh has been hosting the Rohingya refugees since Bangladeshi independence in 1971 and despite having limited resources allowed significant waves of Rohingyas to enter the country on a regular basis notably in 1978, 1991–1992, 2016, and most recently in 2017. In addition to the two officially recognised camps from previous influxes, Kutupalang and Noyapara, the Bangladeshi government constructed 32 temporary camps to house the newly arrived Rohingyas in 2017. Currently nearly a million Rohingya refugees are living in the living in the world's largest refugee settlement in Cox's Bazar, Bangladesh. 52% of this population are children, all of whom are living in dire conditions inside the congested refugee camps being entirely dependent on humanitarian aid and services provided by the United Nations and national and international organizations.

I have worked with the refugee children, women, and communities for more than five years. The refugee communities strive to survive against the adverse circumstances and uncertainty while also dealing with their traumatic past experiences. Even after six years of the influx, the Rohingya are still relying on humanitarian assistance for protection, food, water, shelter, health, and education. Devastating hazards like floods, landslides, and fire are a on-going concern. Camp unrest and escalating security concerns (characterized by frequent abduction, targeted killing, and other incidents) further compound the daily hardships. Reports of forced disappearances, kidnappings for ransom, and sexual and gender-based violence are all progressively rising. Such occurrences are greatly impacting the wellbeing, survival, and coping mechanisms for particularly vulnerable groups including children, youths, and women. A genuine risk exists for children and adolescents who are still out of education, turning into a "lost generation" who can easily be abused by traffickers and others for financial gain or other purposes. Girls and women are especially vulnerable to sexual and other forms of gender-based abuse, such as being pushed into child marriage or being kept home by their parents rather than receiving formal education.

The Rohingya refugee crisis is now referred to as a "protected humanitarian crisis," shifting the global attention and reduction of funds and assistance due to increasing crisis like the Ukraine war and the Israel-Gaza crisis. This has resulted in a decrease in humanitarian assistance for refugees and has sparked worries about potentially catastrophic cascades of events such as an increase in starvation, school dropout rates, child marriage, child labor, and gender-based violence. According to the Joint Multi Sectoral Needs Assessment 2023 report, services have decreased since the crisis between Russia and Ukraine erupted in February 2022. Consequently, the World Food Programme cut food vouchers in 2023, from U.S. $12 to $8 dollars in June 2023. Such a reduction of funds further escalate the miseries of the Rohingya communities in many ways as well as for the humanitarian agencies who have been working relentlessly to provide for this population.

Through The Power of Faces, I would like to urge the international donor communities and philanthropists to continue funding for this vulnerable population residing in Bangladesh. With around 19% of the Bangladeshi population already living below the national poverty line, the Bangladeshi government is unable to support this massive refugee population without sufficient financial assistance. The Rohingya crisis has greatly impacted the economy and living conditions of the surrounding Bangladeshi host community. The shrinking of funds and services will disrupt social cohesion and peacebuilding as both these communities are not yet entirely settled for a peaceful cohabitation mechanism.

A Human Rights Perspective

by Ute Ritz-Deutch

Ute Ritz-Deutch is a human rights educator and lecturer at the State University of New York (SUNY) at Cortland, and a New York State Coordinator for Amnesty International USA.

As a human rights advocate I often refer to human rights documents when analyzing world problems. Many of these had their origin after World War II and the dislocation of tens of millions of people. From the realization that all humans have the same universal rights and that these need to be protected, several declarations, policies, treaties, and international laws were created. I frequently talk about the international human rights framework that has emerged since then. The right to seek asylum is one of these human rights. Article 14 of the 1948 Universal Declaration of Human Rights (UDHR) states "Everyone has the right to seek and to enjoy in other countries asylum from persecution." The UN Refugee Convention and the protocols that followed it specifically addressed the issue of refugees and the obligations states have to determine if someone has a legitimate case.

As a signatory to the UDHR and several international human rights treaties, the U.S. and other countries are therefore required to process asylum applications. Sadly, most countries are not living up to their obligations. We should do better, and we certainly can do better.

I came to this work as someone whose maternal ancestors were among those millions who lost their homes, belongings, and statehood at the end of World War II. My mother, who was six years old when this trauma occurred, was forever marked by the experience. So for me the refugee crisis is personal. And while rational arguments and reference to international law are important, what is desperately needed is understanding, empathy, and political will. At this very moment the world is witnessing the largest refugee crisis since the 1940s. The number of displaced people has risen to more than 110 million, with more than 35 million of them officially recognized as refugees by the United Nations.

Many come from Syria and Ukraine; numerous others are fleeing from African countries. Yet, at a time when solidarity is so important, many countries are shutting their doors and turning their backs on refugees, seemingly blind and mute to their humanitarian and human rights obligations. Anti-immigrant sentiment and xenophobia are increasingly commonplace.

Without a doubt, the situation is dire. In 2023, more than half a million refugees were fleeing their countries and trying to reach the United States, by traveling to South America, and attempting to cross the dangerous Darien jungle between Panama and Colombia. More than 20,000 did so in January of 2024 alone. The journey is perilous and many never arrive at the U.S.-Mexico border. If they do, they face tremendous hurdles, including potential family separation, detention, or deportation. As legal avenues continue to narrow, those who seek asylum are demonized as criminals and undesirables. But who are they and what are their stories?

It is easy to get discouraged about the state the world is in today, because the magnitude of the problems is so great. Still, there is always hope, especially if more people are engaged, willing to educate themselves about these difficult issues, and committed to taking action. Civic engagement is now more important than ever. That is why the "Power of Faces" exhibit is so valuable. It is important to recognize the humanity of the people whose circumstances have forced them from their homes. Through the portraits we can see them as fellow human beings, who are about more than just pain and hardship. They are personable and relatable. They are inspiring. It is not hard to imagine that we could be in their shoes.

Coming from a refugee family, it hits close to home for me. But one doesn't need to have this background to be moved by these faces, who are so caringly captured. Daniel Farber Huang and Theresa Menders have done a beautiful job bringing a glimmer of joy into the lives of the refugees they photographed and sharing the images with the rest of us.

Rohingya Refugees and Their Resilience

by Adem Carroll

For over ten years, until recent retirement, Adem Carroll served Justice for All as UN Programs Director and Team Lead for its long-running human rights program, Burma Task Force. Adem has worked with and within the community since the 1990s, following Peace Corps and AmeriCorps service, with focus areas including civil liberties, refugee rights, interfaith dialogue, and education.

We "humans" can be very cruel to minority communities. This is true of "We the People of the United States of America" but tragically also true around the world. Until a year ago, I served for ten years with Justice for All (JFA), a UN-accredited NGO working on behalf of, and in partnership with, persecuted minorities. Rooted in the diverse Muslim communities in the U.S., JLA programs focused on the plight of mostly Muslim minorities in China, India and Myanmar (formerly Burma). In each case, governments targeted communities through increasingly genocidal policies until suddenly scaled-up massacres and mass displacement catch the world's attention, at least briefly.

Between 2013 and 2019, Justice For All's main program focus was "Burma Task Force" (www.burmataskforce.org) — with the genocide of the Rohingya minority taking place in August 2017, and the Burmese military coup taking place later in February 2021. With so many now displaced as refugees, and many historical buildings destroyed, Rohingya struggle to pass their cultural traditions, their pride, and their history to young people.

It is humbling to witness Rohingya resilience despite the brutality of soldiers and the heartlessness of bureaucrats. In Bangladesh, half a million Rohingya refugee children were denied education for several years, and many restrictions remain. Employment is forbidden. It is outrageous how refugees are treated in the nations that offer them safe haven: at first with some generosity, then with hostility and exclusion.

No wonder so many refugees put themselves in the hands of traffickers, risking death for hundreds of miles in dangerous, leaky boats—and yet, wherever they land, the survivors continue to be treated as an underclass, as "less-than-human."

Rohingya were vilified for their Islamic beliefs and for their skin color. The mass rape of 2016 paved the way for even more widespread crimes against humanity in 2017. With over 300 villages in flames, nearly a million Rohingya fled the country into Bangladesh, joining earlier waves of refugees. After a delay of almost five years, the U.S. Government formally recognized the Rohingya genocide in March 2022. The U.S. State Department was convinced that the Myanmar government's intent to erase the minority population was demonstrated by the comprehensive nature of persecution in the years leading up to the mass displacement, including denial of citizenship rights and severe restrictions on education and employment, denial of free movement as well as marriage rights.

The power-sharing, civilian government of Aung San Suu Kyi was unwilling to take a stand against the genocide when it was challenged in the International Court of Justice (ICJ). The ICJ issued a provisional finding aimed at preventing further genocidal actions and holding perpetrators accountable. Unfortunately, Burmese military leaders staged a bloody coup in early 2021, jailing civilian leaders including State Counsellor Suu Kyi. Inspired by a form of Burman Buddhist supremacist nationalism, the military junta has failed to cooperate with the international court or with the "Five Point Consensus" of the ASEAN countries. Indeed, in 2024, the situation in Rakhine State has worsened, with numerous civilians caught between the local Arakan Army and the Burmese military and murdered by both sides. Bangladesh is resisting allowing more Rohingya to escape. Dreams of an internationally patrolled "safe zone" seem forgotten.

Armed by Russia, China and India, the Myanmar military continues to bomb villages, not only in the Rohingya homeland but also in other ethnic states. It has now instituted a draft to continue its fight against its own diverse people, which comprises well over 100 ethnicities (the count is highly politicized, and the Rohingya are excluded). Mass displacement now affects hundreds of thousands besides the Rohingya. It is impossible for refugees to return at this time: safety and rights must be restored first. Homes have been destroyed and in many cases the land has been stolen and developed by vast military-owned industries.

Faced with an extremist military, the population of Myanmar has generally become more understanding of the Rohingya plight. The civilian government in exile, the National Unity Government, has made some outreach to Rohingya leaders, but more trust building is needed. Rohingya hope to return some day when it is possible.

But throughout the last five years Bangladesh has tried to coerce Rohingya refugees to return across the border. A series of mysterious destructive fires has destroyed various refugee camps. The Bangladesh government has pushed to relocate Rohingya to a desolate, inaccessible island called Bhasan Char. Floods and cyclones threaten the future of all these camps. Corrupt police threaten and harass Rohingya but ignore the gangs that proliferate and that murder local Rohingya leaders. For almost five years education for children was severely limited. Even now, schools run by Rohingya teachers are opposed by government officials and from time to time are bulldozed to the ground.

Imagine living in such conditions, with fires, floods, and murders along with the memory of trauma. Rohingya deserve our deepest solidarity. I remain in daily contact with Rohingya partners in the camps. They regularly send WhatsApp pictures of all these catastrophes, including dead bodies and burned homes. Government restrictions limit NGO access, especially after dark. In Bangladesh, the Camps of Cox's Bazar are like "the wild west" at night. Gun battles are not uncommon. How are guns being brought into the camps?

A Rohingya journalist I know reports in detail on trafficking and corruption, while authorities harass his family, and his father died from lack of medical care. Family money that was collected to provide his father care in a private facility outside the camps was "confiscated" by the local police force.

Another long-term colleague was taken hostage by a gang. As a talented photographer, who happens to be Rohingyan, he had won two international awards during the last year, but authorities would not allow him to travel to receive the awards, even with the UN agency for refugees (UNHCR) arranging travel. Rohingya do not like to be called "stateless," but this is how the world treats them.

Over the last several years, the U.S. government has given over one billion dollars to the million displaced Rohingya for food, medicine and for shelter, but there are many "middlemen" and little of this money goes directly to the refugees. Now, new crises compete for the world's attention and the World Food Program has dramatically reduced food allocations. Rohingya would like to work to earn their living but are not permitted to. Bangladesh makes a difficult situation more difficult. And in the U.S., certain political forces even wish to cease all foreign aid. Instead, humanitarian assistance needs to be increased, but provided more honestly and more directly.

The Rohingya inspire with their efforts to mutually support. Despite hostility from officials, volunteer-run schools provide education to girls and boys. I frequently receive photos of their sports activities, their test scores and their lessons. These children learn, just like all children, and their drive to succeed is moving. They are the future hope of their people. And yet they live in a sort of prison.

My sincere thanks to Daniel Farber Huang and Theresa Menders and their important work to show the human face of refugees.

Much more might be said of the displaced Rohingya. I would like to name them. And yet, the situation does not seem safe, especially for young leaders who interact with the world on a regular basis. Besides Bangladesh, the over 150,000 Rohingya in Malaysia also face popular hostility and worsening conditions. Scattered among many other nations, survivors of human trafficking undergo unfathomable ordeals. It boggles the mind. There are over 110 million displaced people in the world today. But please don't forget the Rohingya.

Documenting the Ukrainian Refugee Crisis

Interview by Braden Kelner

Braden Kelner is Associate Editor at Wharton Magazine. This article originally appeared in Wharton Magazine, May 12, 2022.

The United Nations estimates that roughly six million people have fled Ukraine since Russia began its invasion of the country in late February. Of those seeking safety, more than 3.25 million refugees have crossed into Poland. Moving swiftly in the face of the crisis, Daniel Farber Huang and Theresa Menders traveled to Poland to bring greater awareness to the situation as part of their Power of Faces project. Through the ongoing initiative, Menders and Huang have sought over the years to shed light on the broader global refugee crisis by photographing individuals who have fled their home countries around the world.

In Poland, their pictures at relief centers, transportation hubs, and a border checkpoint serve to provide a firsthand sense of the invasion's devastating impact on Ukrainians. Huang and Menders shared some of their photographs and insights from their time in Poland — as well as a little-known secret about their own lives — with Wharton Magazine.

Wharton Magazine: What has your journey as photographers looked like since graduating from Wharton, and what specifically led you to start the Power of Faces?

Daniel Farber Huang: We've been working as a wife-and-husband photo team for over 20 years. Our earlier work focused heavily on New York City's post-9/11 recovery, and much of that work has been archived in the permanent collections of several museums and historic institutions. We've had an ongoing focus on women's and children's issues and the alleviation of poverty around the world, having worked in Colombia, Haiti, Honduras, China, India, the Republic of Vanuatu, and several other places. When the global refugee crisis began in 2015, we wanted to understand what was happening as millions of people were being displaced due to conflict and persecution. Over the ensuing years, we have documented the plight of displaced people in refugee camps across Greece and in Turkey, Bangladesh, and Mexico.

At the refugee camps, people may be living there for weeks, months, or even years. Inside the camps, we are granted permission to set up our makeshift photo studio to take and give proper photographs to people. Given the fast-moving nature of the situation in Poland, we weren't able to plan for a studio or distribute photos as we normally would. Instead, our intention was to raise awareness of the challenges and dangers Ukrainians are facing as they flee the violence in their homeland.

Theresa Menders: We'll let you in on a little secret: We both have full-time day jobs. I am a chief of staff at a pharmaceutical company, and Daniel is a strategy consultant. Our documentary work is done whenever and wherever we can fit it between our jobs, our four children (which is a whole other story!), and the demands of daily life. We plan our time accordingly because this is important to us. What we've learned from our experiences is that focusing on helping people does not take away from the other parts in our lives; it truly does open up so much more — not just on an emotional or spiritual level, but in the way we prioritize and spend our waking minutes.

WM: What do the paths of the people you've met on the Poland-Ukraine border look like? What typically are their options after crossing the border?

Huang: There are enormous practical considerations displaced people have to navigate, from things as immediate as finding water, food, and shelter to obtaining information (such as where they are currently located, what is happening back in Ukraine, what their next options are) and communications (such as practical needs like obtaining a new SIM card that works in Poland) to continuing on their journey (obtaining transportation, deciding to stay inside Poland or venturing further).

Fortunately, at present, there is an outpouring of compassion in many parts of Poland, where resources are being directed to help Ukrainians, such as basic relief supplies from NGOs, temporary shelter in state-run reception centers, free SIM cards being offered by cell operators, and free train and bus tickets offered by the Polish government. For anyone who is fleeing for their safety, having to figure all of this out and more — when they're exhausted, scared, and responsible for the safety and well-being of their families — must be terrifying day after day. Furthermore, everybody has someone — a husband, father, brother, son — who is back at home in Ukraine, and they are fearful for their lives in the war.

WM: What are some of the greatest needs of the refugees you've met in Poland?

Menders: Psychological first aid and survivor mental health is extremely important but is often an afterthought or ignored in these situations. That's partly due to different stigmas or misunderstandings around the world attached to the concept of mental health. Another challenge is that mental health is simply not included as part of the conversation around humanitarian relief and recovery, but it is one of the critical elements that can help people heal and move forward, not only mentally but physically and emotionally.

I've been interviewing with field doctors, and there seems to be general consensus that psychological first aid and psychosocial support is highly important and additive, but there simply aren't enough, if any, resources directed to it: trained practitioners, information dissemination and education, and dedicated resources that can be placed when and where needed. The sooner these services can be provided to traumatized individuals, the better the longer-term mental health well-being and overall health implications. I'm surveying the disparate resources that may currently be in place around the world and also working to confer with universities, medical centers, practitioners, and advocates to see what resources or services may be aggregated or scaled for future crisis situations.

WM: Unlike some of your previous work, in which you had ample time to plan your arrival at long-existing refugee sites such as those in Greece and Bangladesh, you arrived in Poland within a matter of weeks of the crisis's onset. What did that process look like, and why was it important to get on the ground quickly?

Huang: An important part of what allowed us to be on the ground so quickly in the current crisis are the lessons we've learned covering other situations around the world, so our ability to respond immediately is built on experience. In any crisis situation, we try to be as prepared as possible to ensure we have clearly defined plans, objectives, and access to locations and individuals, as well as personal safety considerations. We do also know that, once we are in-country, the landscape can shift rapidly and we have to be flexible and willing to improvise to document the situations. Sometimes, we are able to have advance written authorization from government entities to gain access; other times, we frequently have to navigate bureaucratic and other obstacles once we land.

Menders: In the weeks and days prior to Russia invading Ukraine, we were seeing actions and events compounding, which were all moving closer to the likelihood of war and the humanitarian crises that unfortunately always arise. We know that raising awareness of humanitarian crises can spur action. The faster we can document the situation and share objective information with the public, the faster at-risk people can be helped.

WM: Out of all of your work through the Power of Faces, is there a particular place you've visited, or a person you've photographed, that especially continues to resonate with you?

Menders: I spent a significant amount of time with a Ukrainian mother and her two-year-old son at the Medyka crossing in southern Poland. After crossing the border, she was able to obtain a temporary location in a makeshift "women and children" safe area within a tent set up by Sauveteurs sans Frontières (Rescuers Without Borders). It is apparent that many refugees are suffering from PTSD, as we all would if placed in a comparable situation. She became frightened whenever she heard police sirens or other loud noises because of the horrors she had witnessed. She also had to worry about not just herself but her child. She kept asking whether she was safe there and was visibly shaking. Fortunately, she was able to obtain the medicine she required, and her son could get some rest. I sat with her for a few hours, attempting to converse with her as her exhaustion set in. The tent was only able to provide one night's temporary relief, allowing her to spend the night with her son there, but her journey was far from over, and she would have to go on.

Huang: At the Poland border, a mother with two children — a teenager and a toddler — was visibly distressed, appearing pained and tearful as she entered Poland through the checkpoint. I intentionally did not take her photo because it didn't feel right. Then she came over and wanted to start a conversation with me. Lyudmilla, the woman, told us that her home and neighborhood about 35 miles to the east was bombed with her family inside. Her 17-year-old son, Slava, pulled her and her infant out of the rubble. Her parents built the house. Her husband stayed behind in Ukraine to fight. Tears flowed down her face as she said, "Bombs started detonating. Everything started exploding, destroying itself. I was afraid. It was terrifying… They were dropping bombs on our children, such tiny children…"

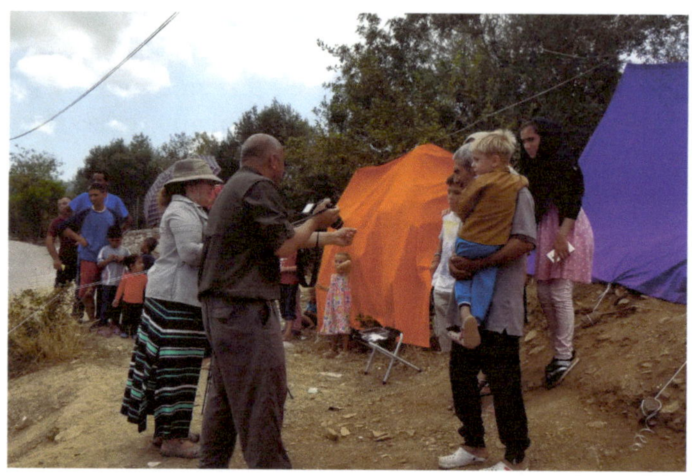

PARTNERS

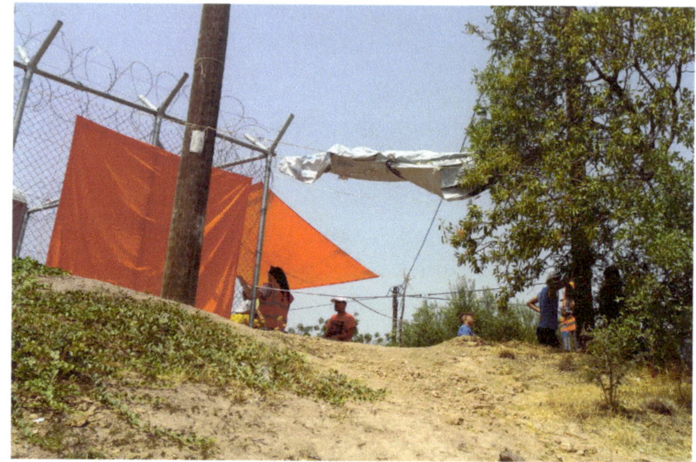

Greece 2017
In-Country Team
Daniel Farber Huang
Theresa Menders
Ratha Lehall - Production Manager
Mohammed - Translator

Greece 2018
In-Country Team
Daniel Farber Huang
Theresa Menders
Alexander Huang-Menders
Celeste Huang-Menders
Quincy Huang
Nina Garcia Wright
Sanjana Kowshik
Lavanya Narishma Murthy

Special Thanks to
Pothiti "Toula" Kitromylidi
Christian Huang
Yuki Zhang – Website Design

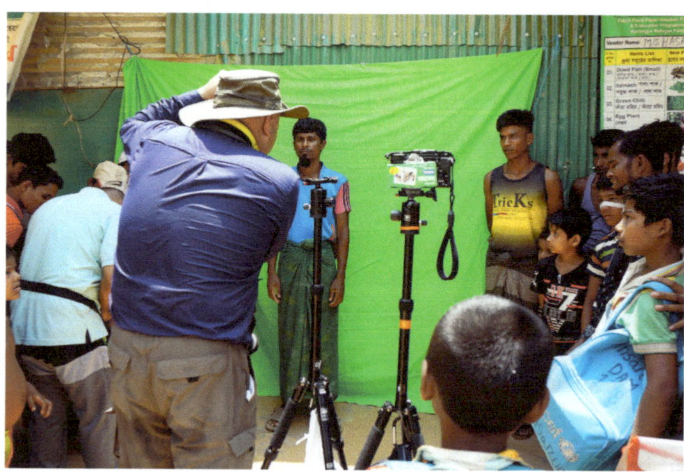

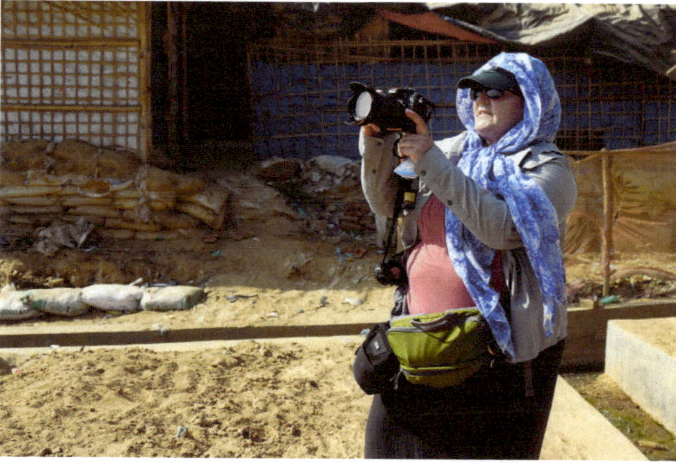

Bangladesh 2019
In-Country Team
Daniel Farber Huang
Theresa Menders
Tahmina Akter
Mohammed Salim - Translator

Special Thanks to
Amy L. Moyer, Ed.D.
Samanjar Chowdhury
Marie Louise Menders
Justina Menders

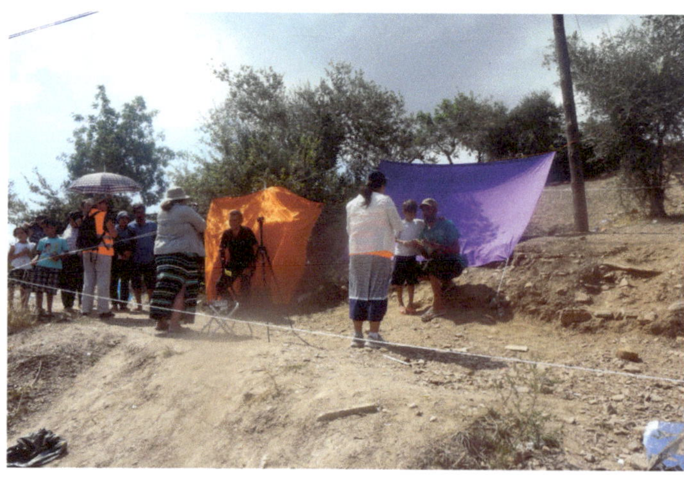

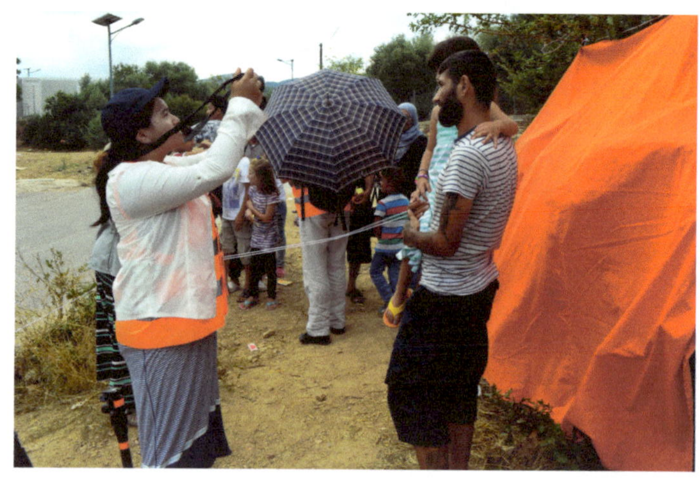

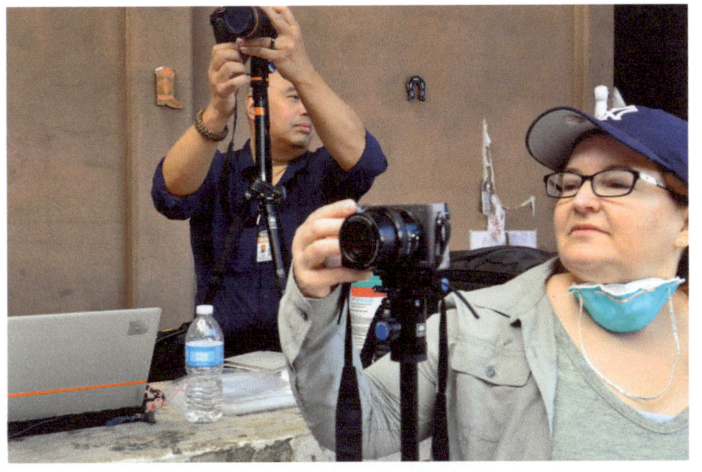

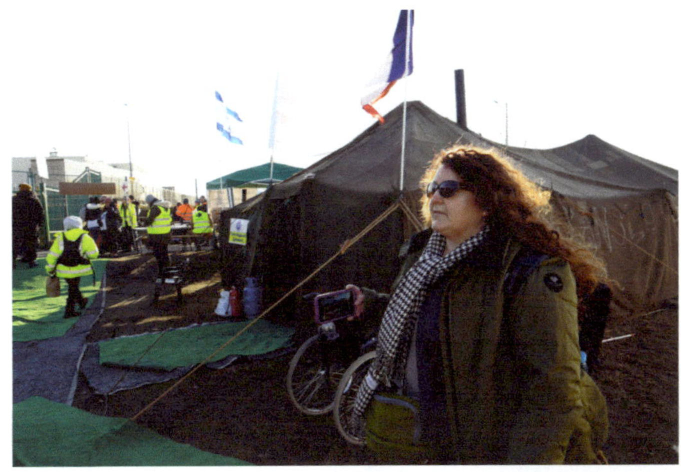

Mexico 2018 and 2019
In-Country Team
Daniel Farber Huang
Theresa Menders
Alexander Huang-Menders
Celeste Huang-Menders
Christian Huang

Special Thanks to
Martha Alvarez Romero
Hugh Wright
Christian Romero
Caroline Villel
Jose Alberto Garcia
Nina Garcia Wright
Quincy Huang

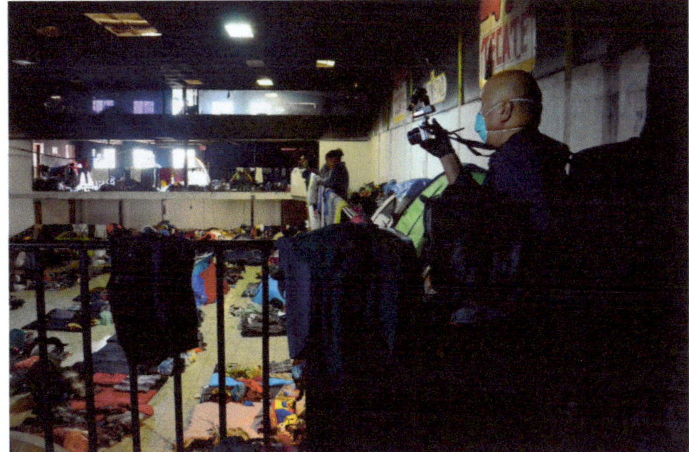

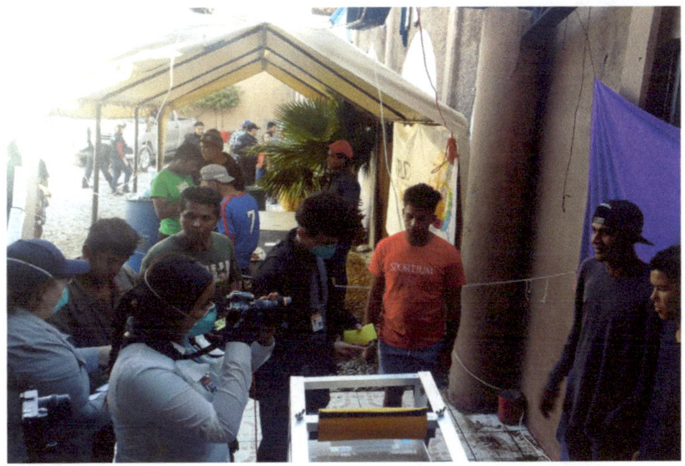

Ukraine 2022
In-Country Team
Daniel Farber Huang
Theresa Menders

Special Thanks to
Michael Wyrick

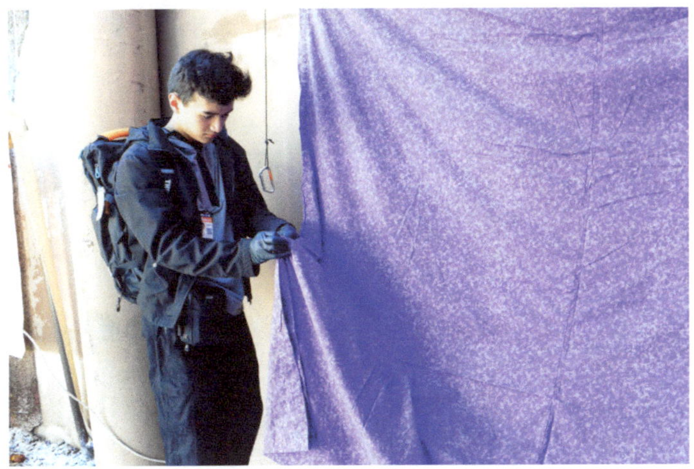

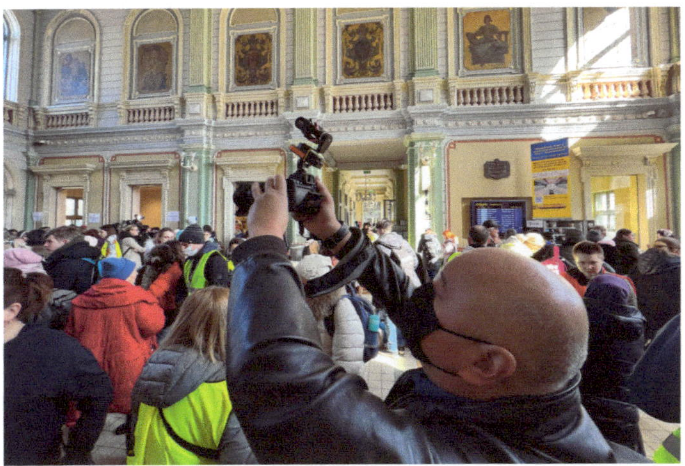

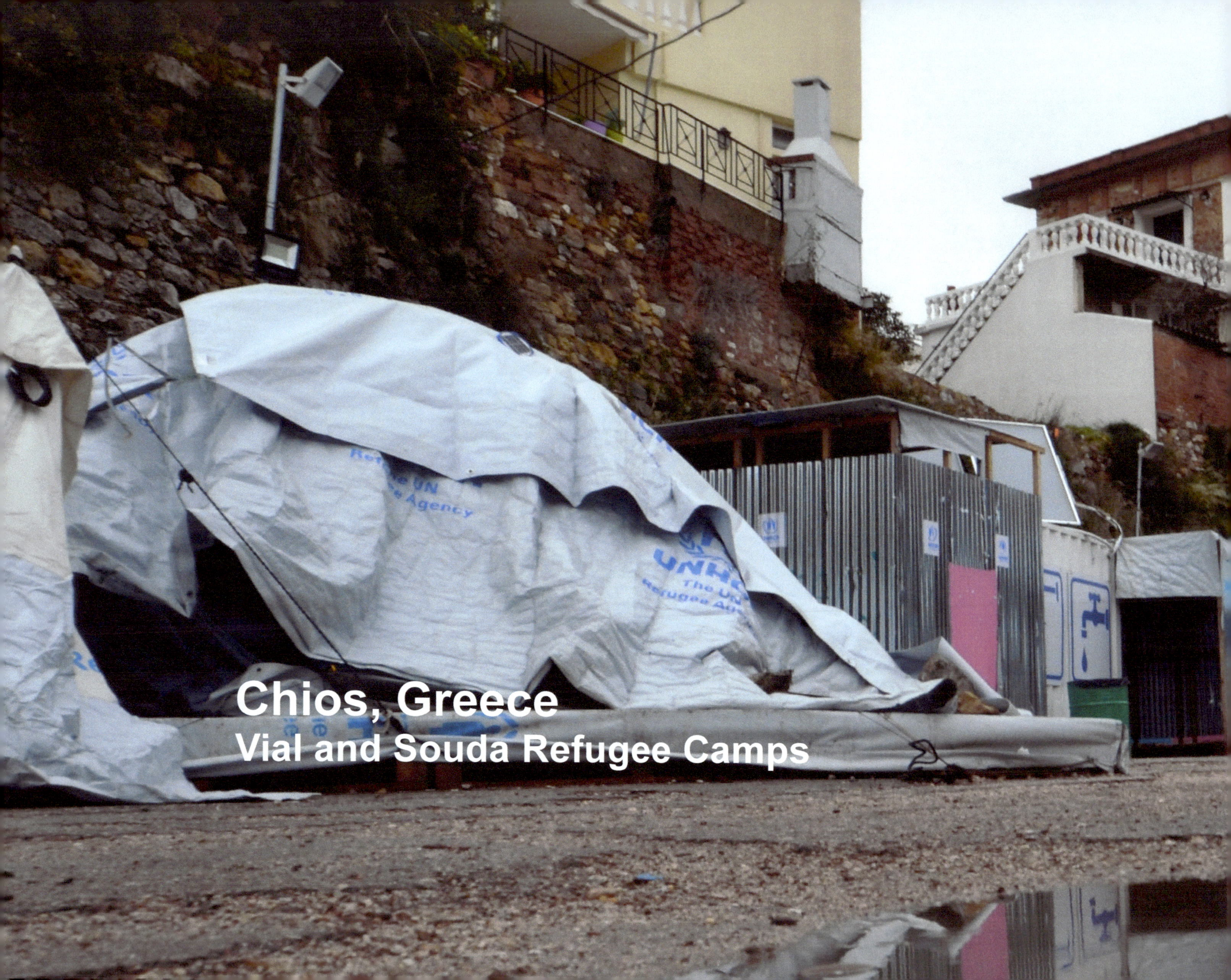

Chios, Greece
Vial and Souda Refugee Camps

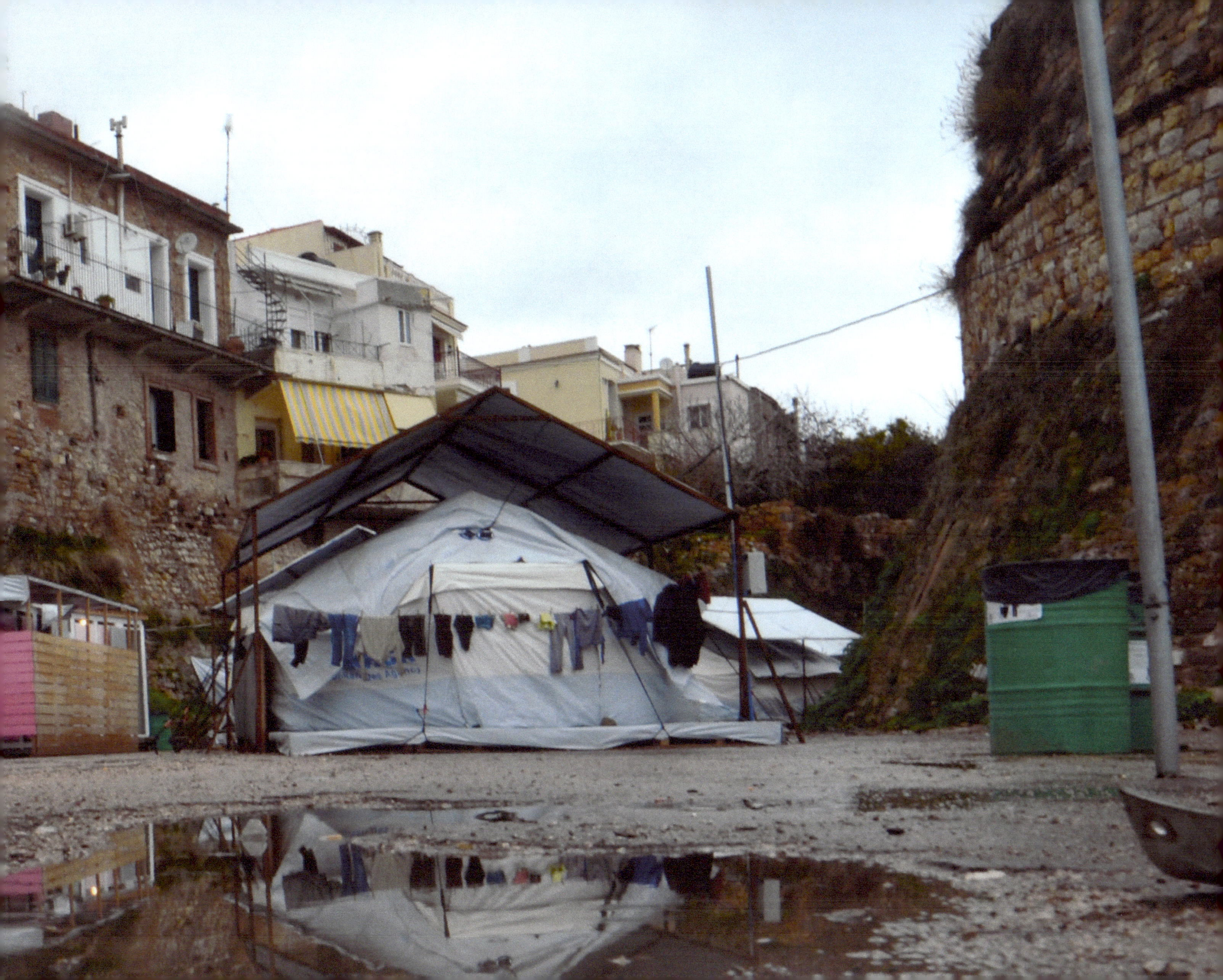

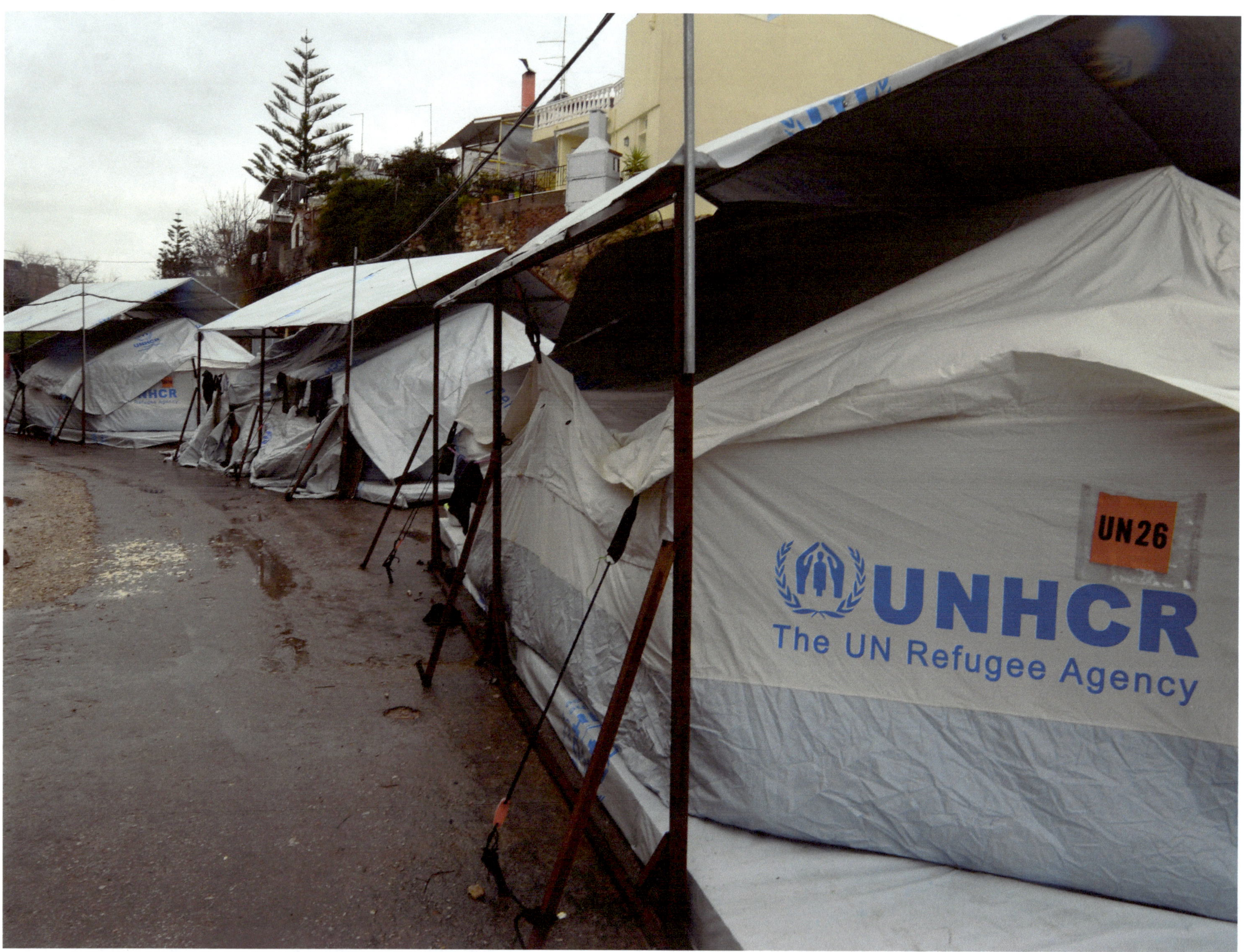

UN26
UNHCR
The UN Refugee Agency

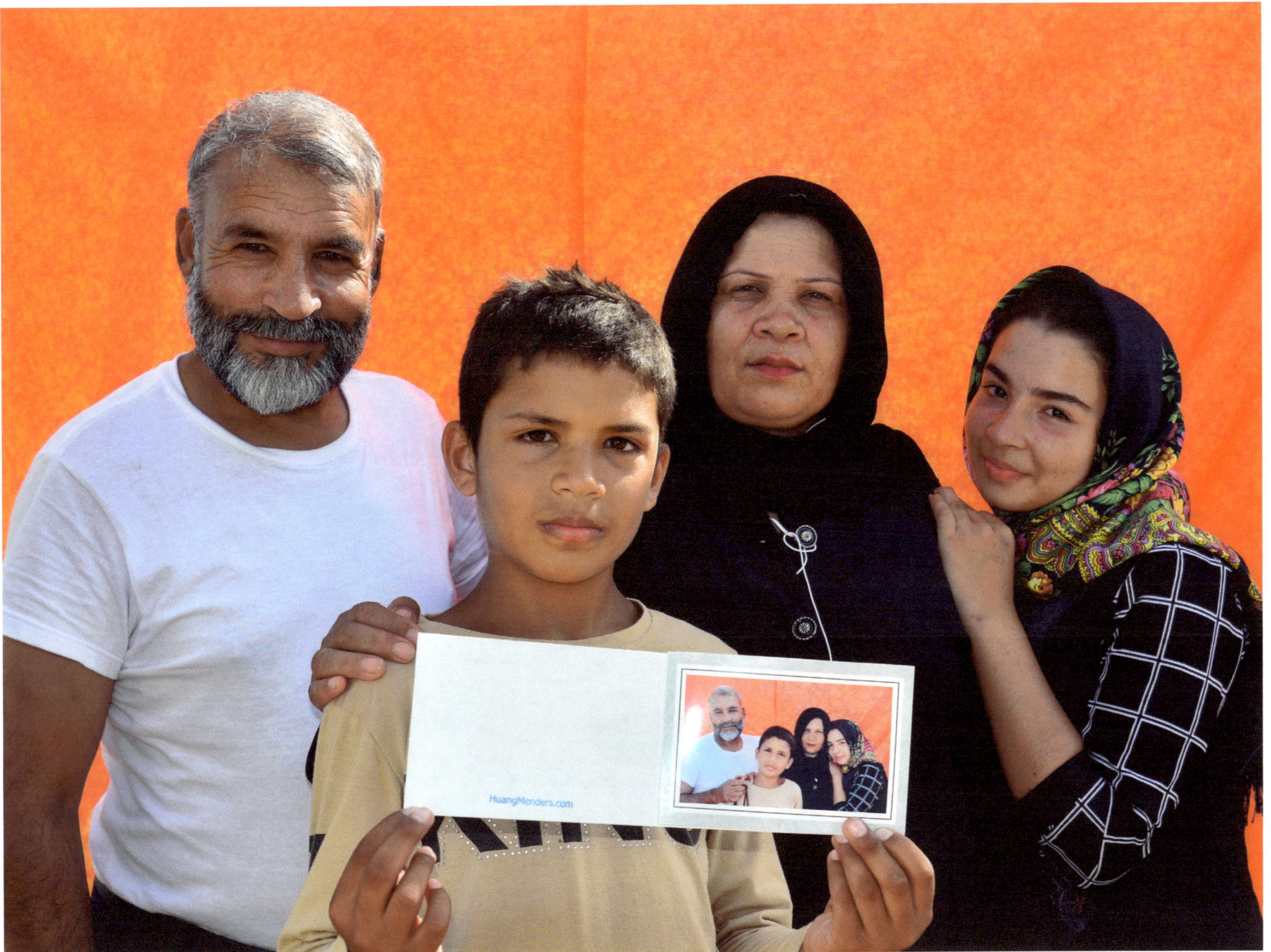
HuangMenders.com

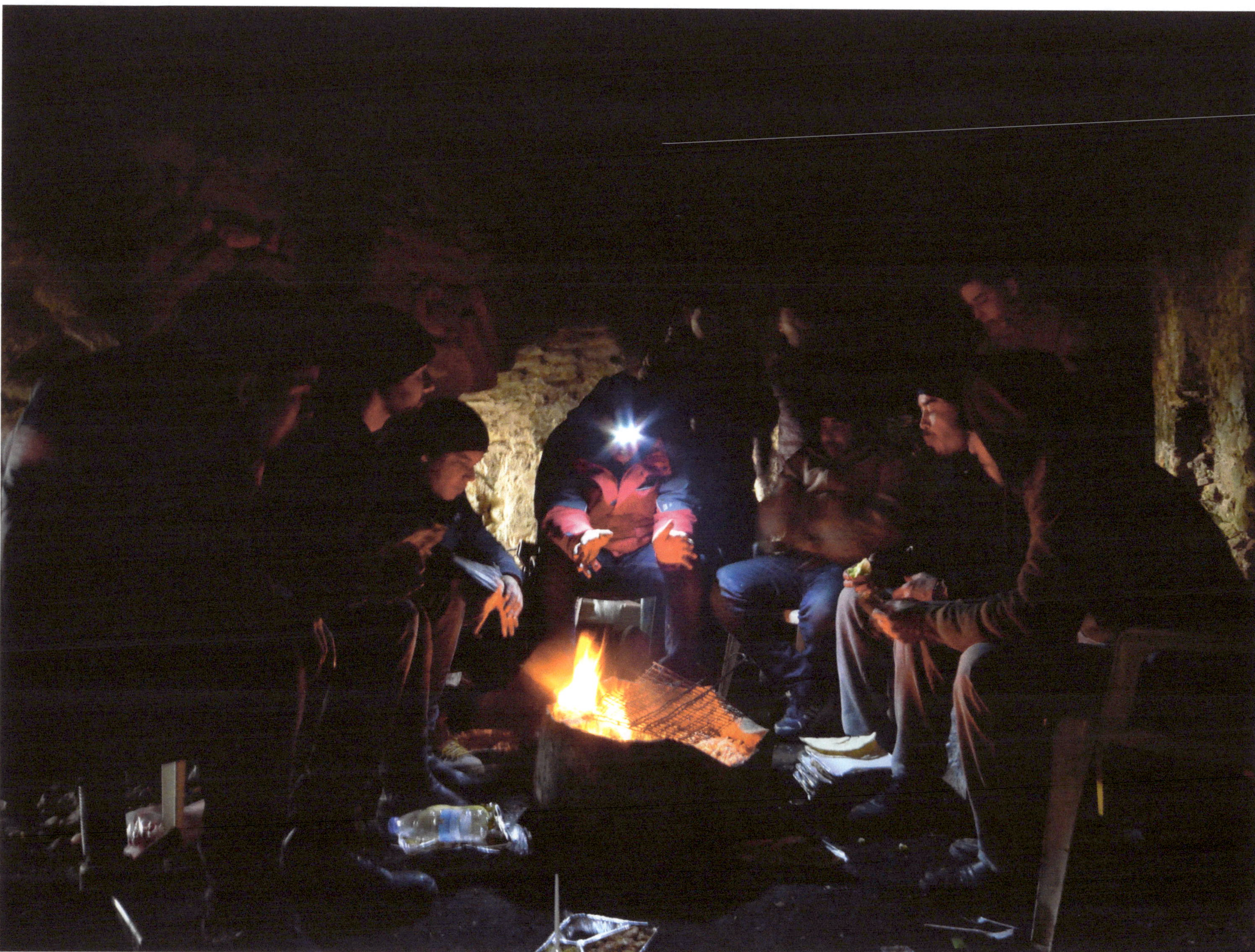

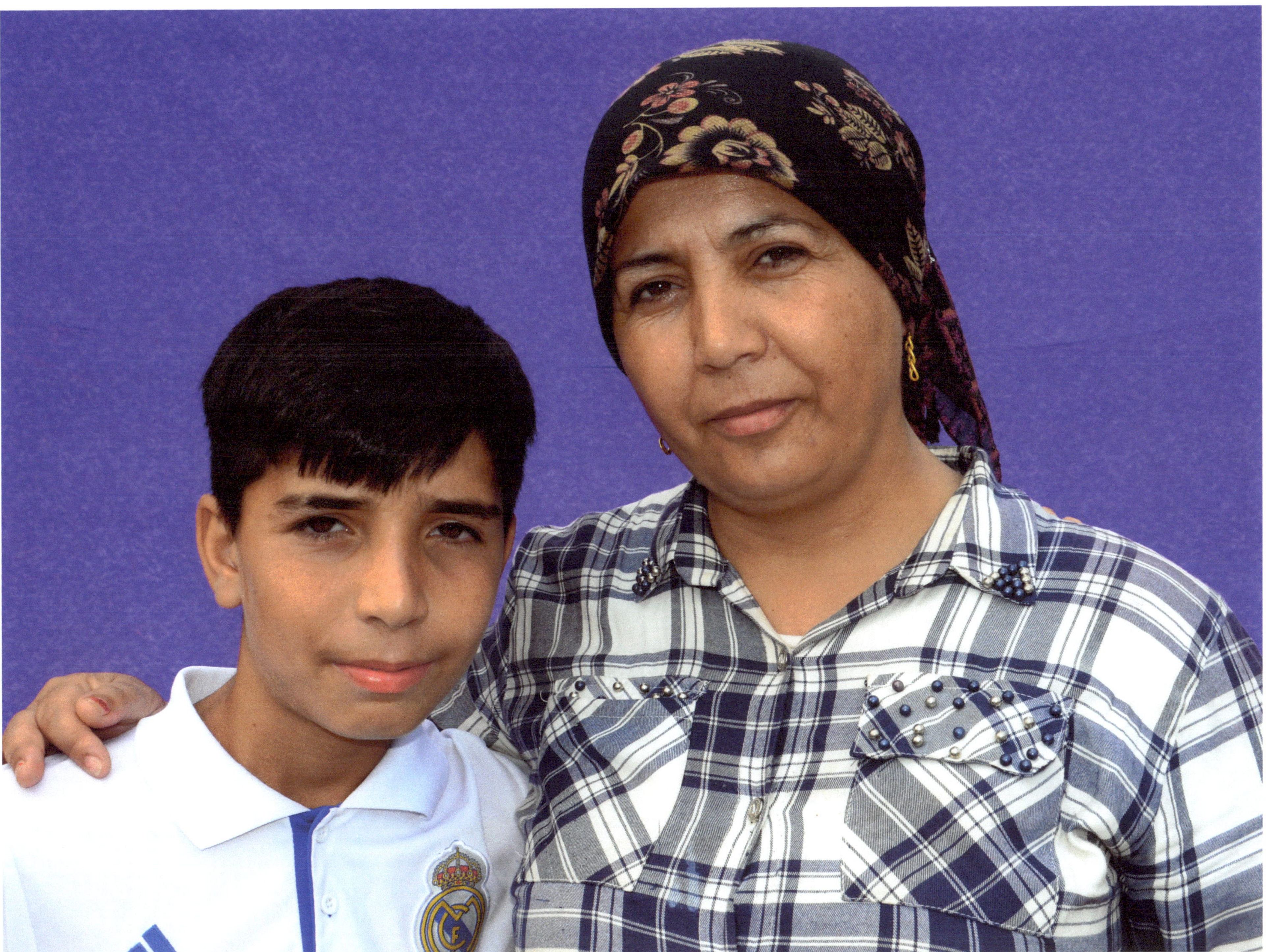

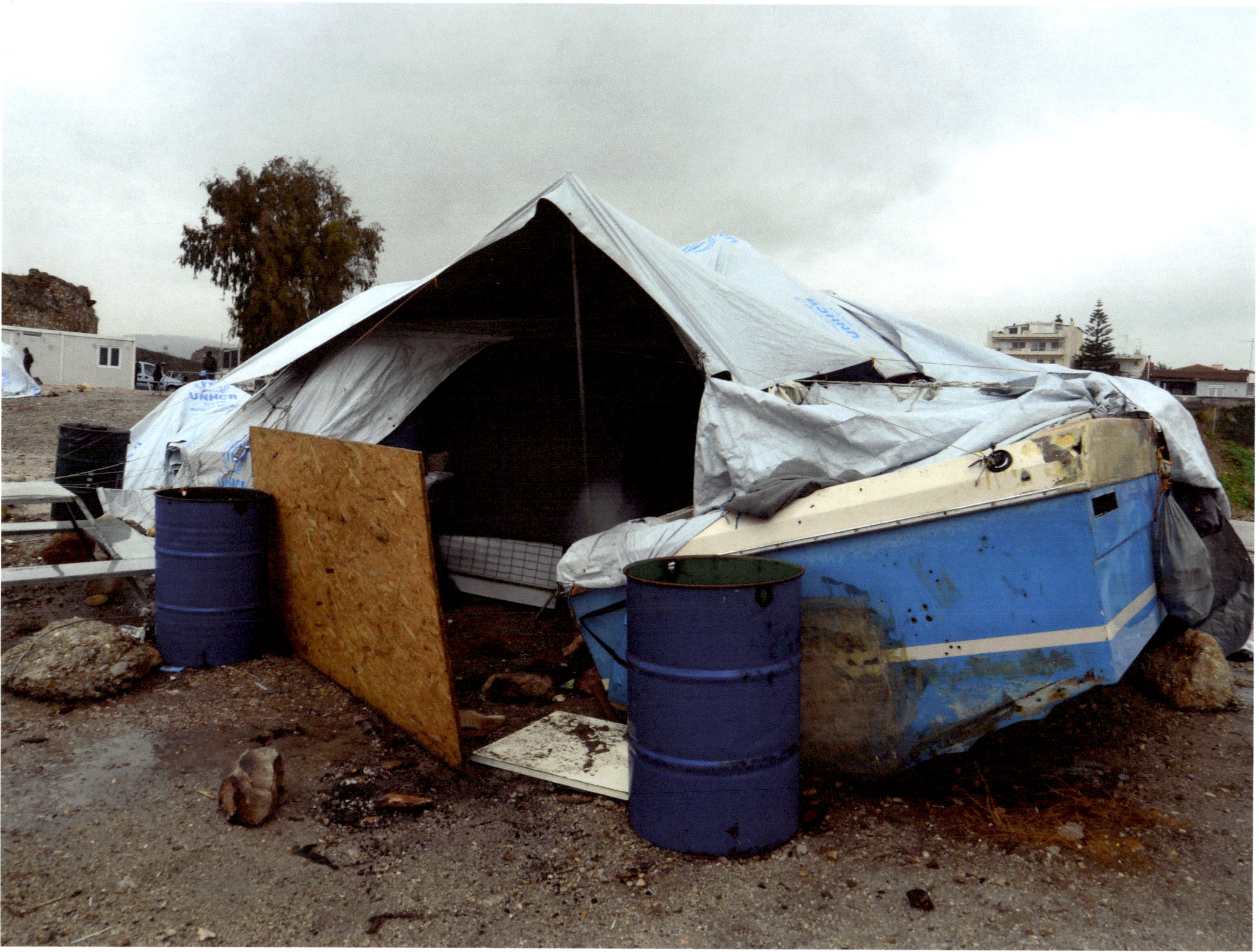

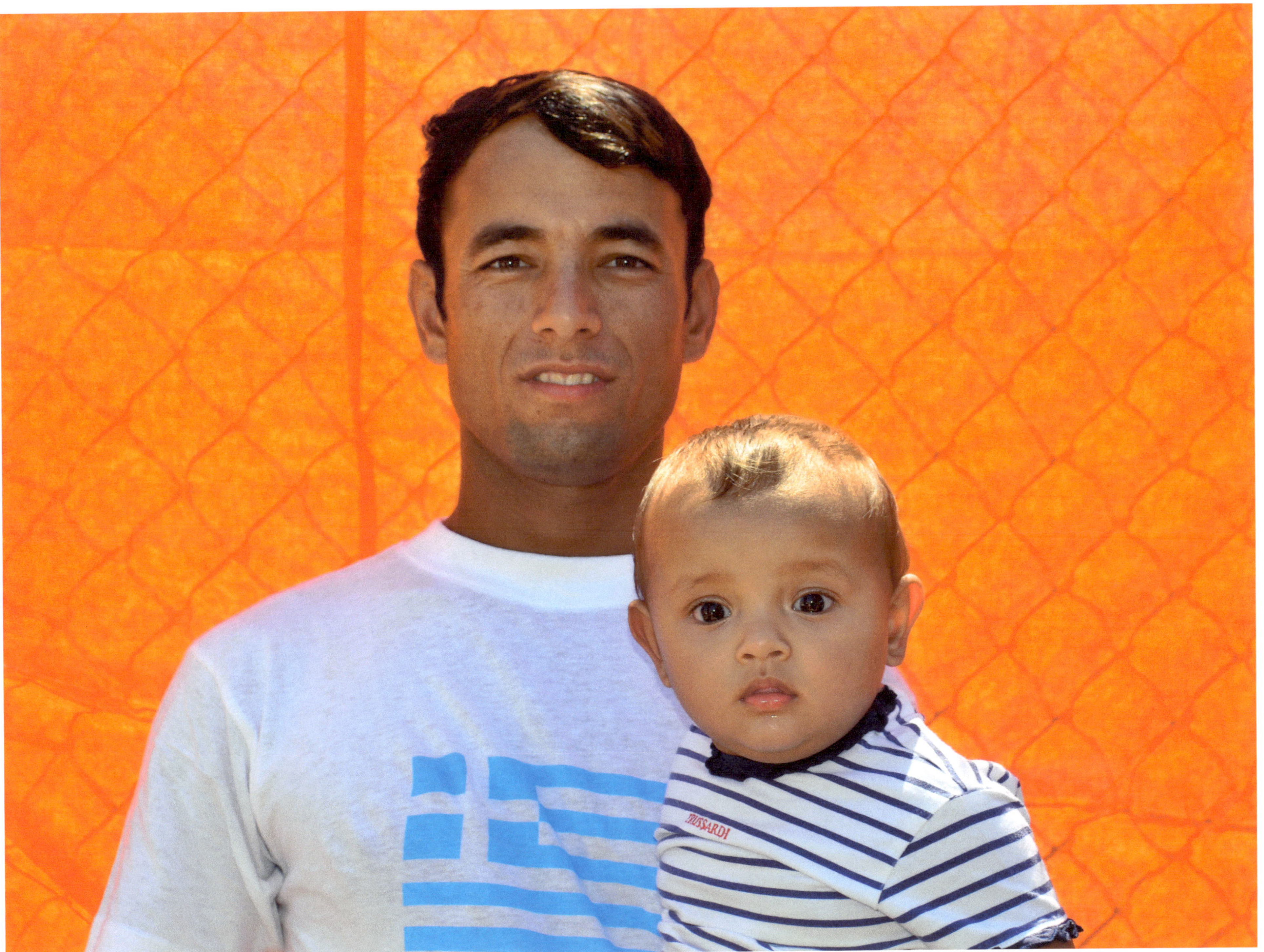

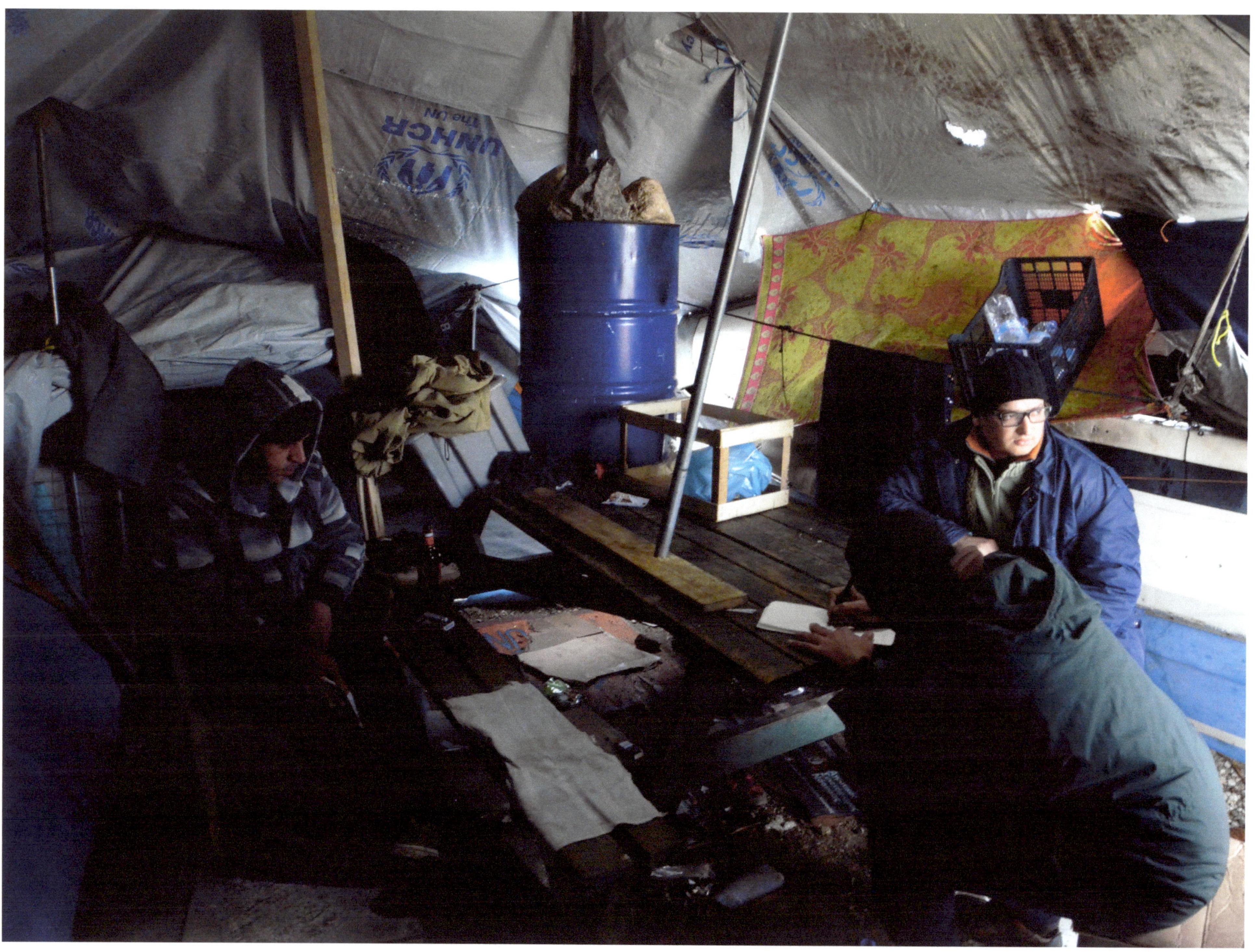

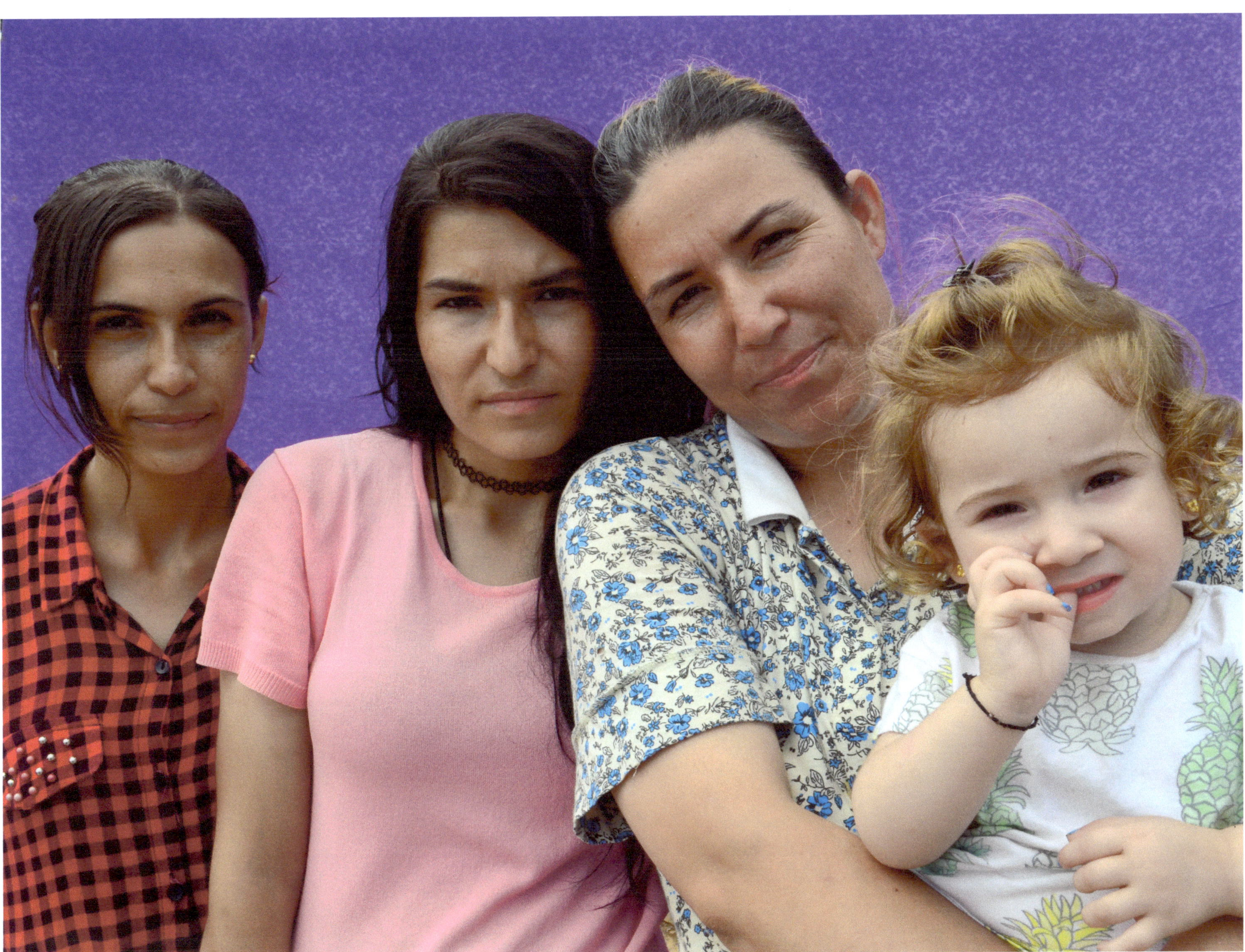

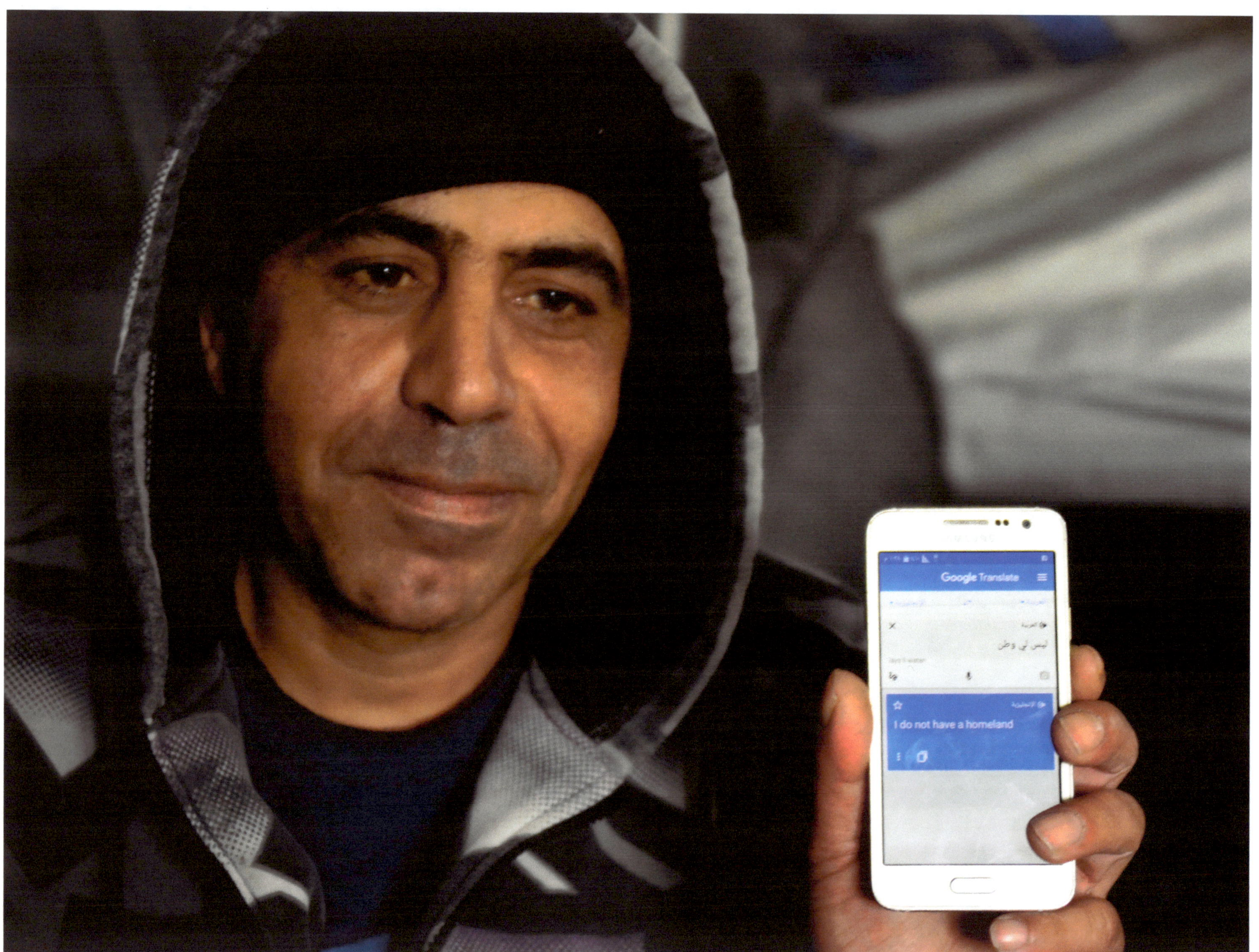

Google Translate
العربية
ليس لي وطن
I do not have a homeland

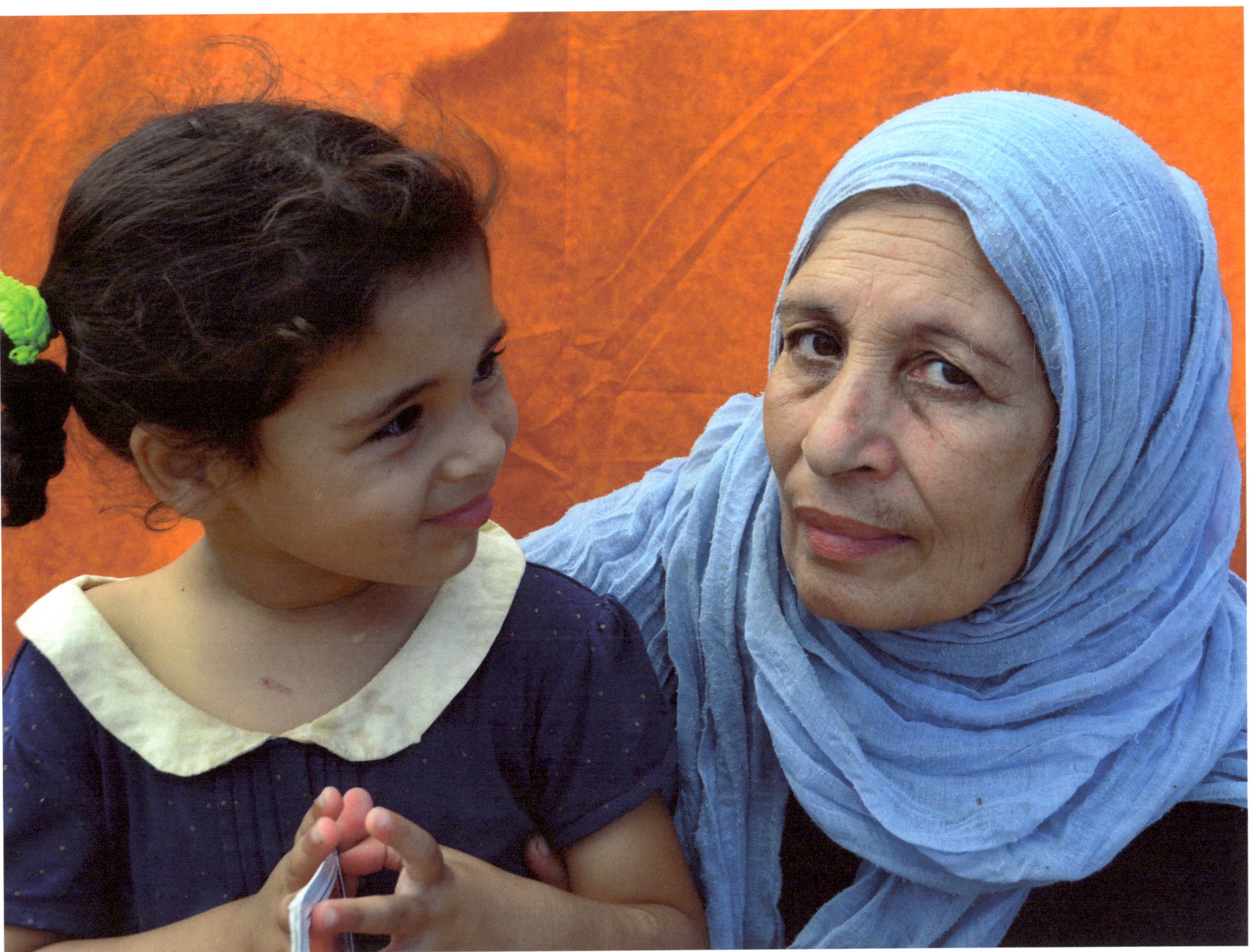

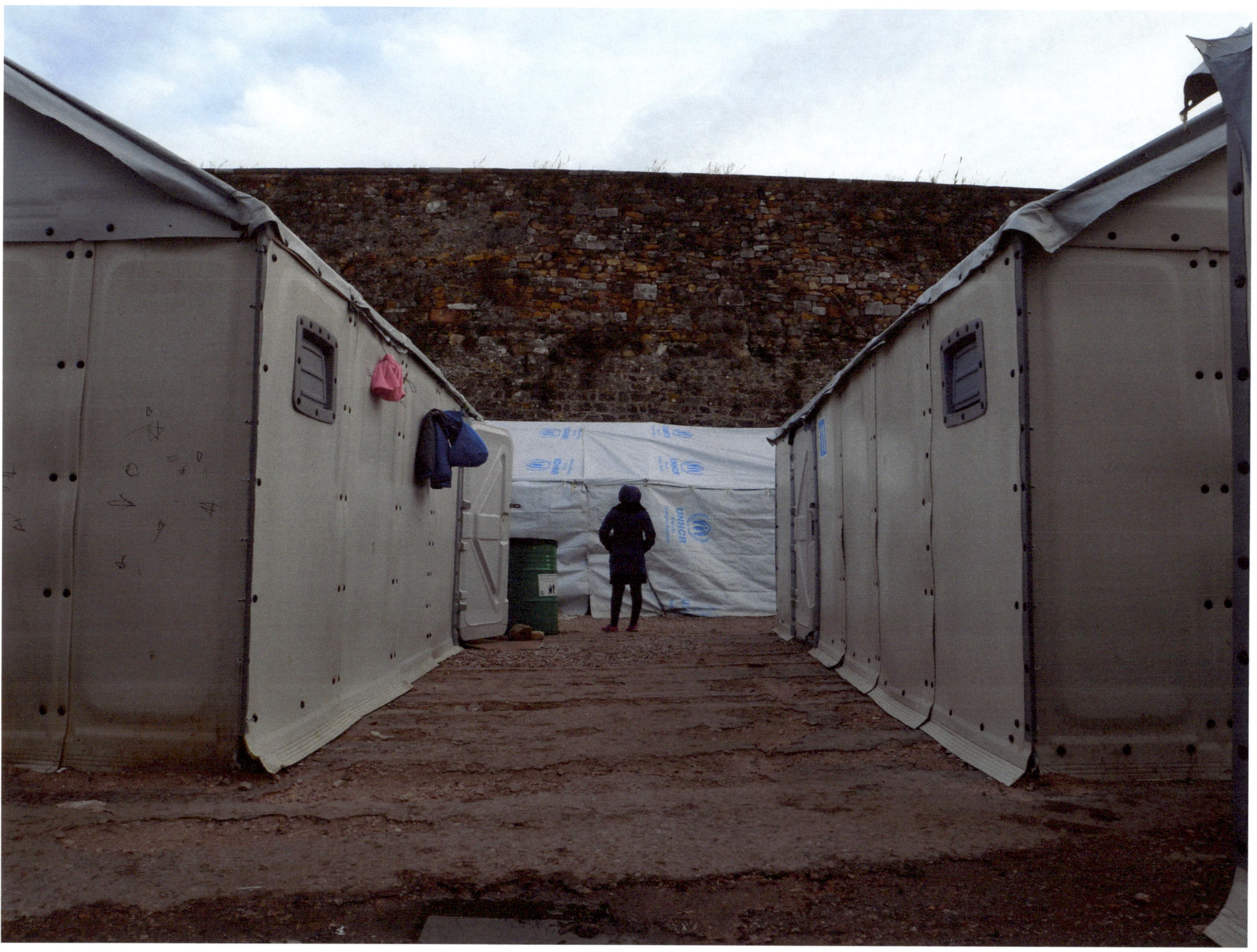

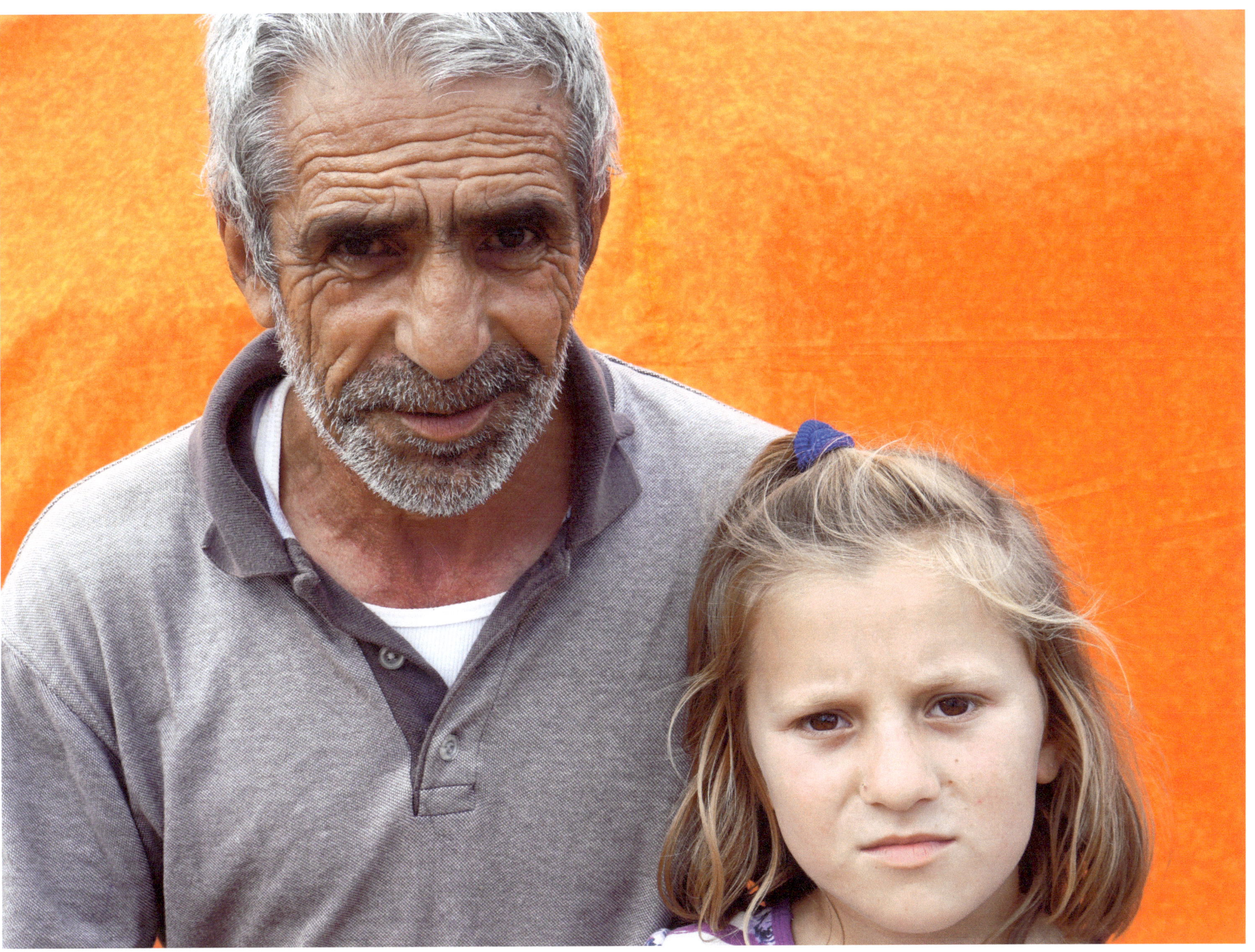

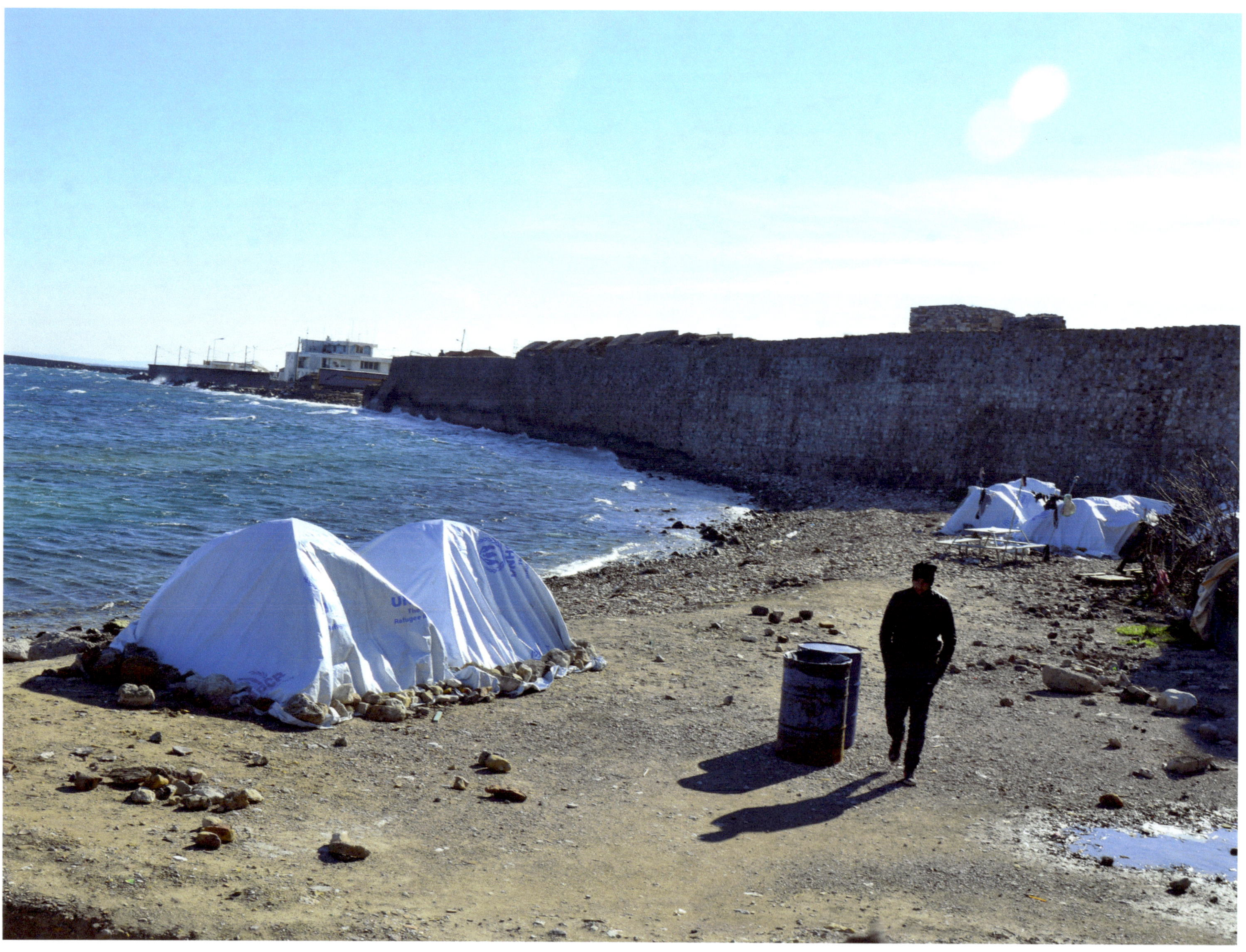

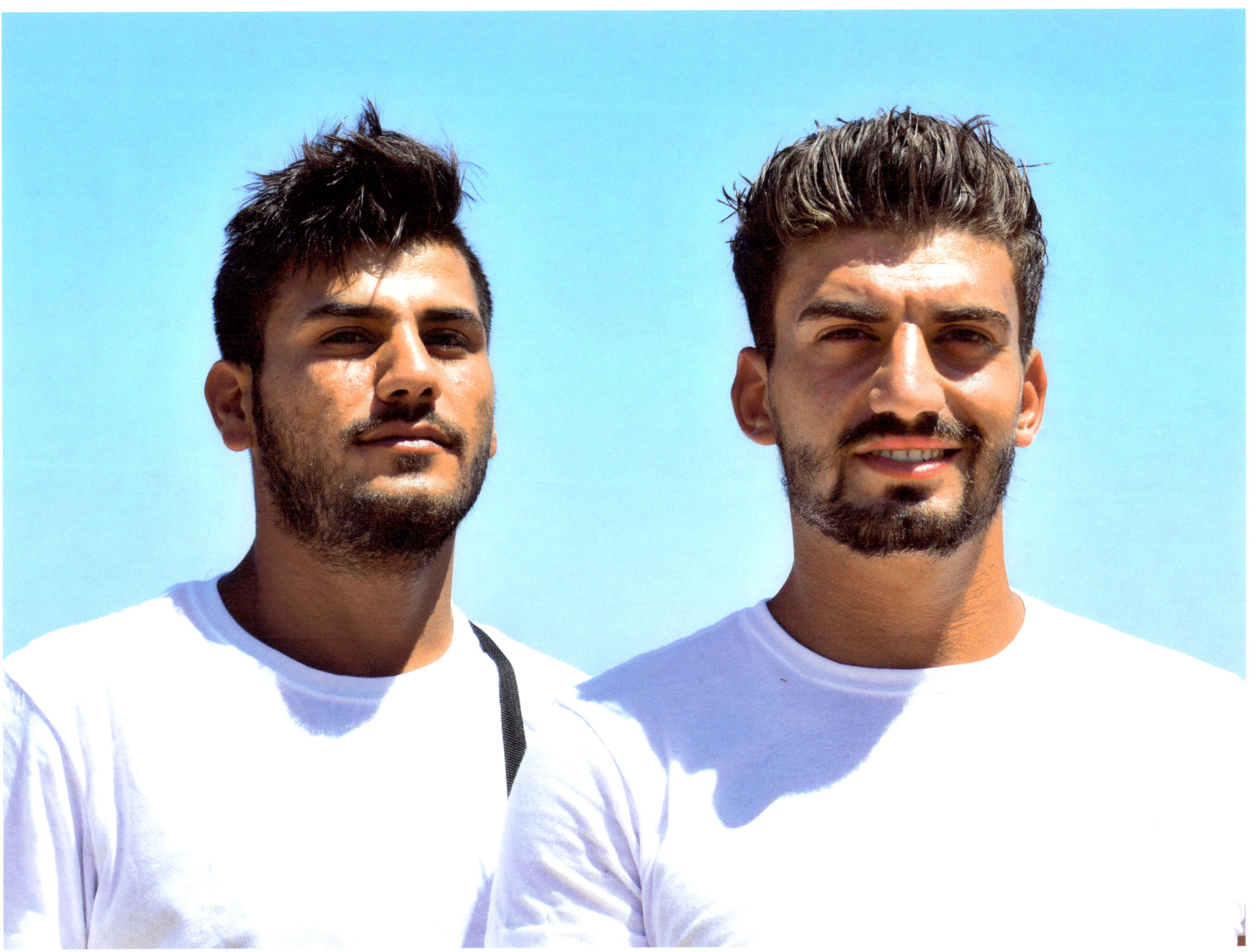

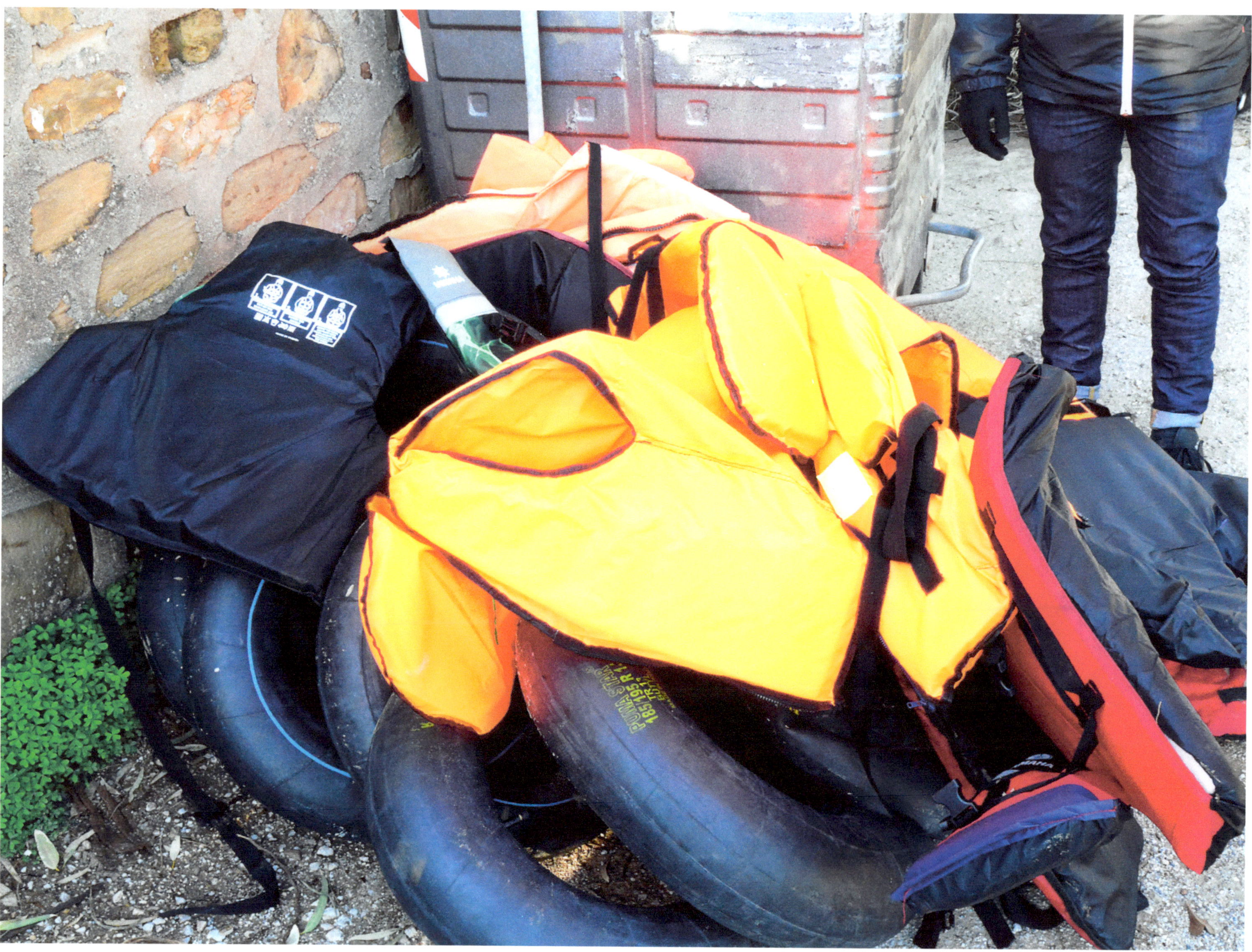

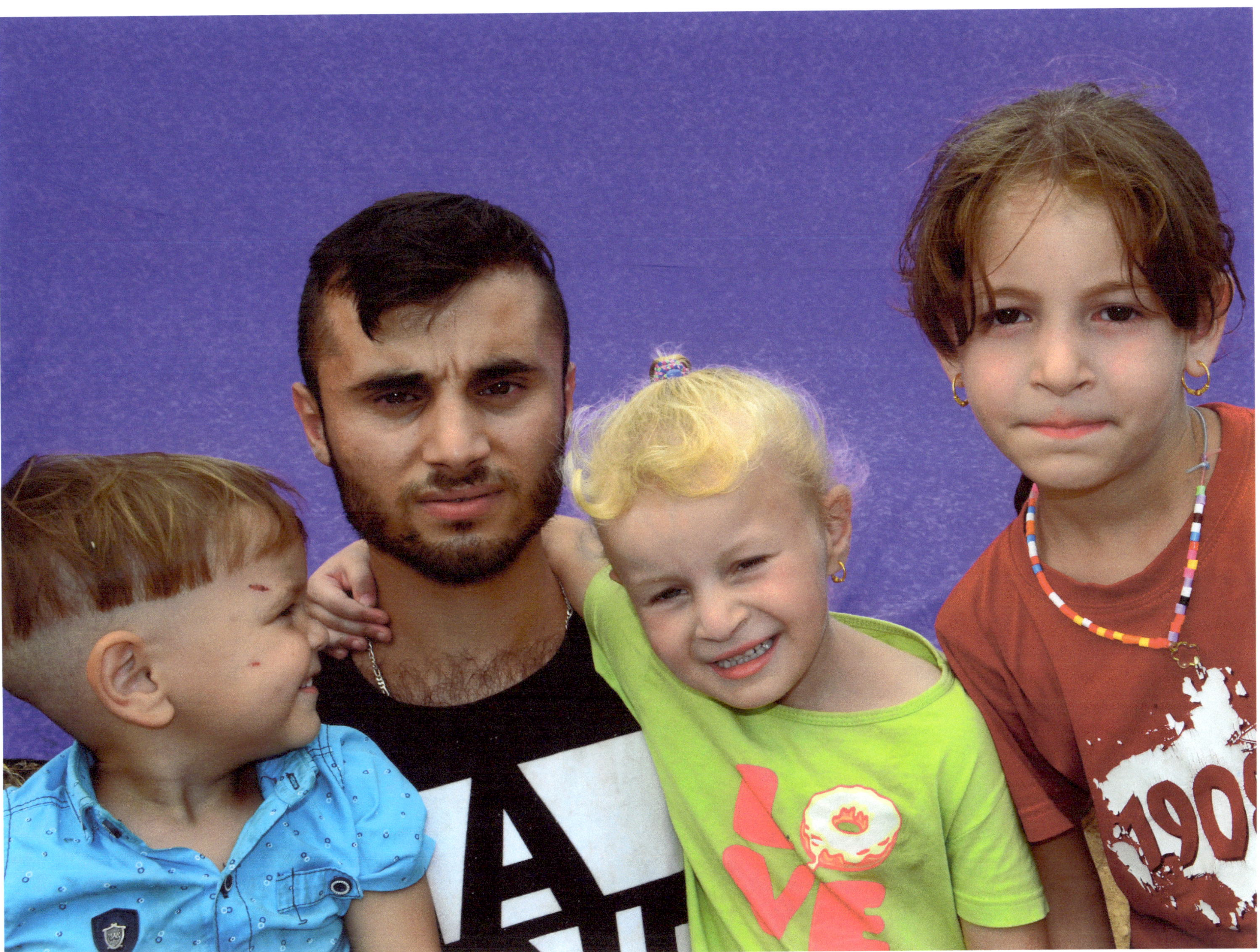

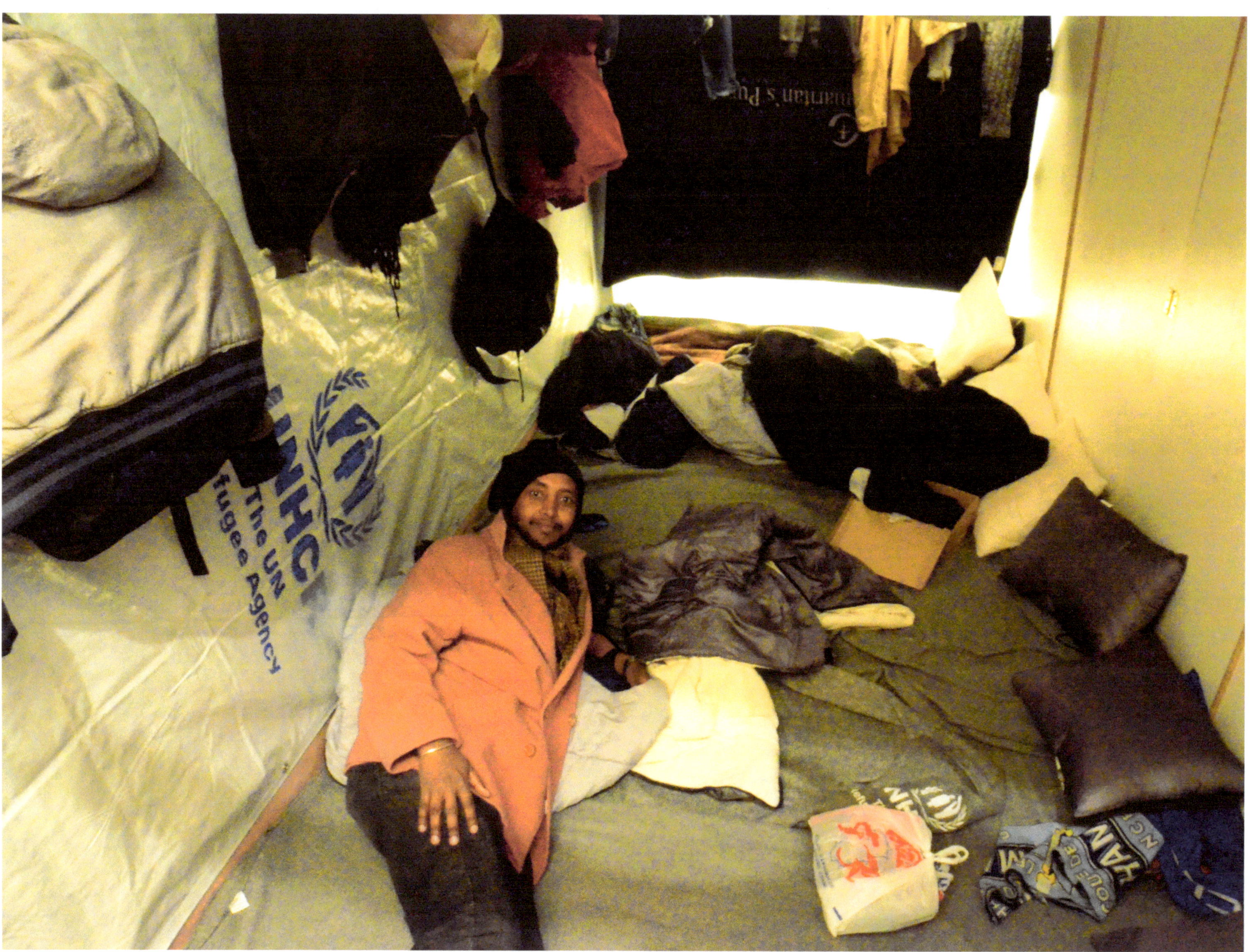

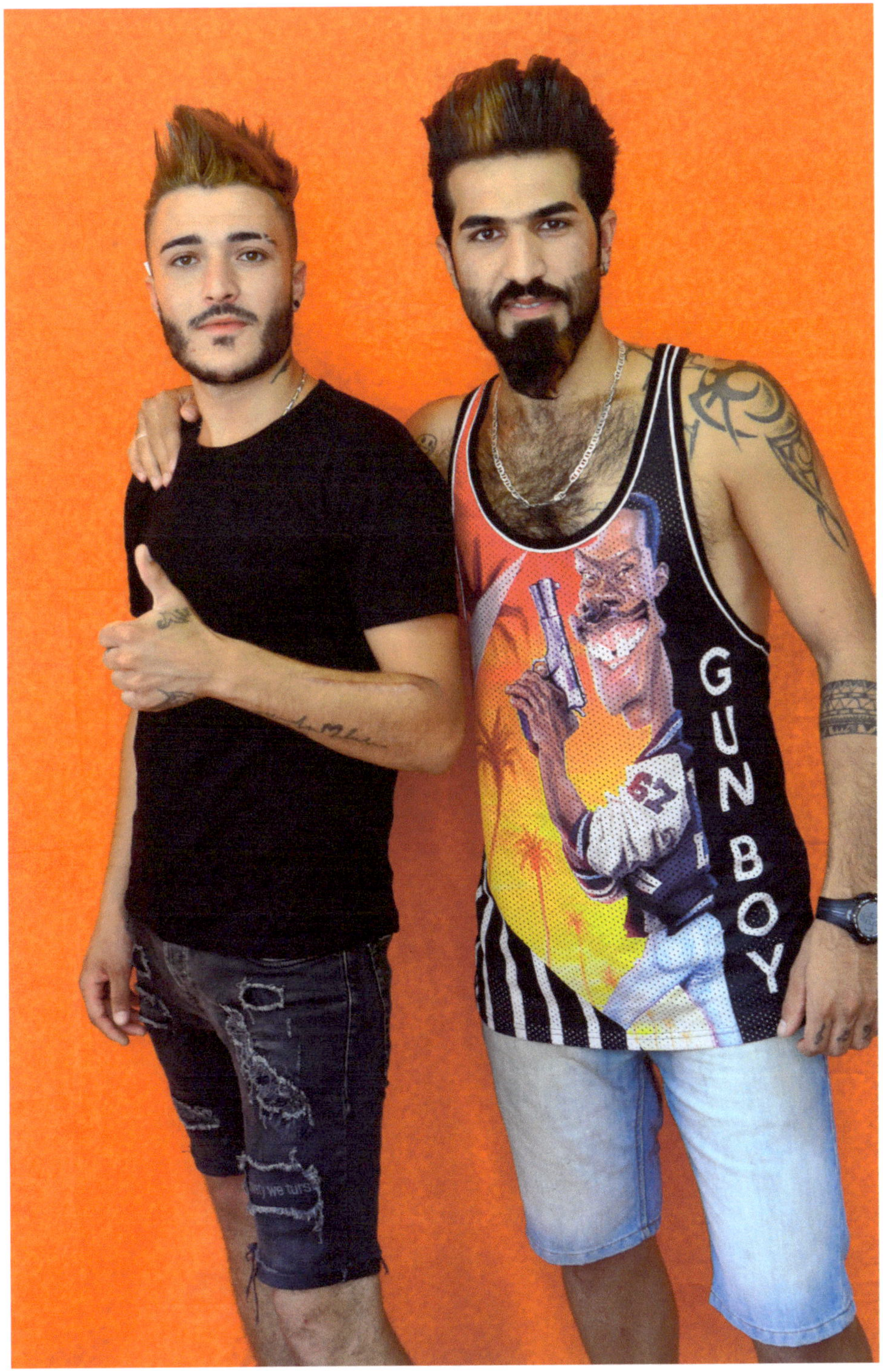

GUNBOY

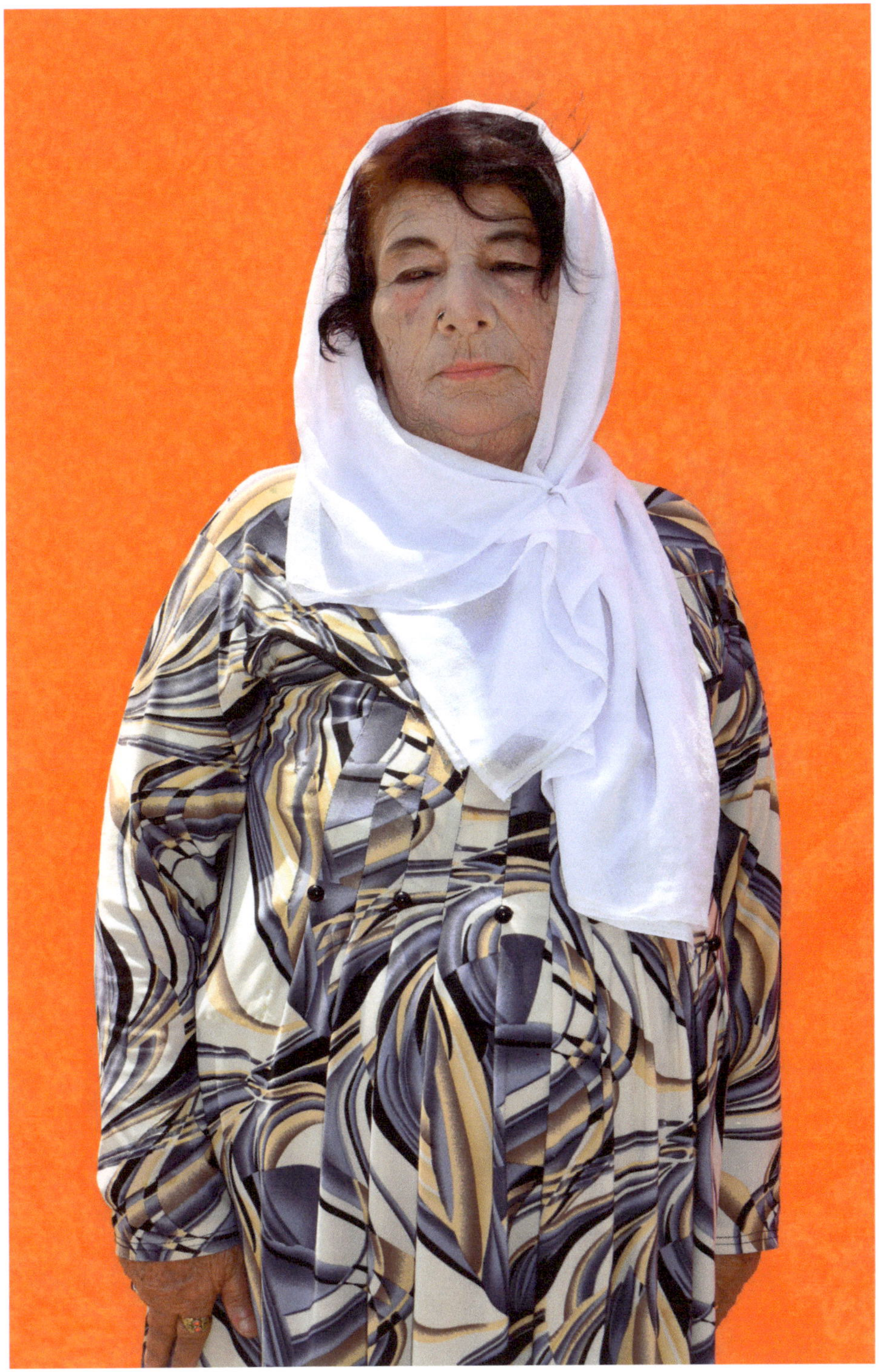

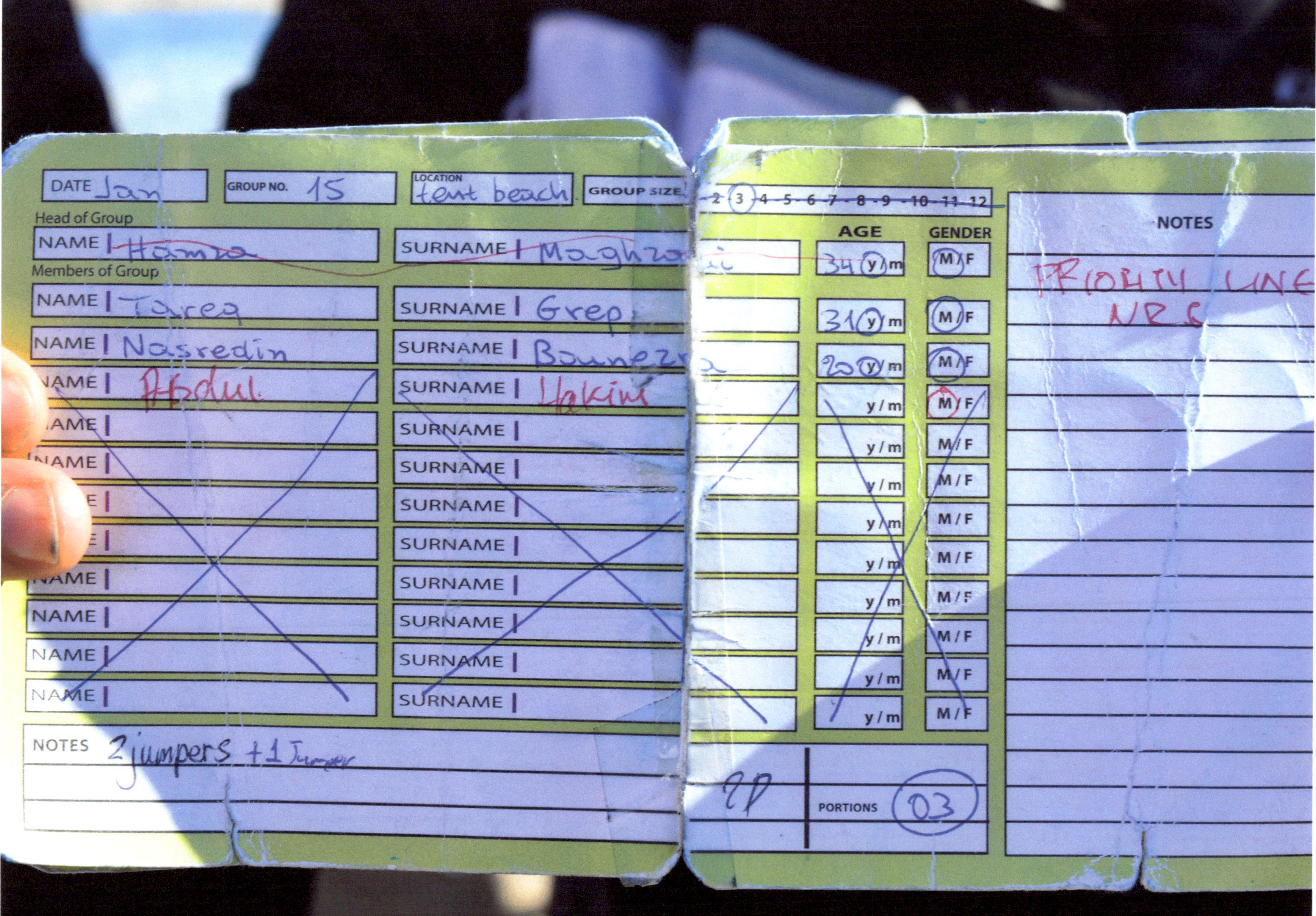

DATE Jan
GROUP NO. 15
LOCATION tent beach
GROUP SIZE
Head of Group
NAME Hamza
SURNAME Maghzaoui
Members of Group
NAME Tareg
SURNAME Grep
NAME Nasredin
SURNAME Bounezra
NAME Abdul
SURNAME Hakim
NAME
SURNAME
NAME
SURNAME
NAME
SURNAME
NAME
SURNAME
NAME
SURNAME
NAME
SURNAME
NAME
SURNAME
NAME
SURNAME
NOTES 2 jumpers + 1 Jumper
2 3 4 5 6 7 8 9 10 11 12
AGE GENDER
34 y / m M / F
31 y / m M / F
20 y / m M / F
y / m M / F
y / m M / F
y / m M / F
y / m M / F
y / m M / F
y / m M / F
y / m M / F
y / m M / F
y / m M / F
PORTIONS 03
NOTES
PRIORITY LINE
NRC

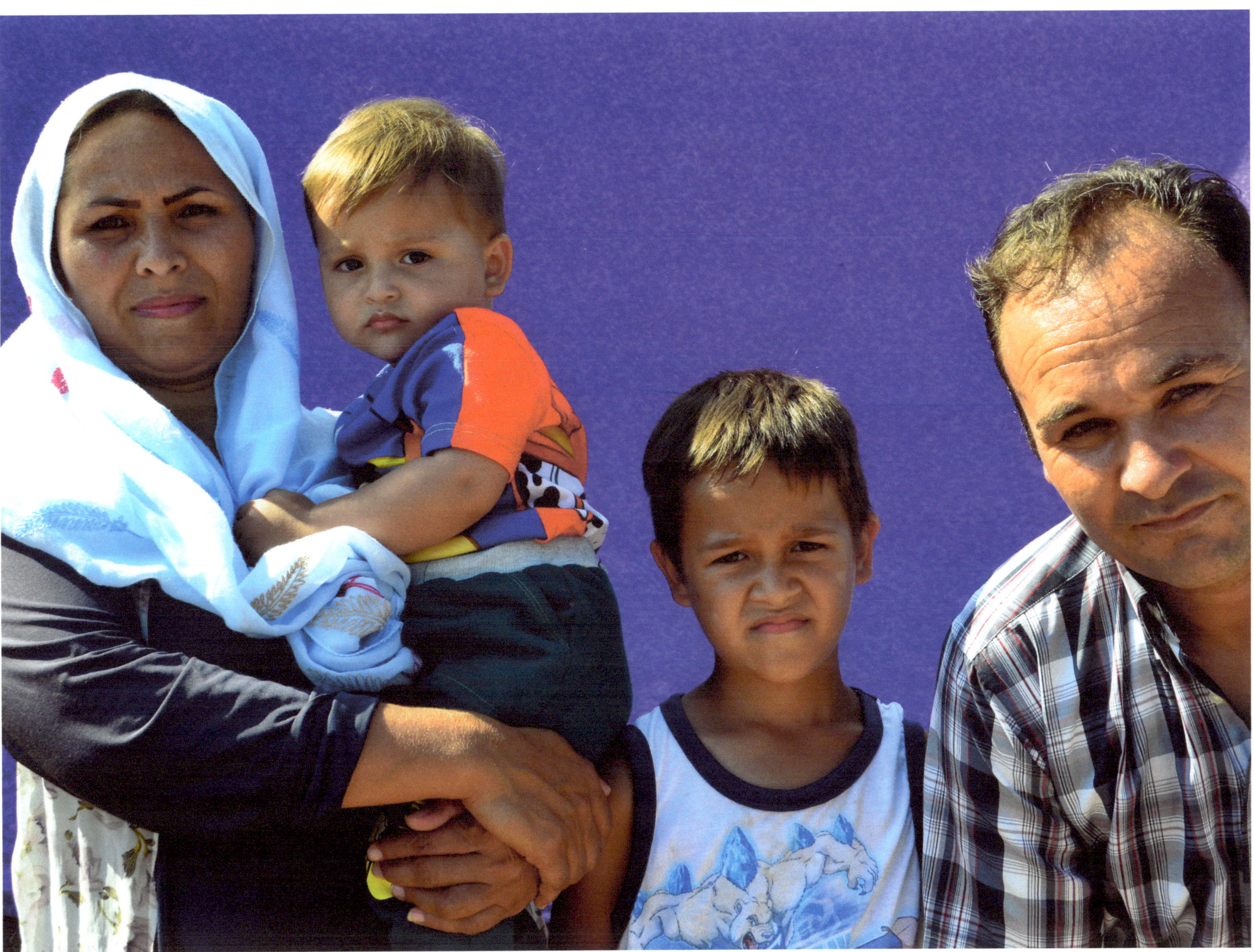

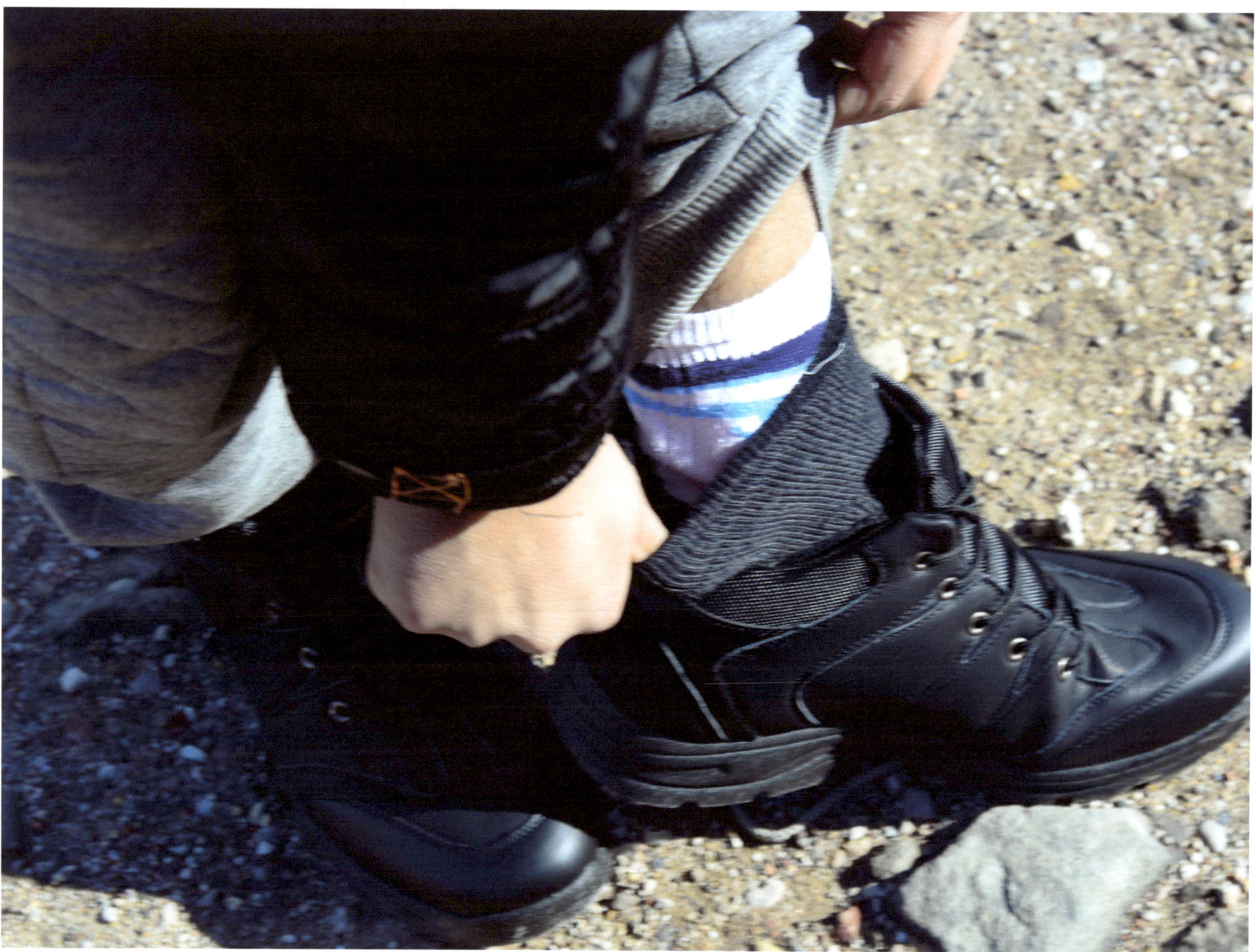

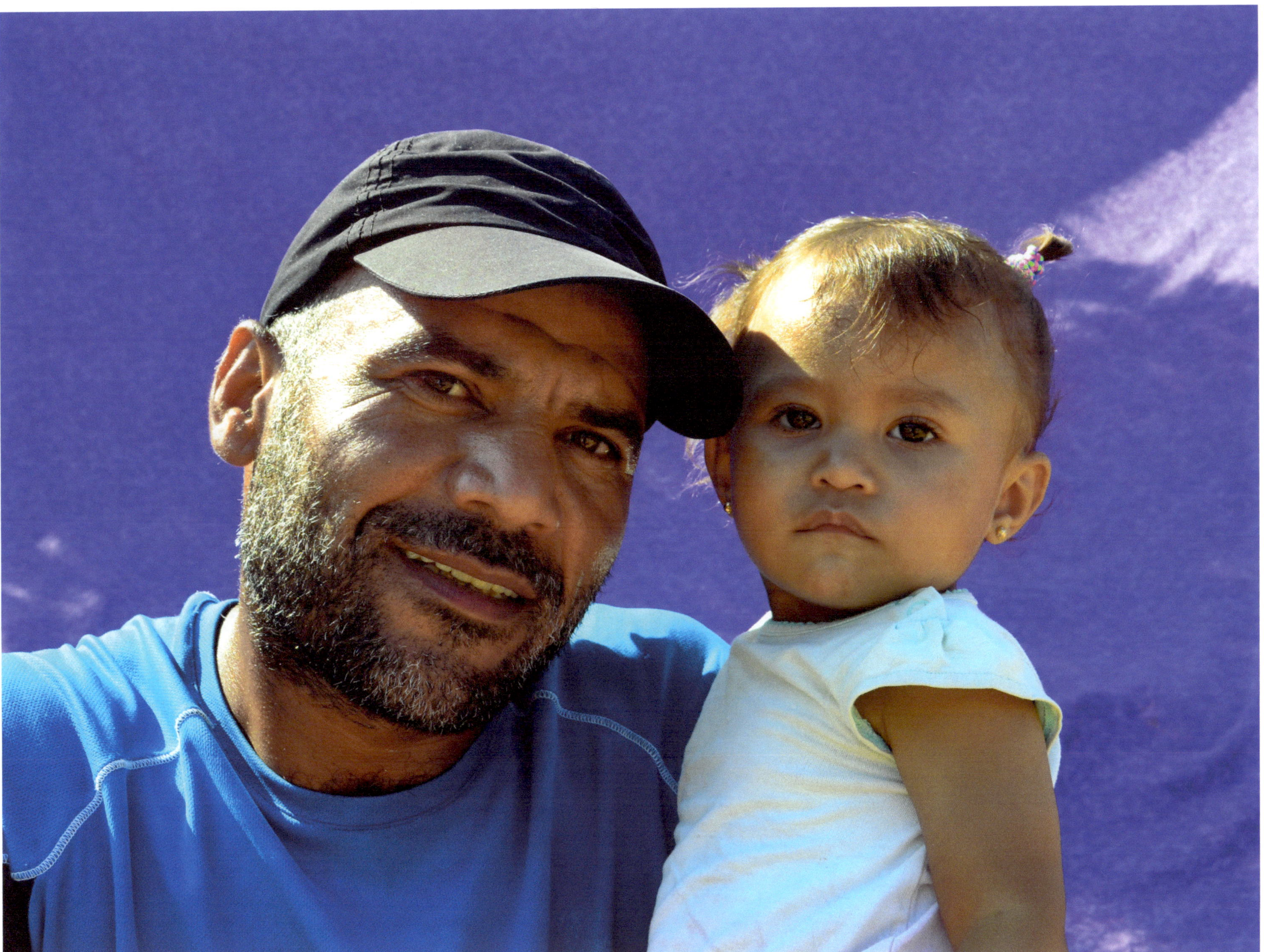

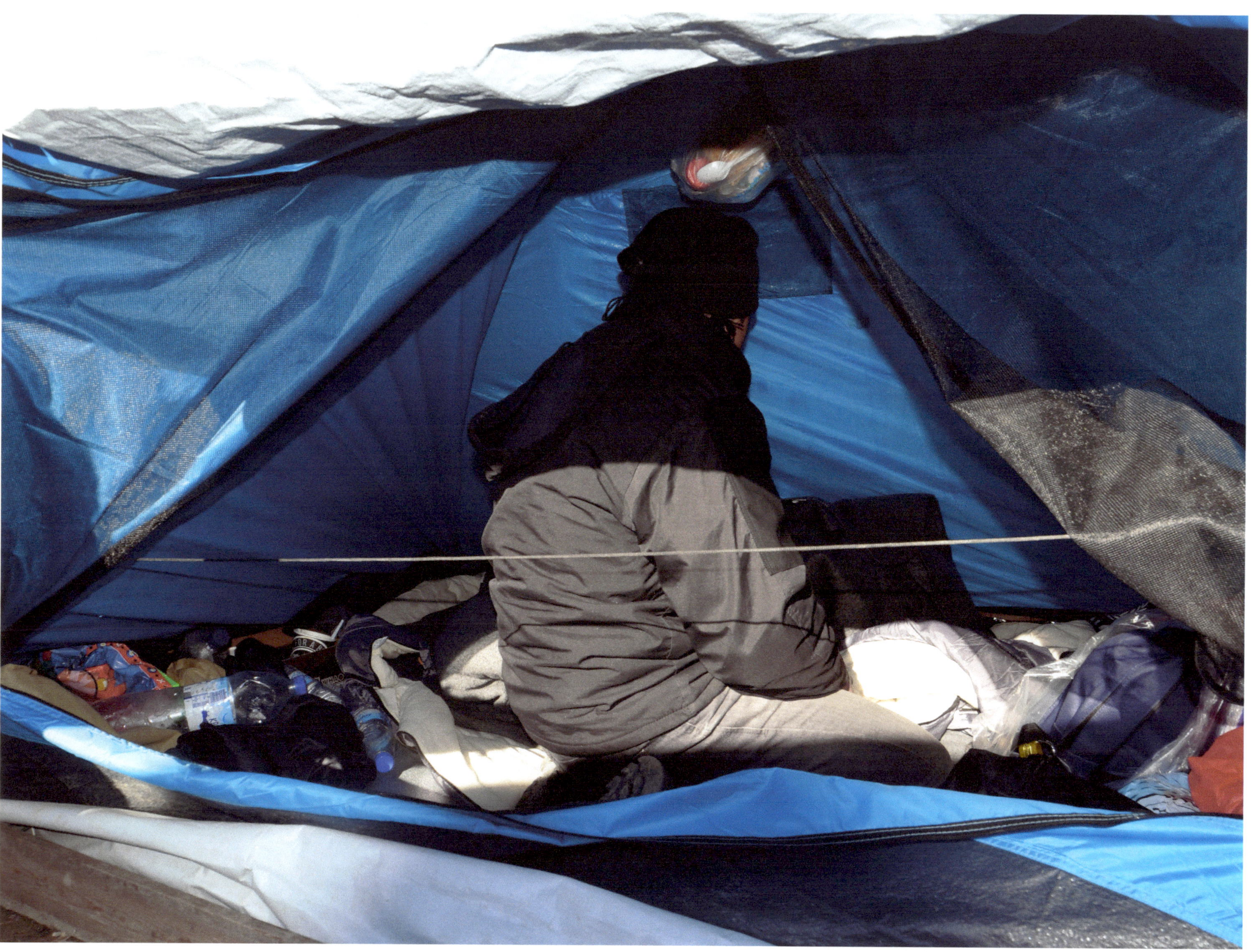

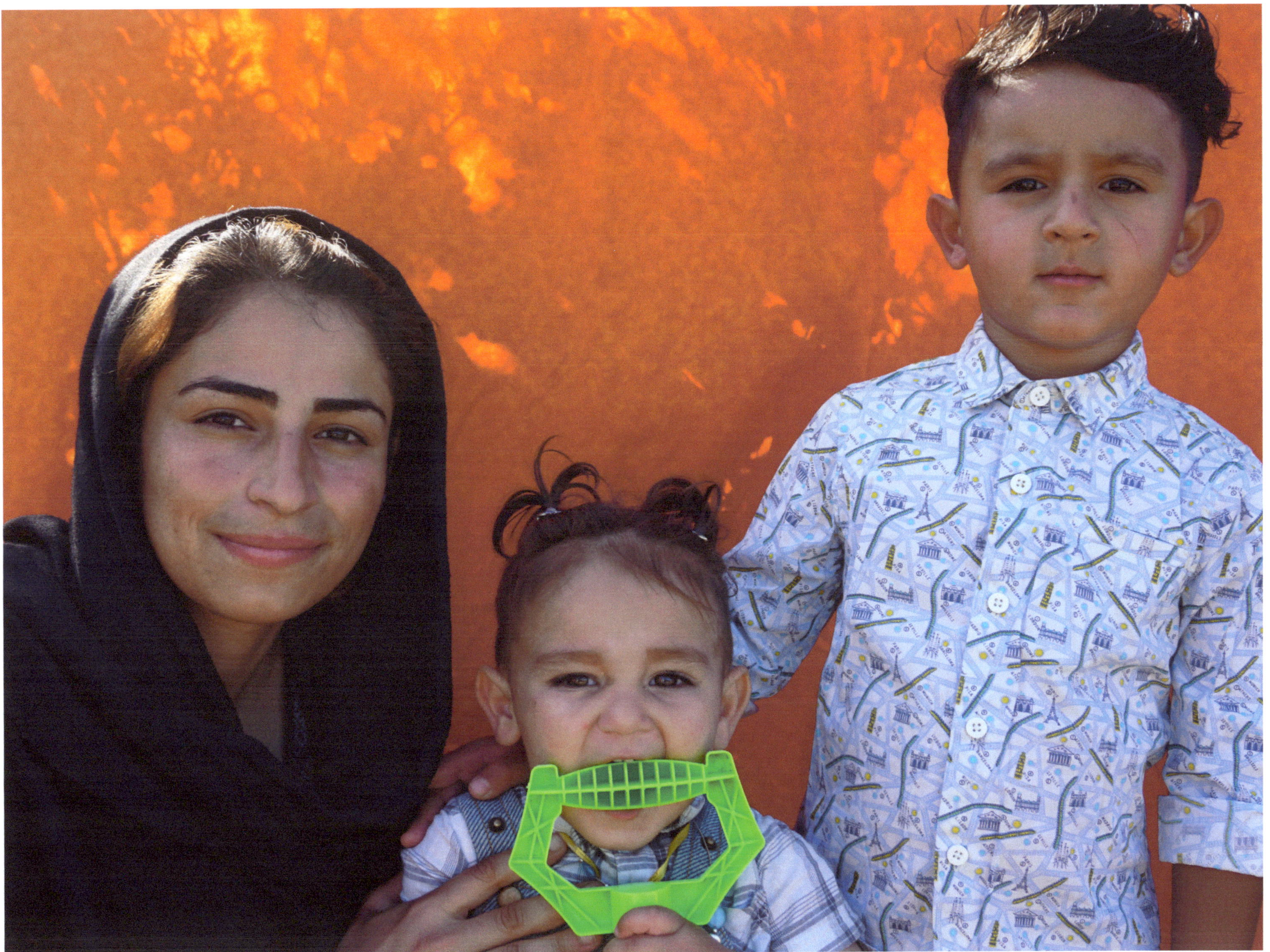

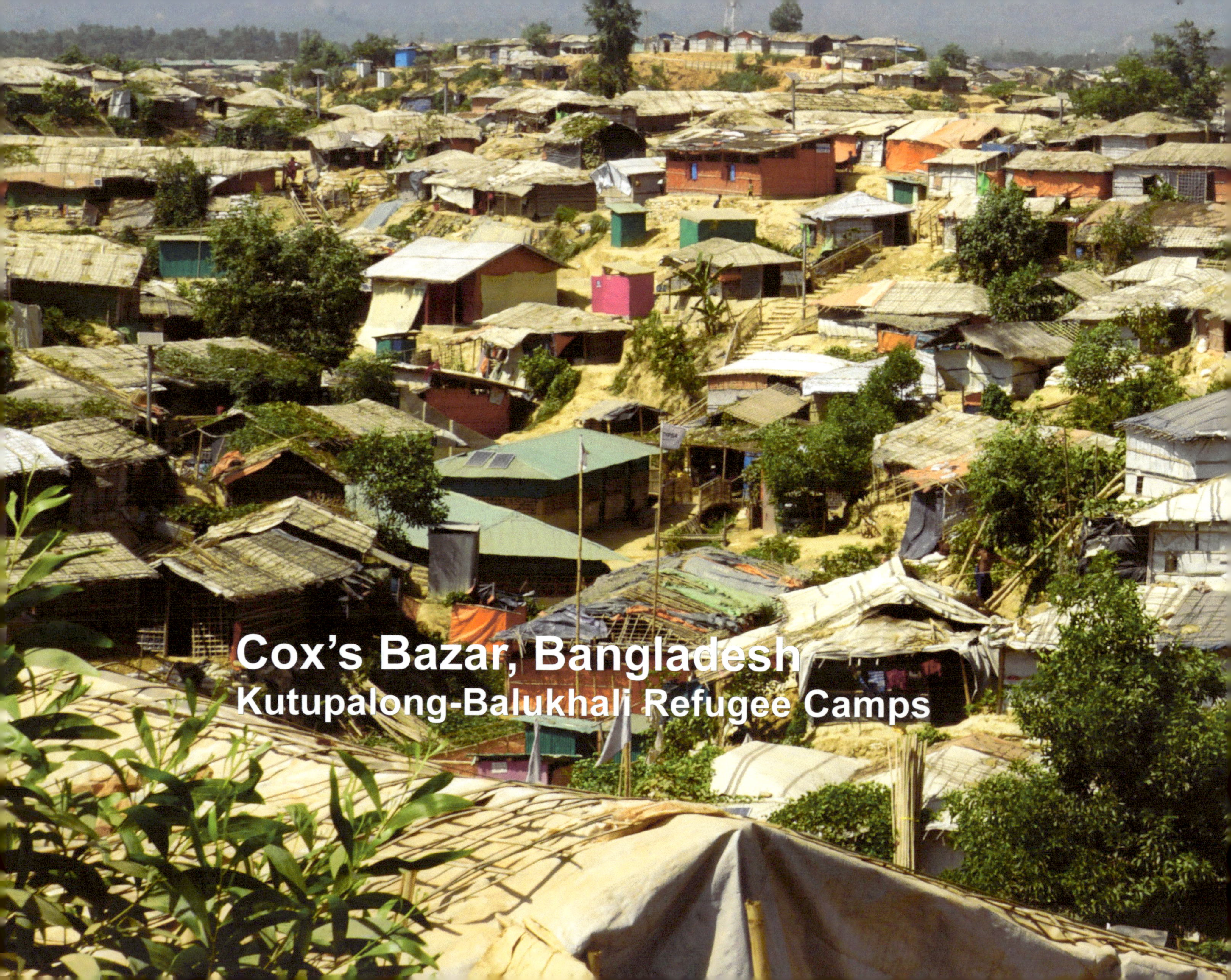

Cox's Bazar, Bangladesh
Kutupalong-Balukhali Refugee Camps

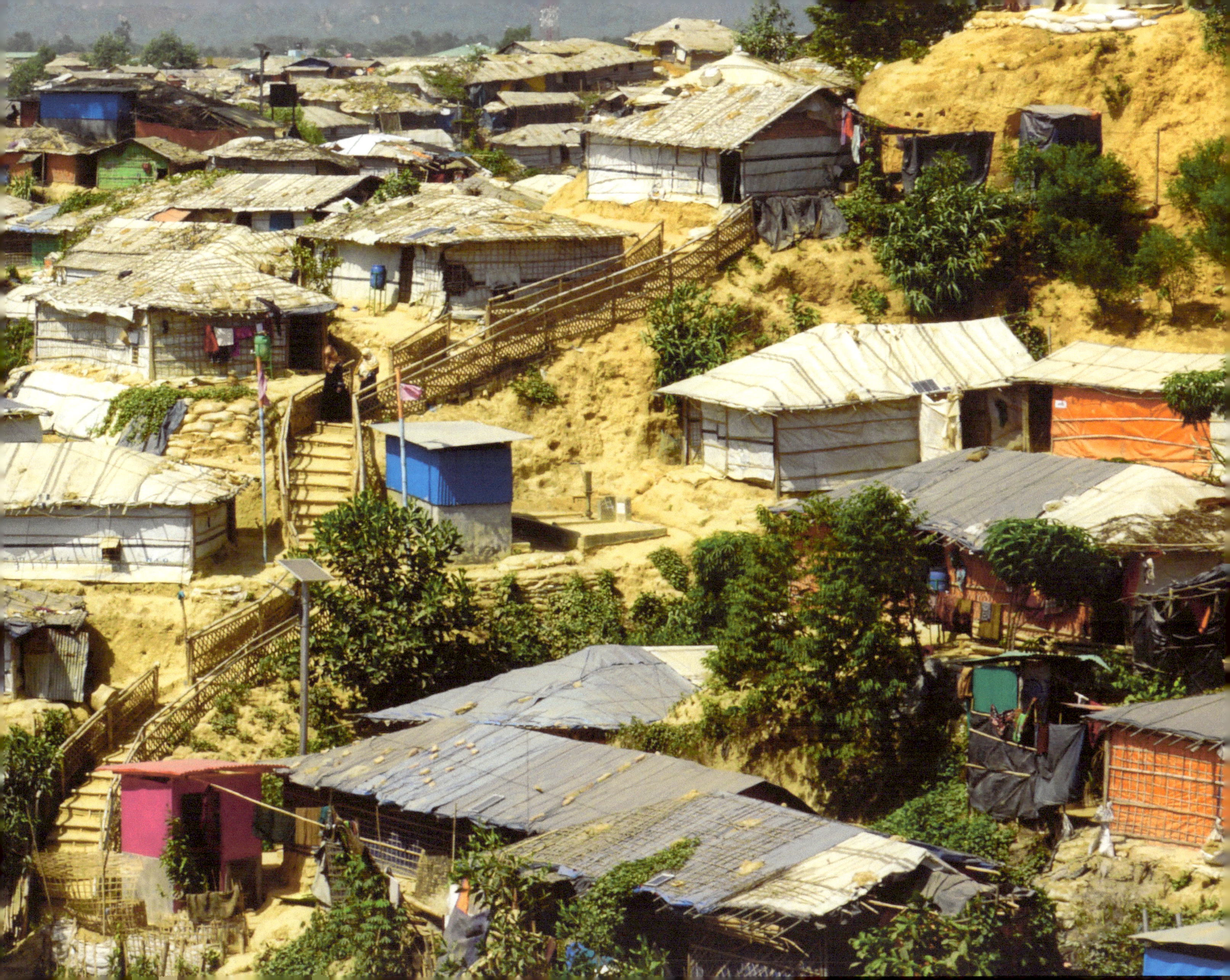

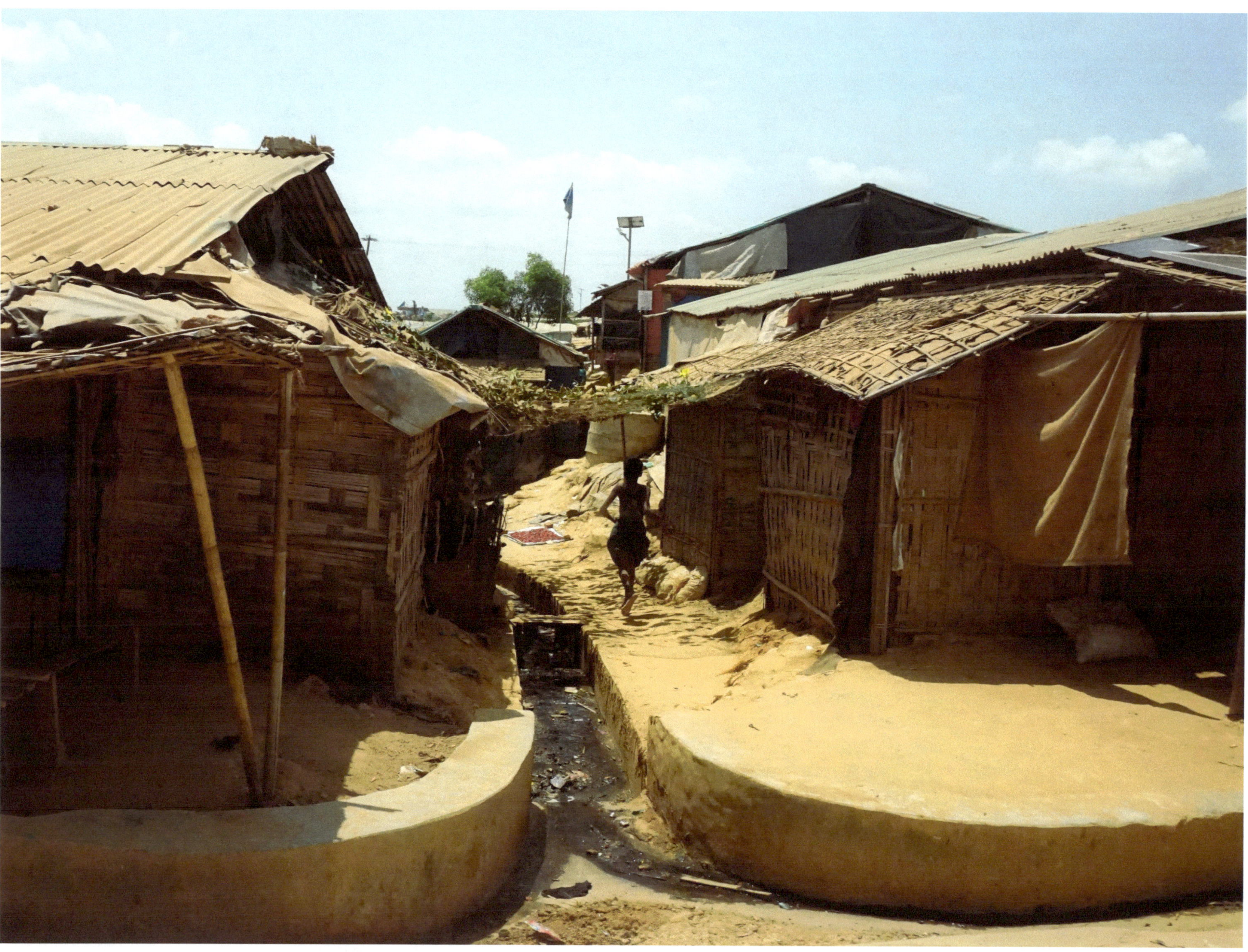

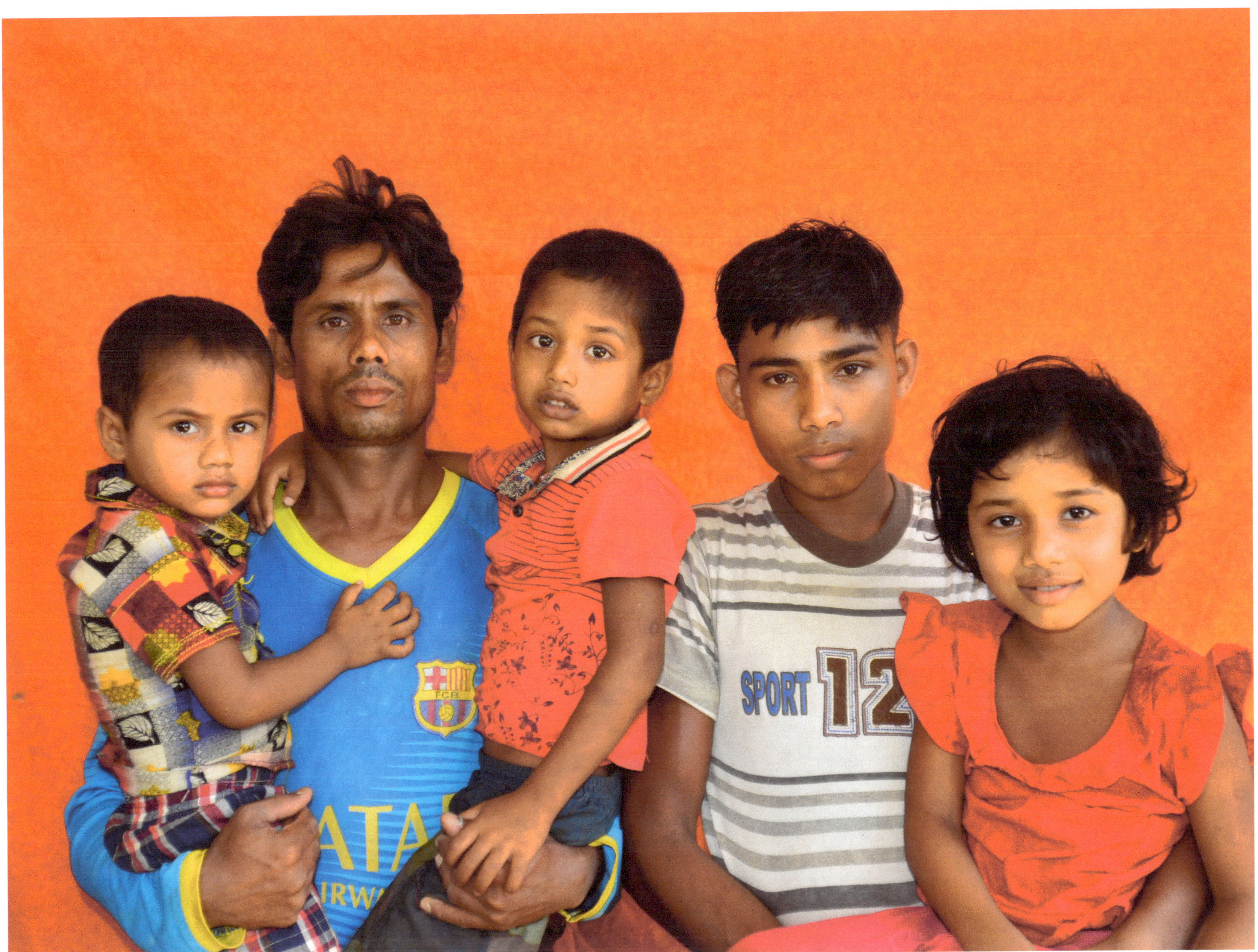

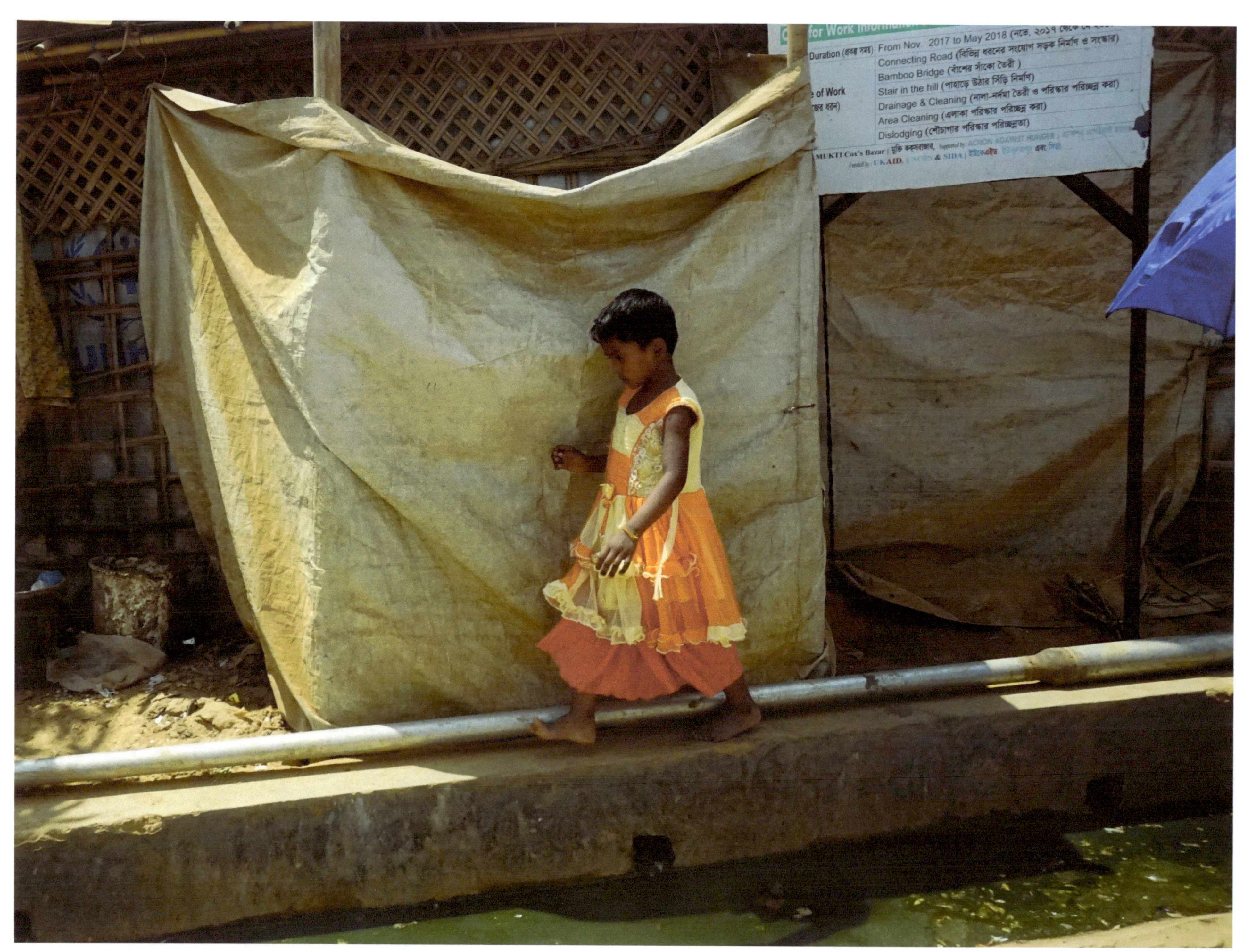
for Work Information
Duration (প্রকল্প সময়) From Nov. 2017 to May 2018 (নভে. ২০১৭ থেকে মে ২০১৮)
Connecting Road (বিভিন্ন ধরনের সংযোগ সড়ক নির্মাণ ও সংস্কার)
Bamboo Bridge (বাঁশের সাঁকো তৈরী)
Stair in the hill (পাহাড়ে উঠার সিঁড়ি নির্মাণ)
Drainage & Cleaning (নালা-নর্দমা তৈরী ও পরিস্কার পরিচ্ছন্ন করা)
Area Cleaning (এলাকা পরিস্কার পরিচ্ছন্ন করা)
Dislodging (শৌচাগার পরিস্কার পরিচ্ছন্নতা)
MUKTI Cox's Bazar | মুক্তি কক্সবাজার, Supported by ACTION AGAINST HUNGER
Funded by UKAID, UNOPS & SIDA | ইউকেএইড এবং সিডা

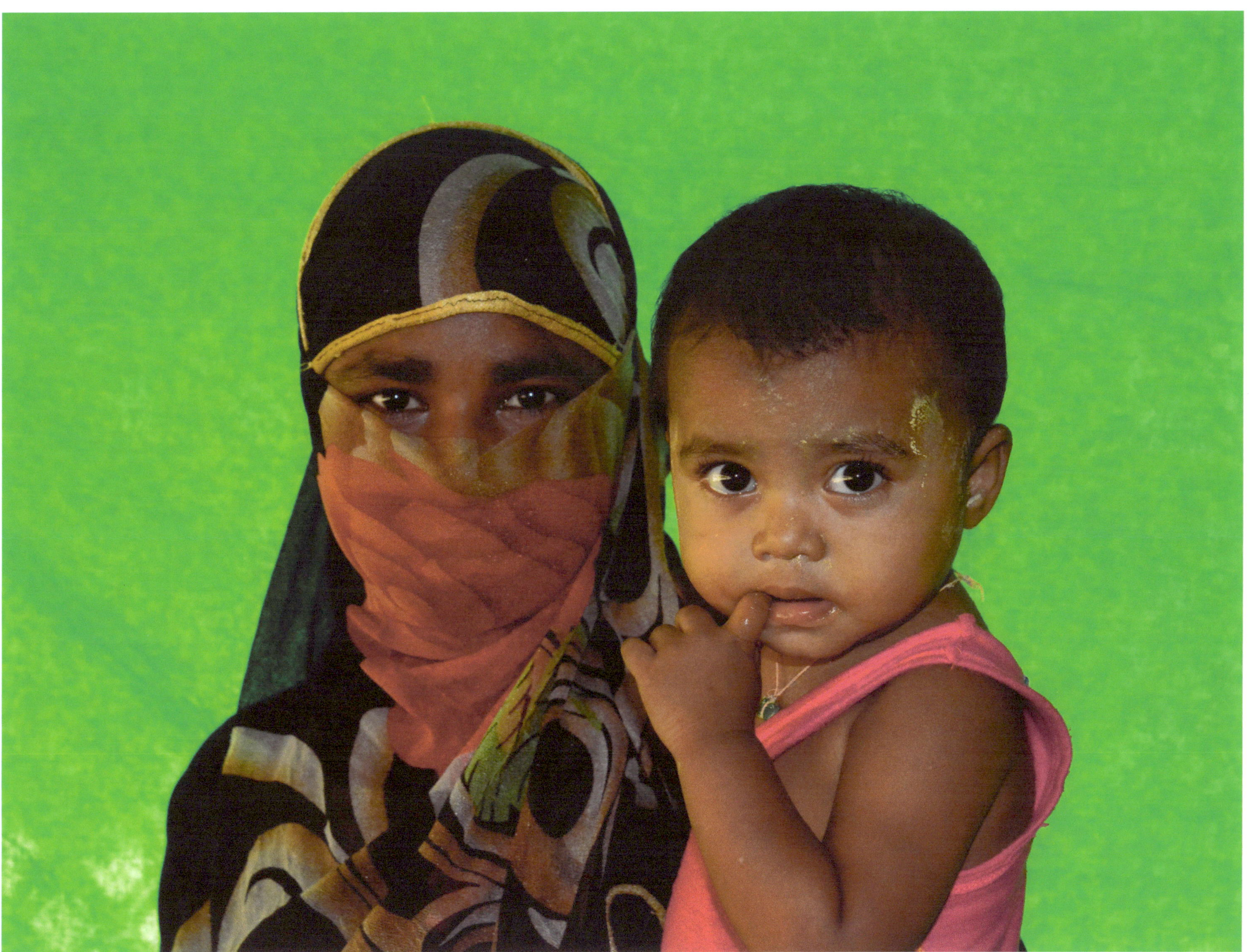

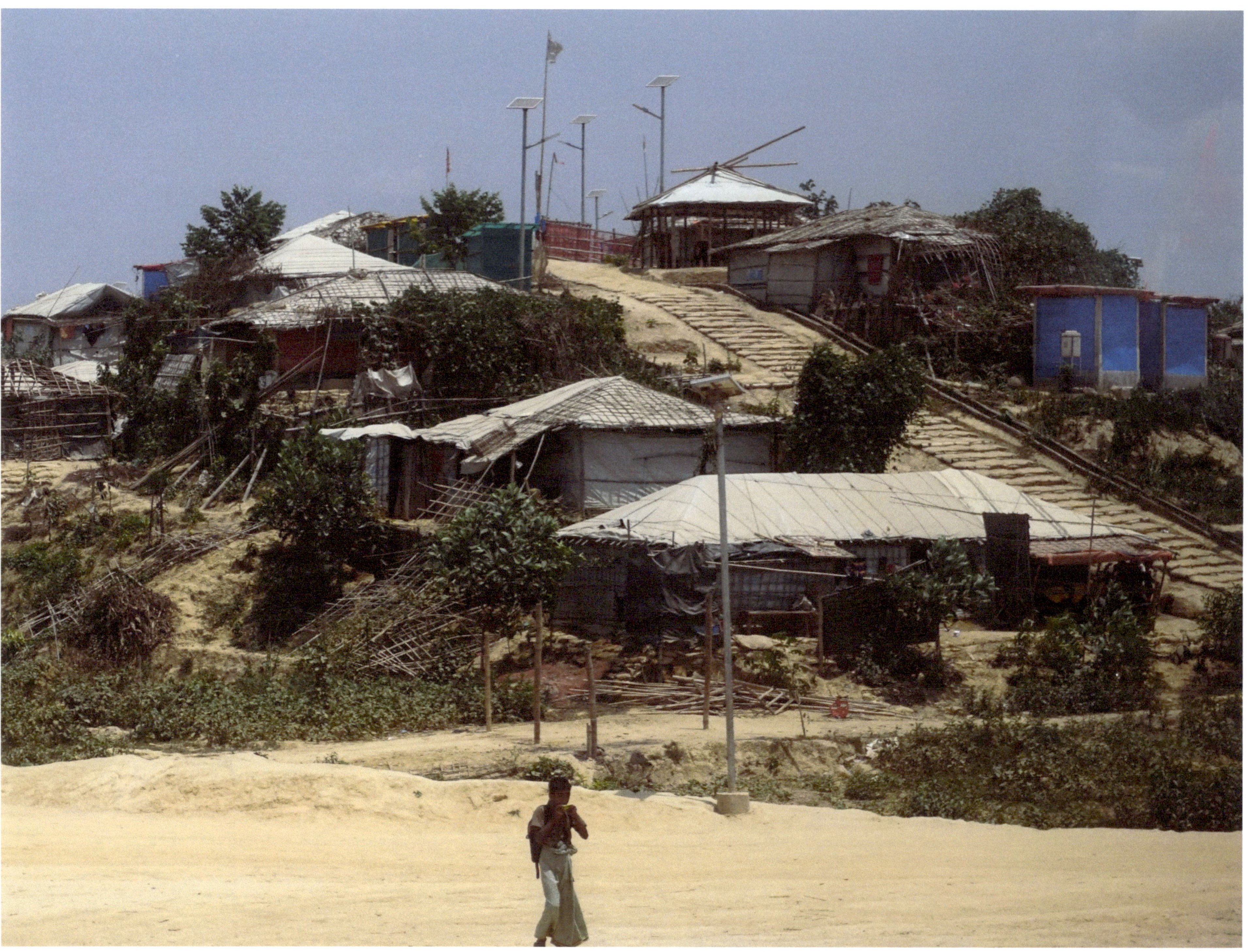

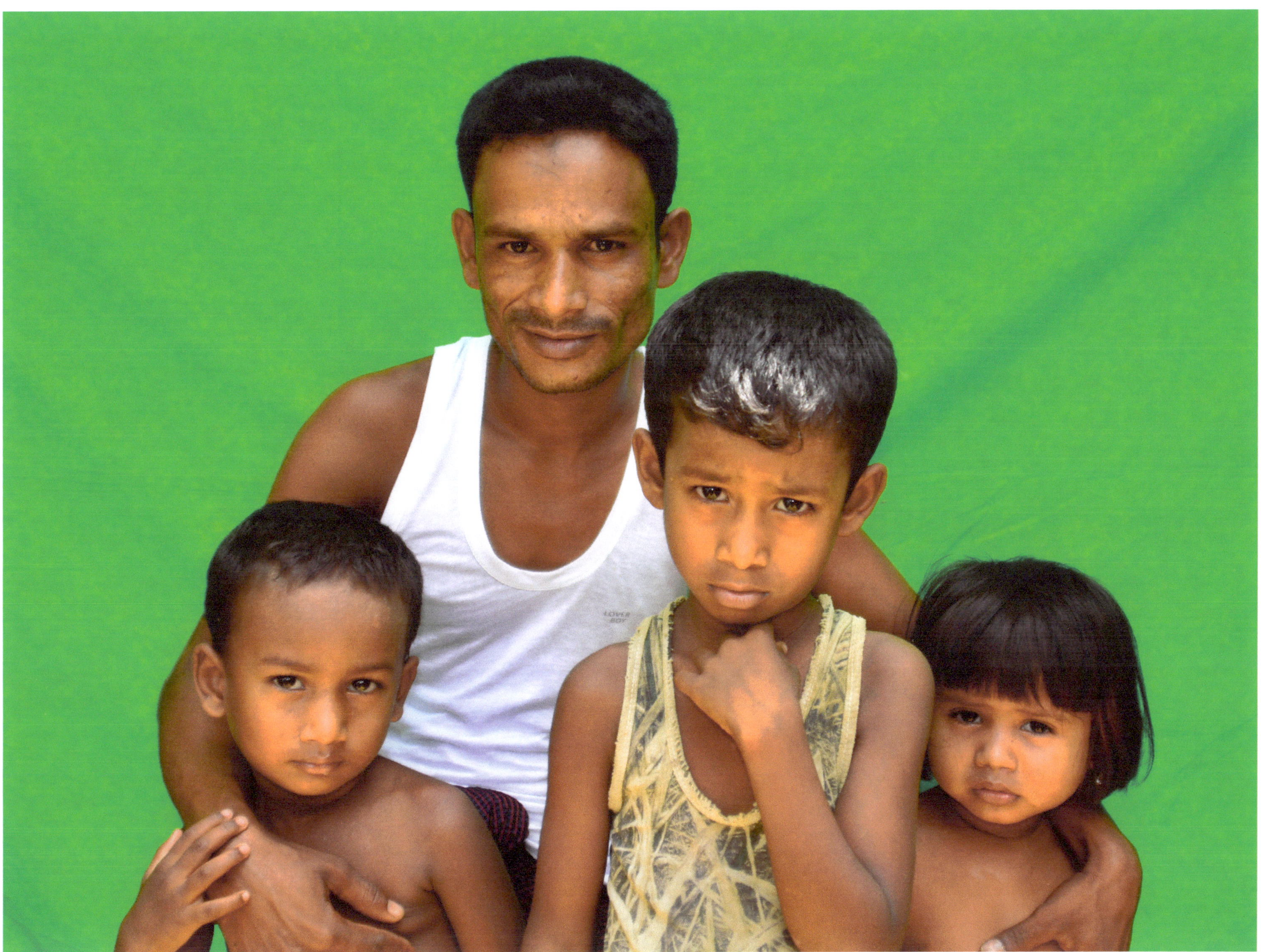

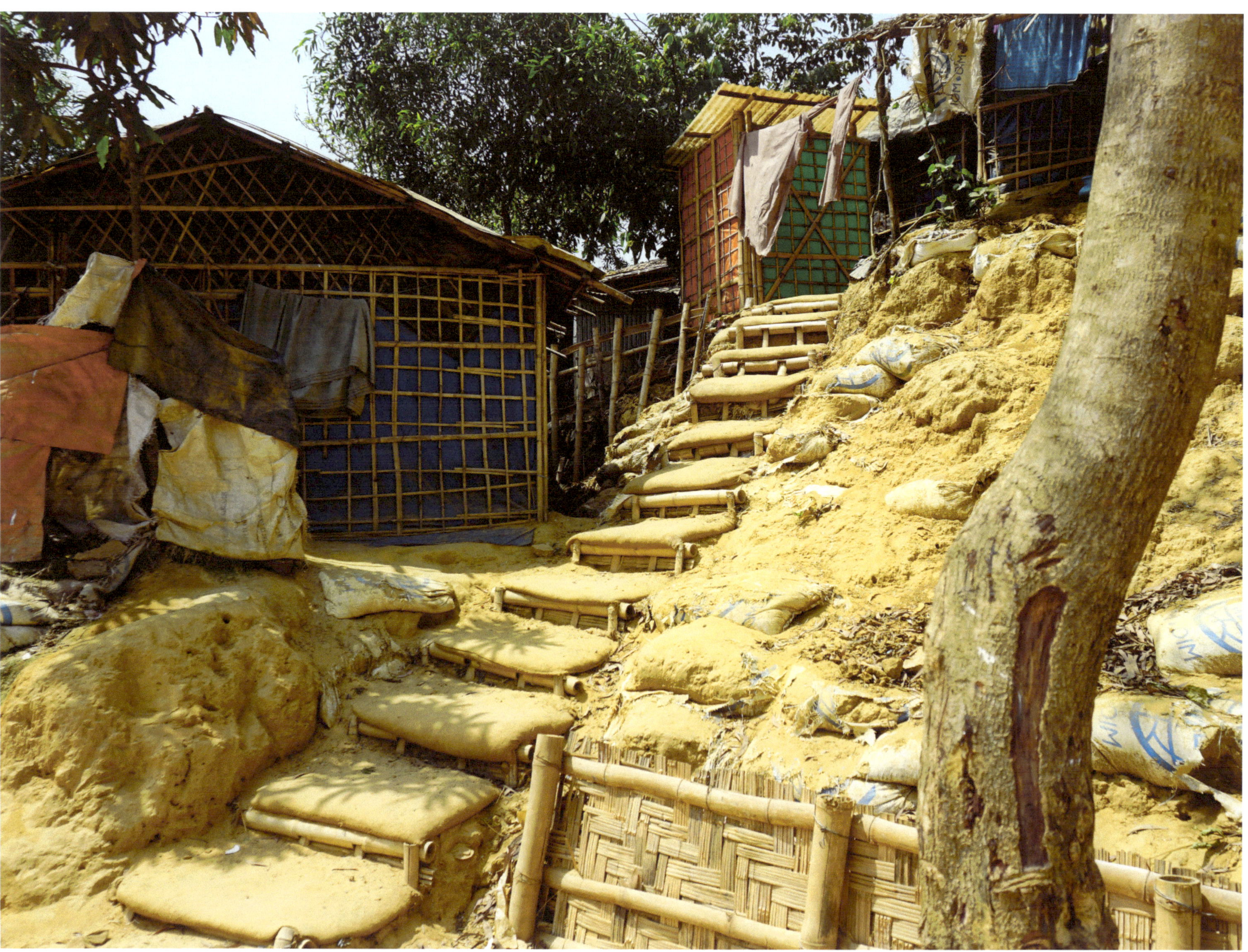

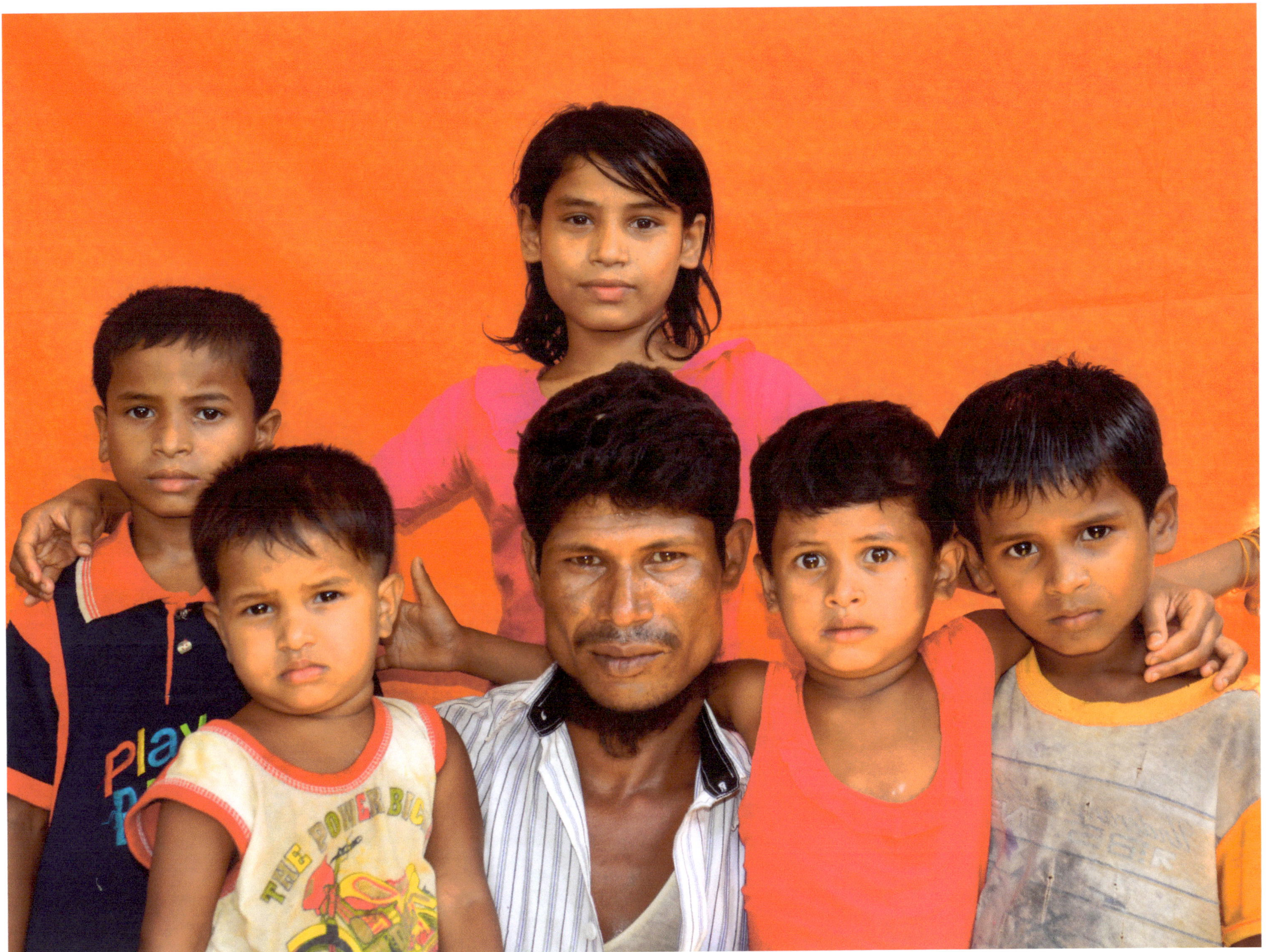

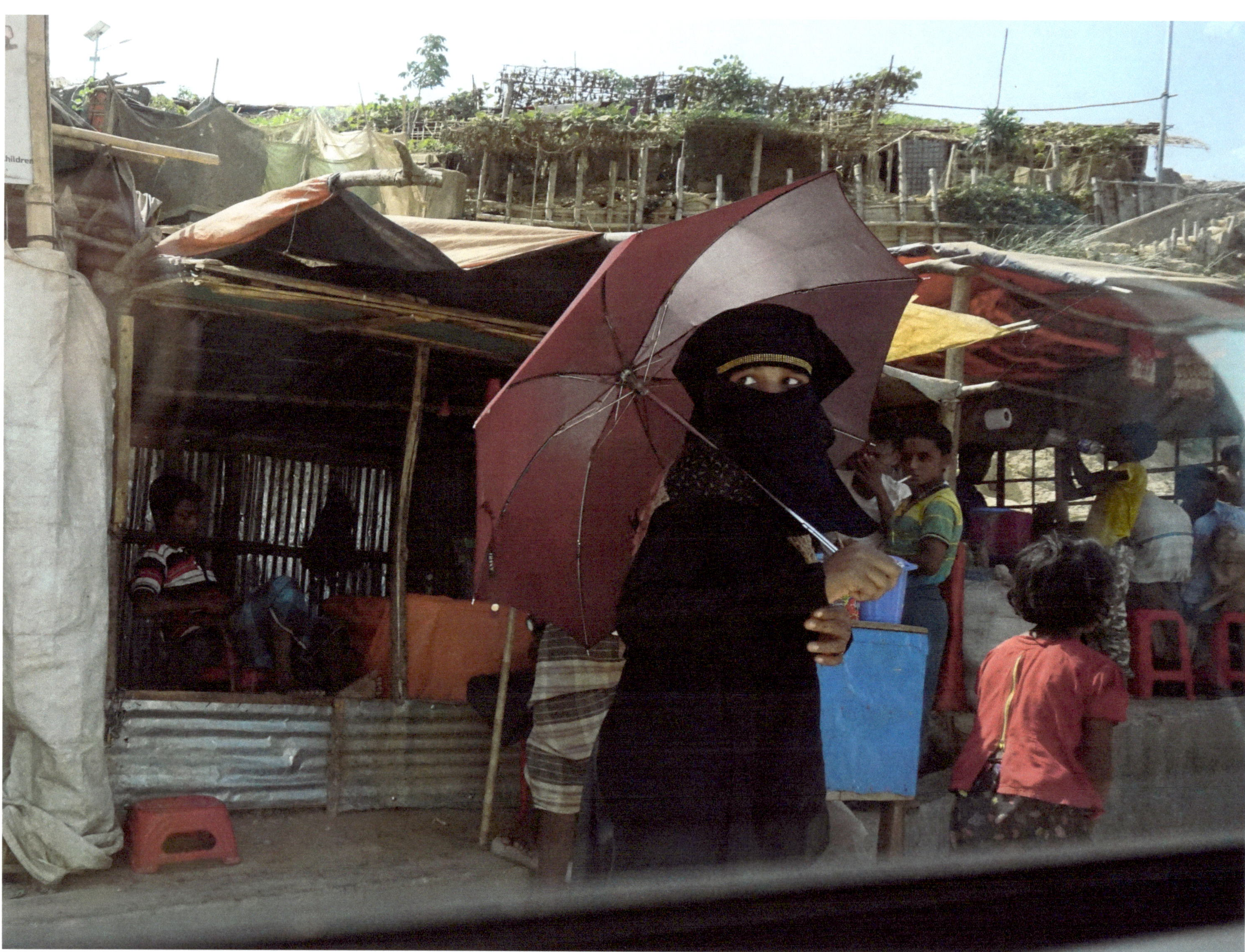

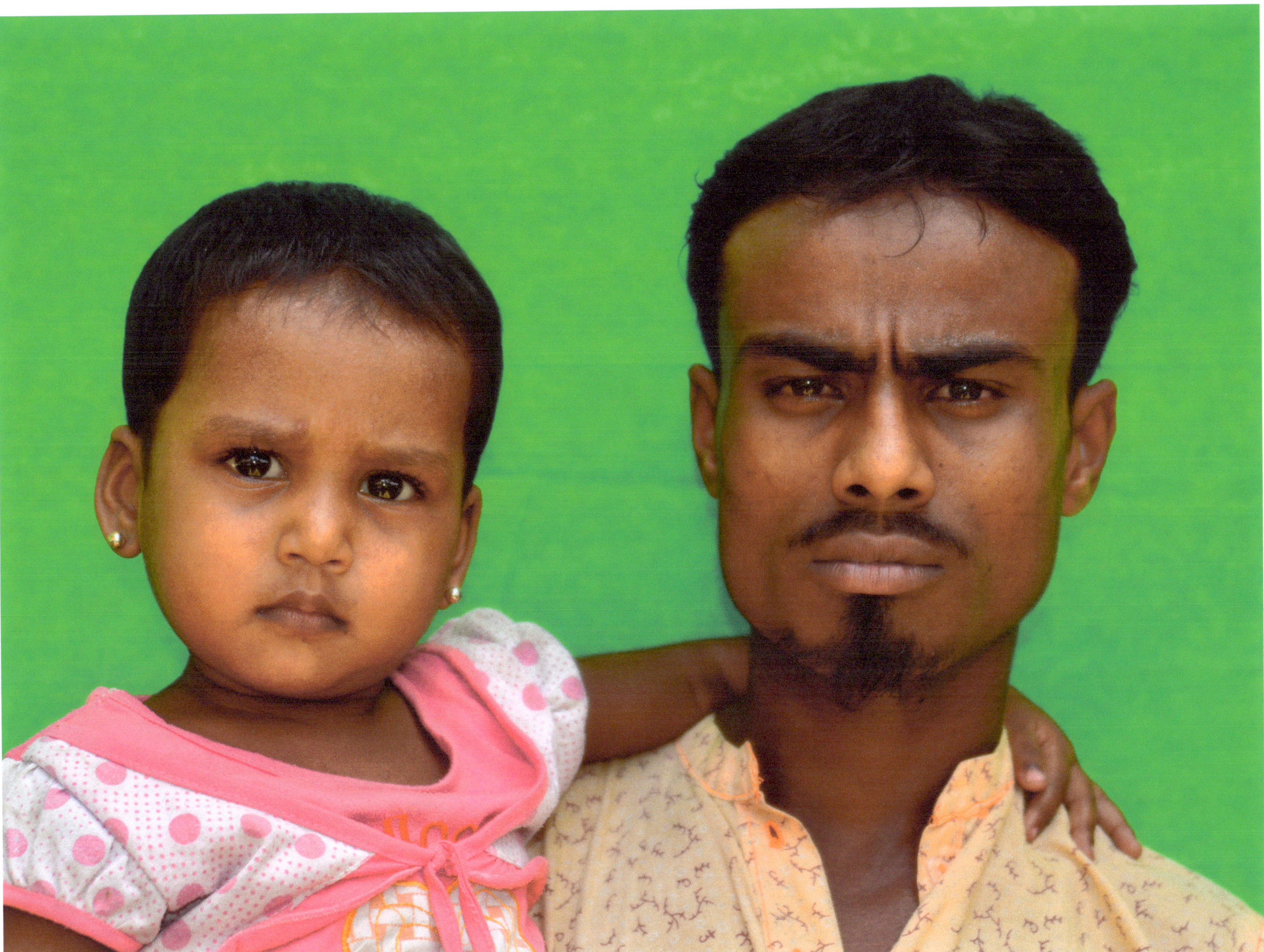

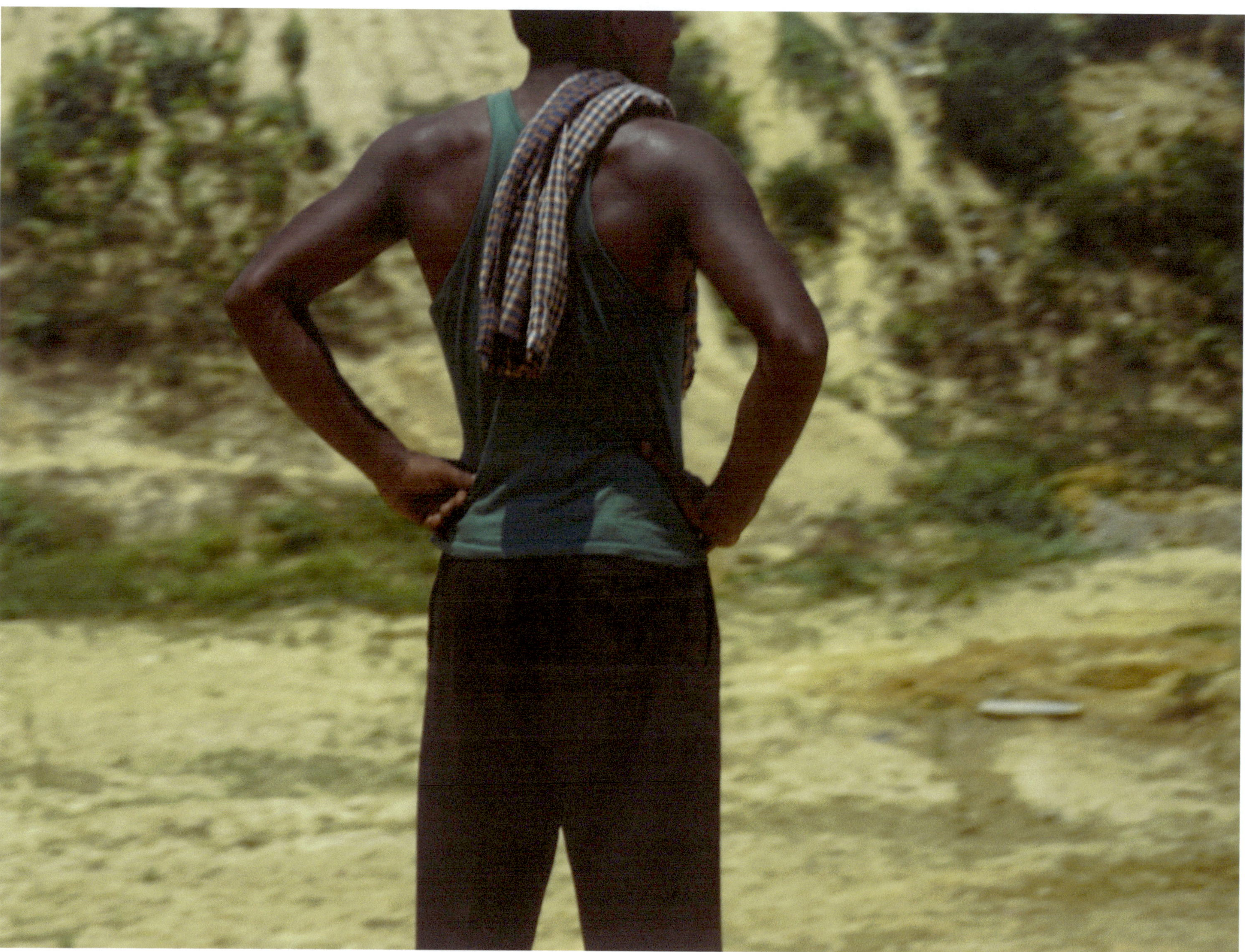

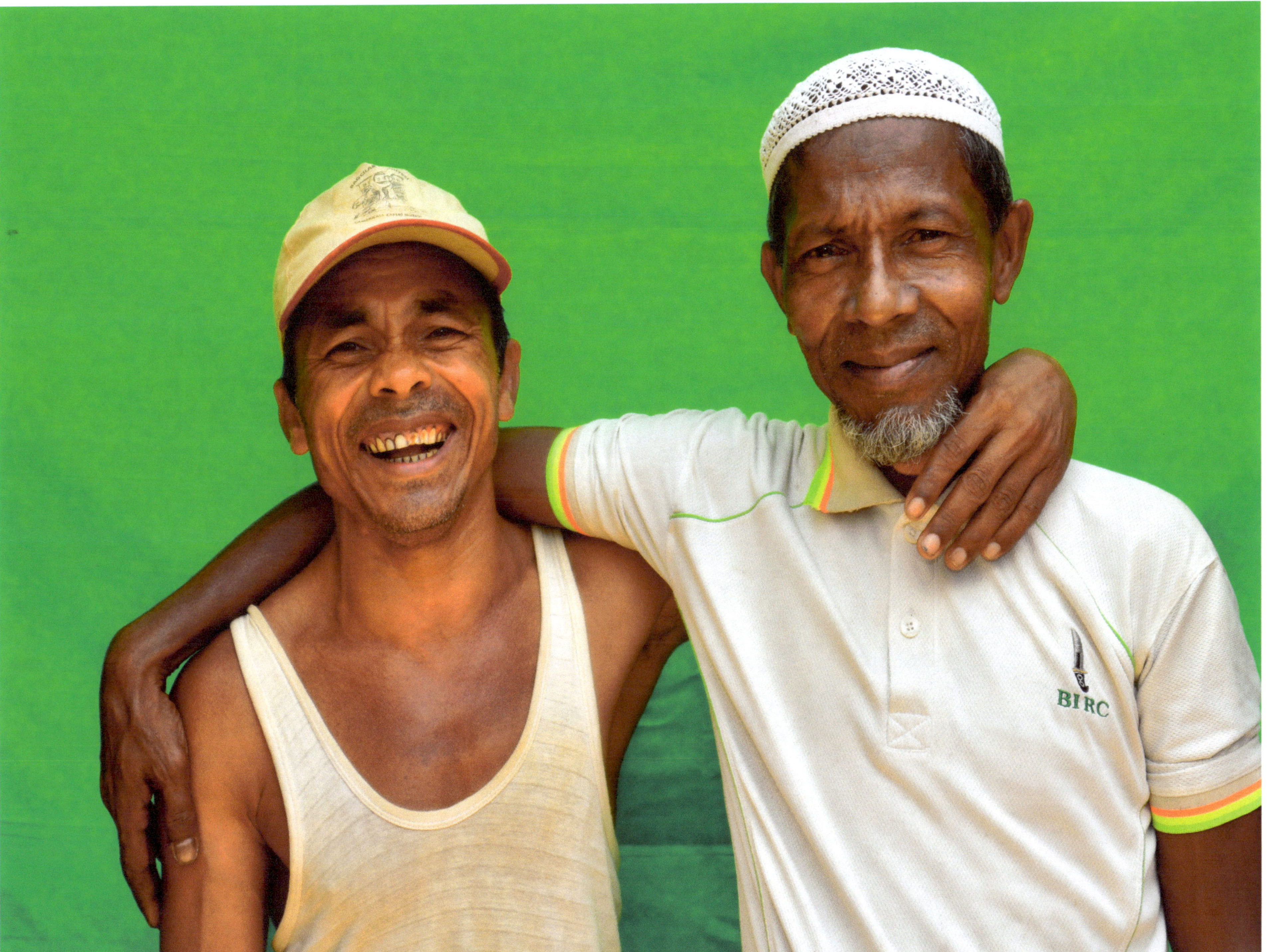
BIRC

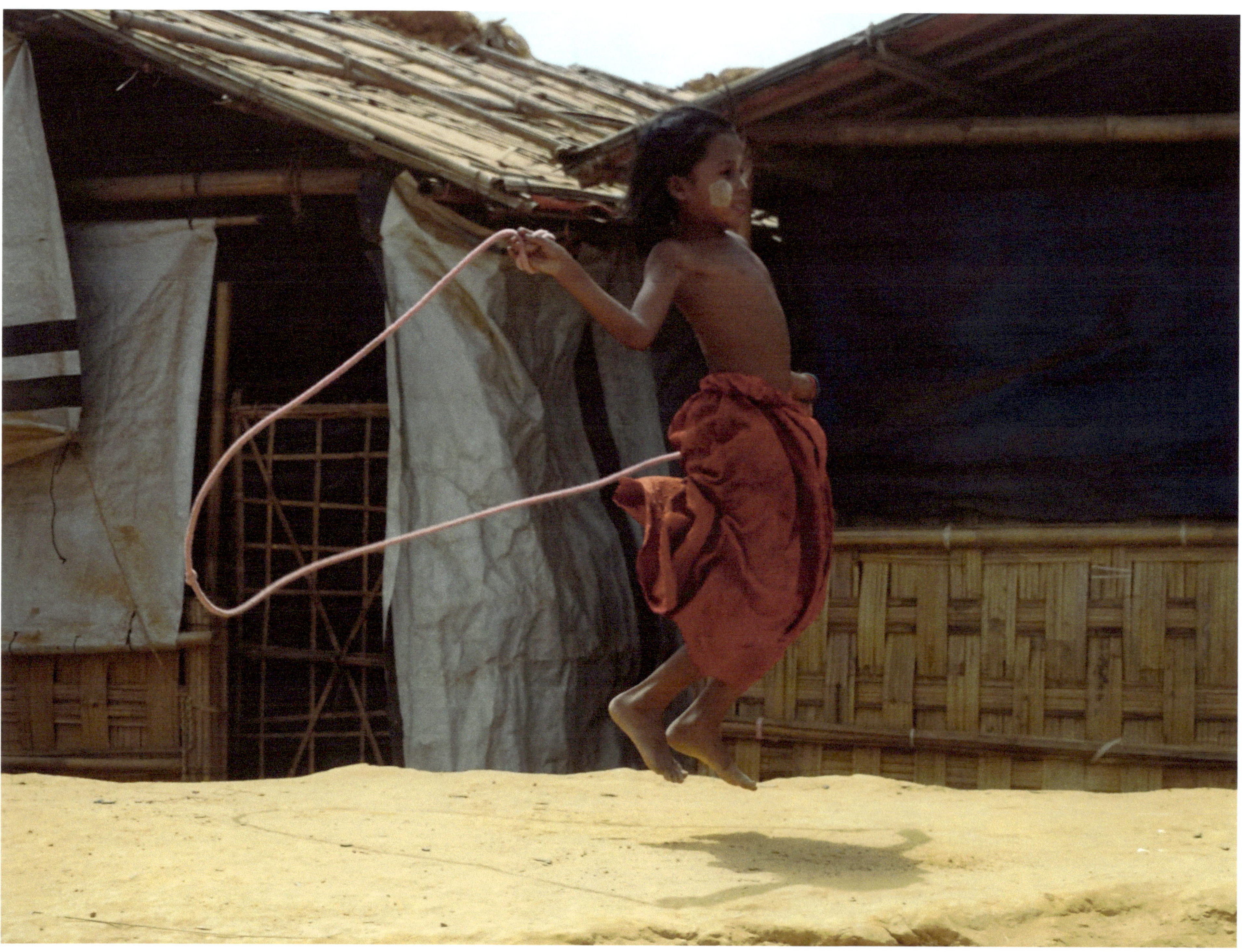

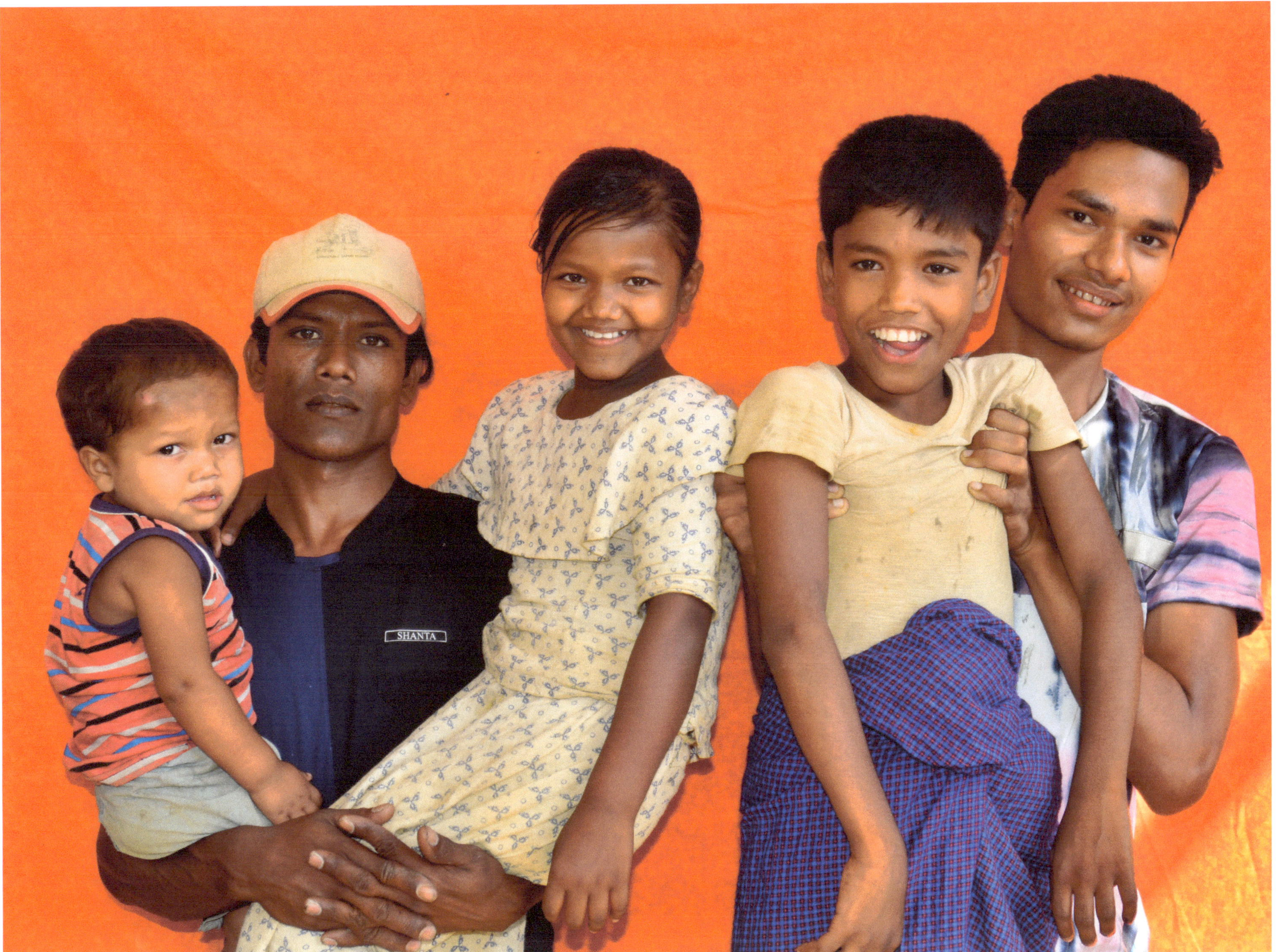
SHANTA

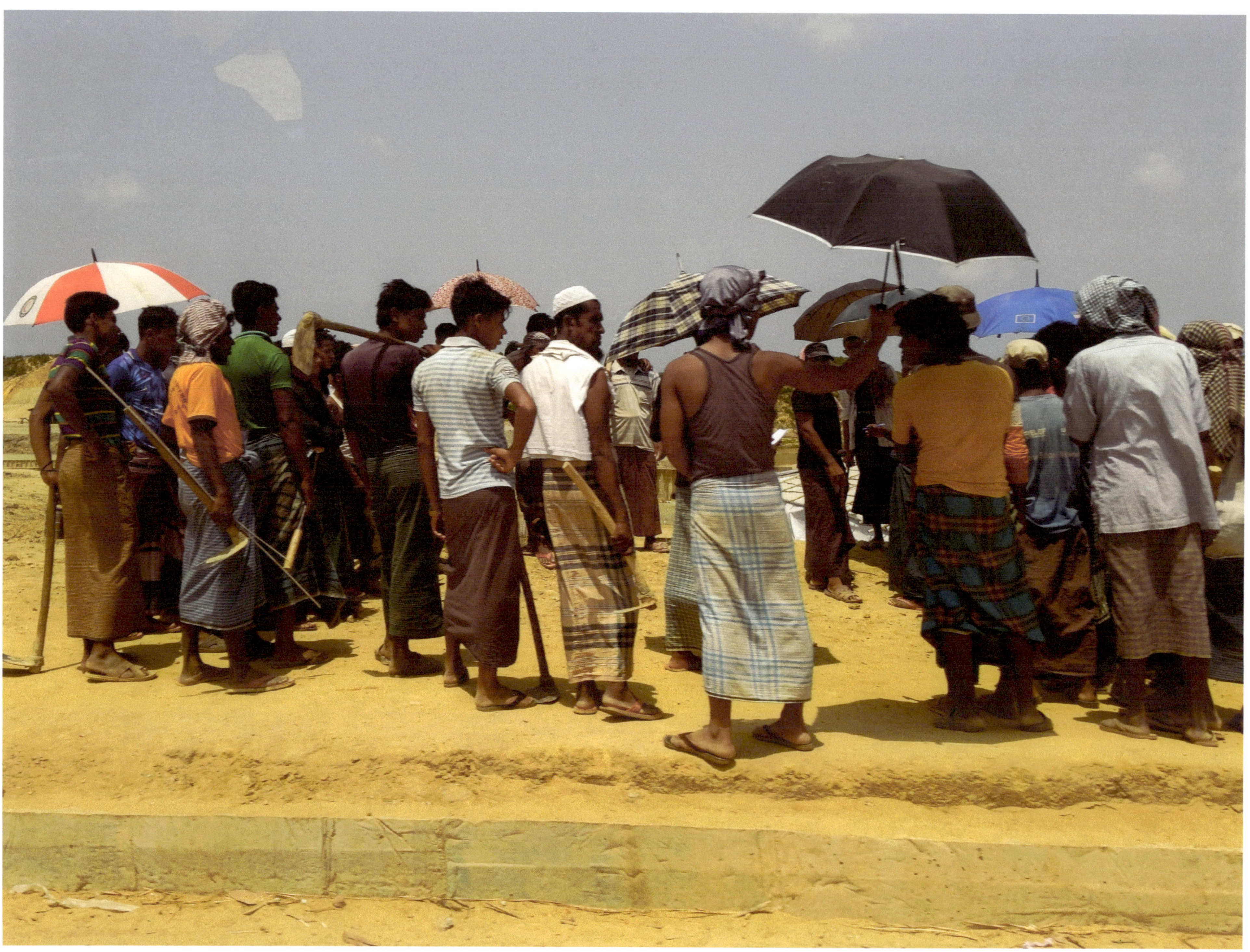

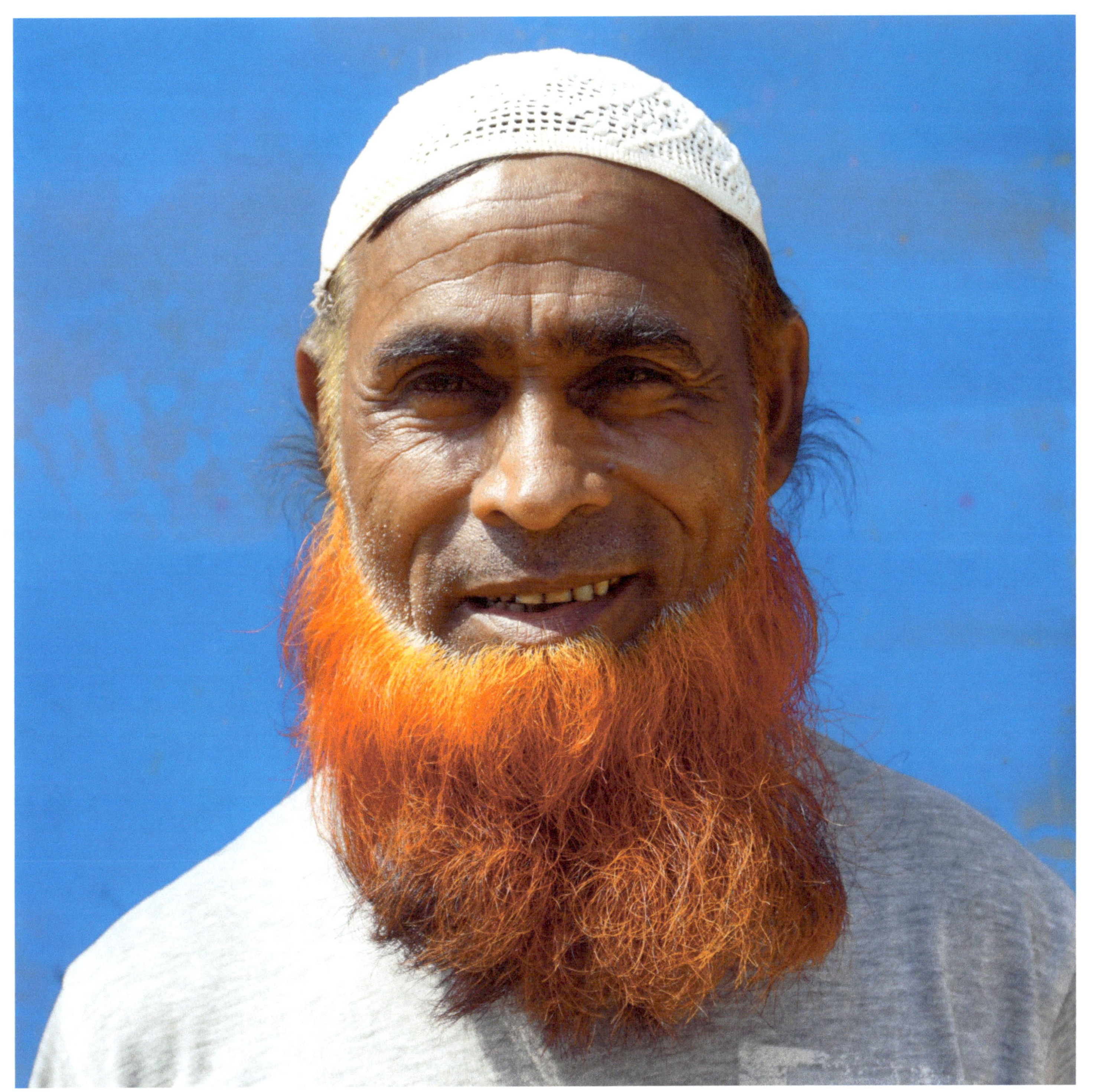

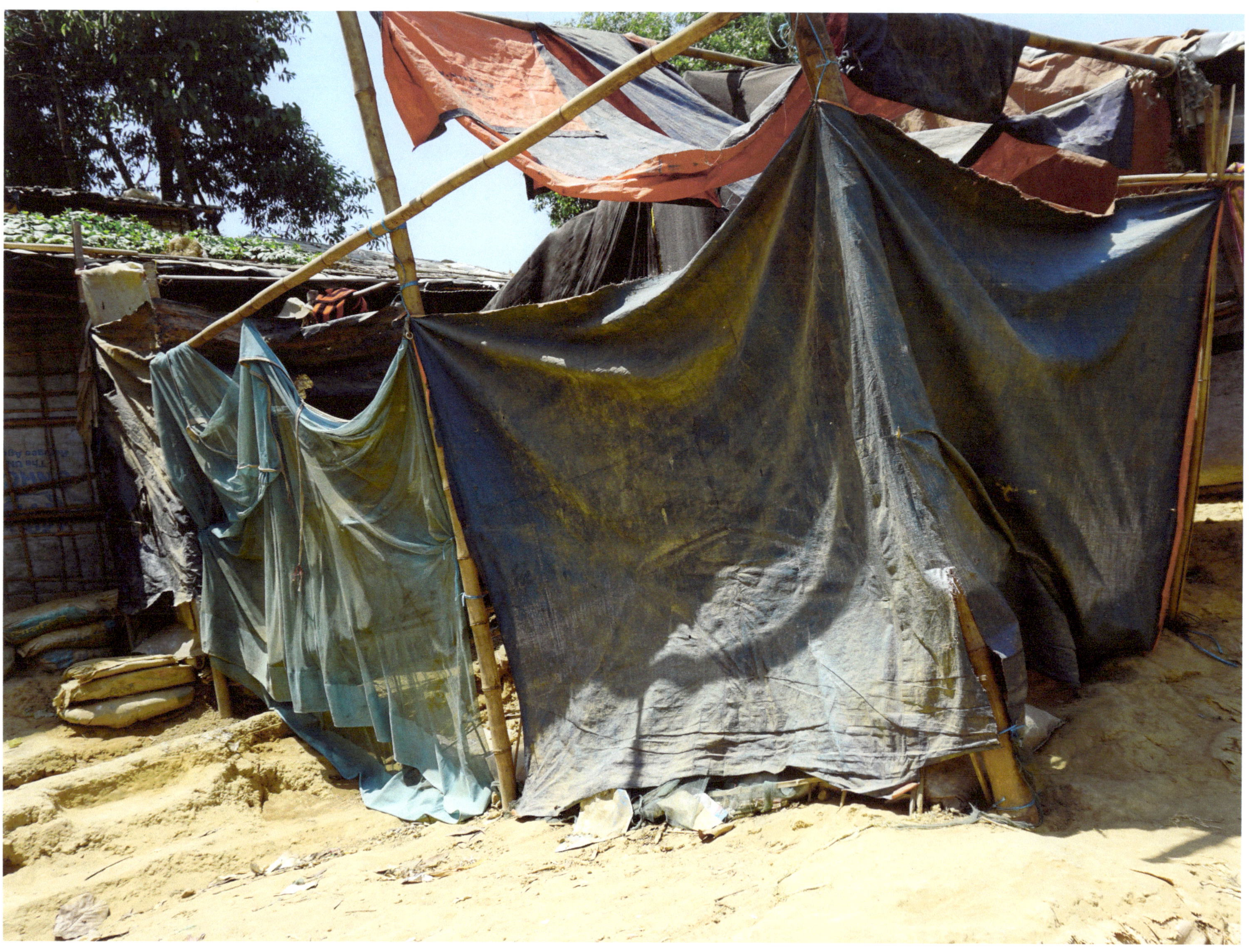

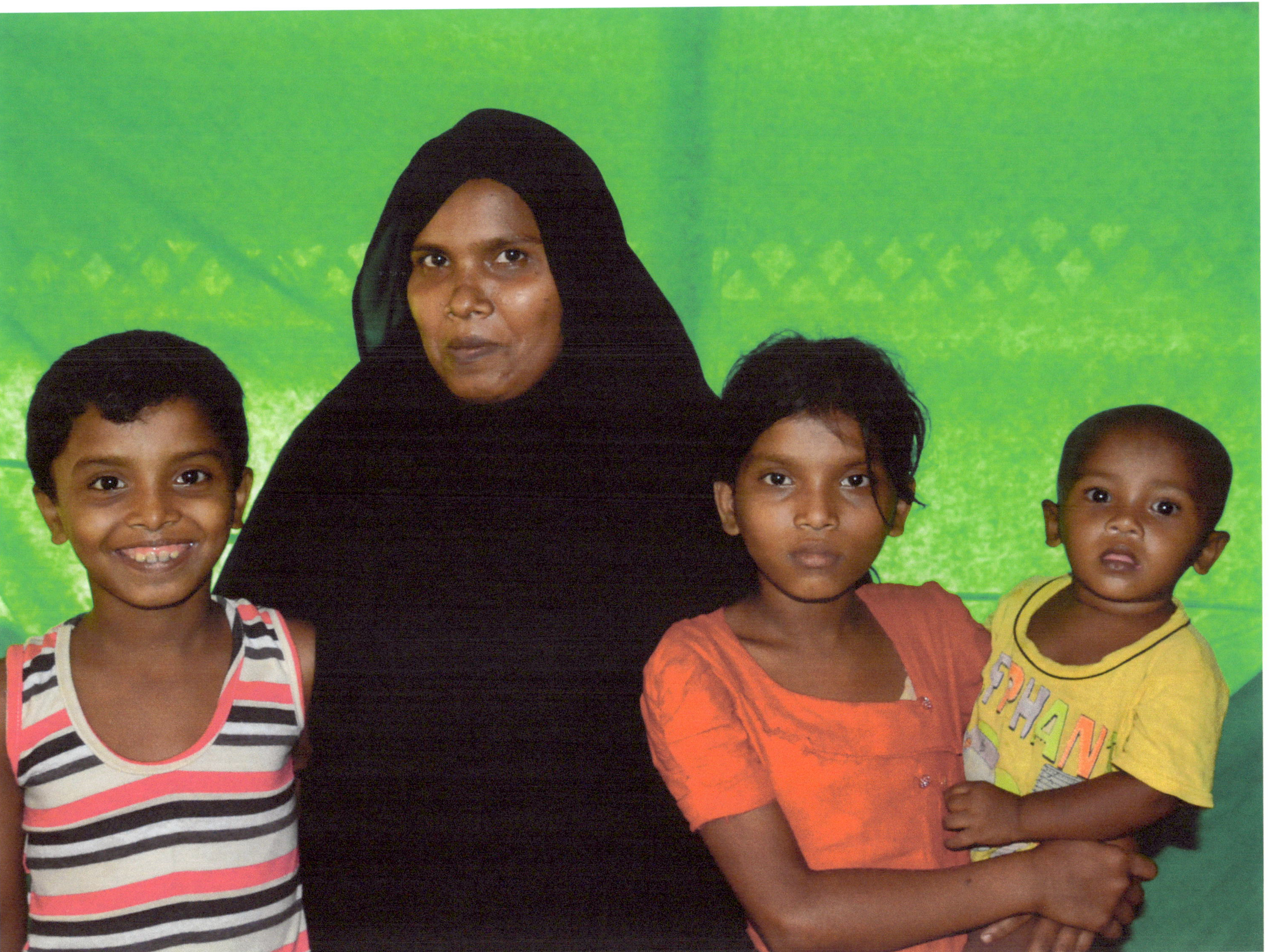

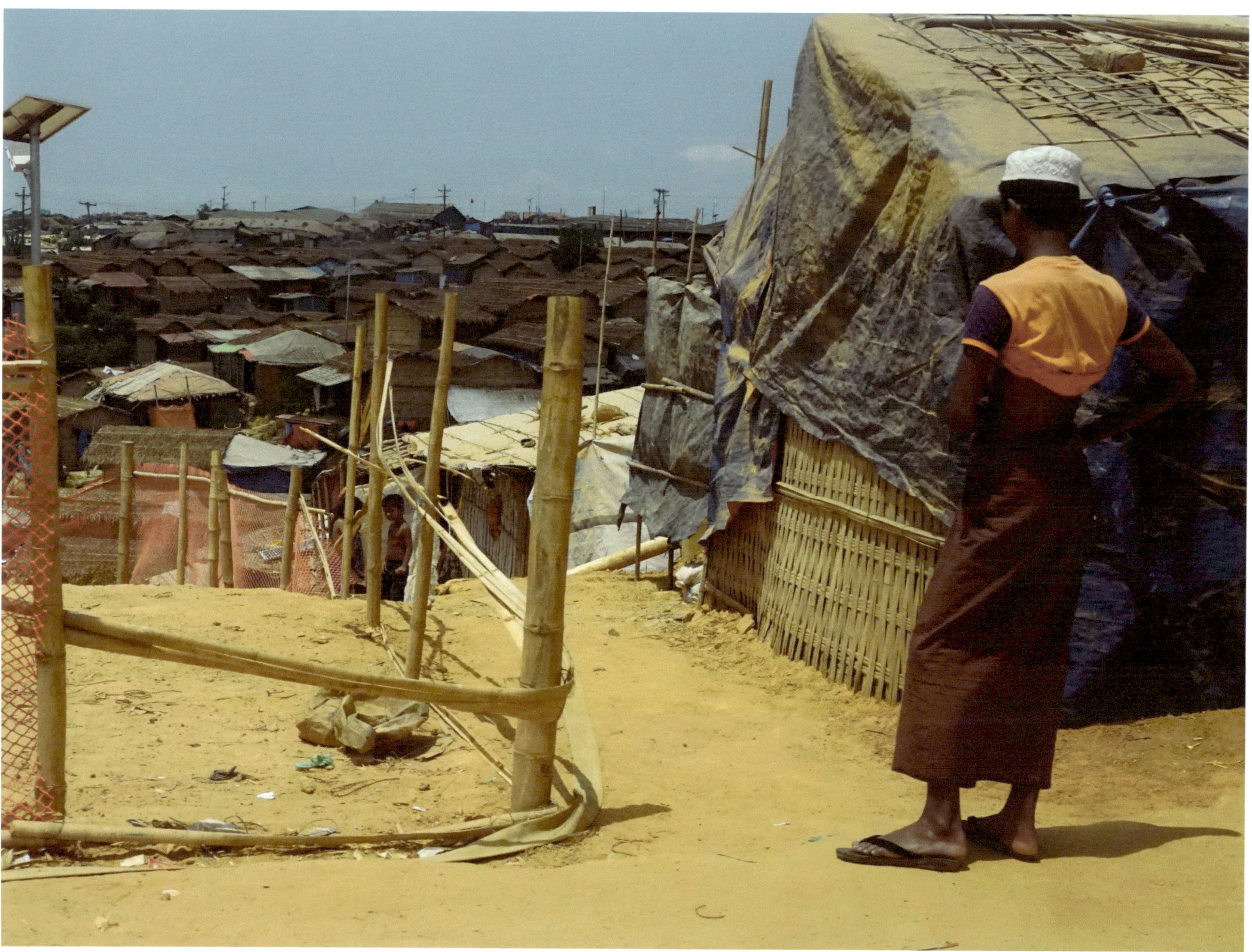

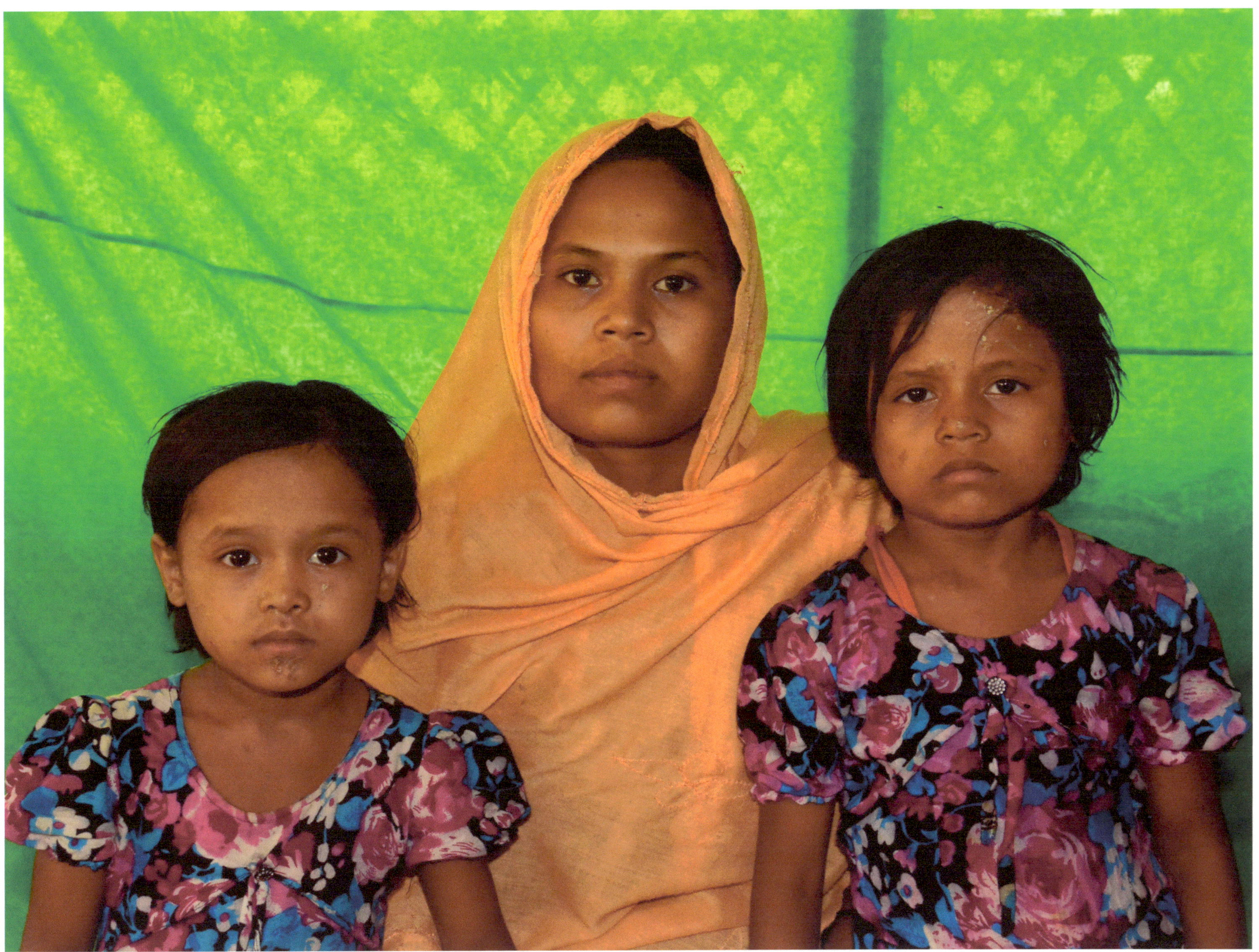

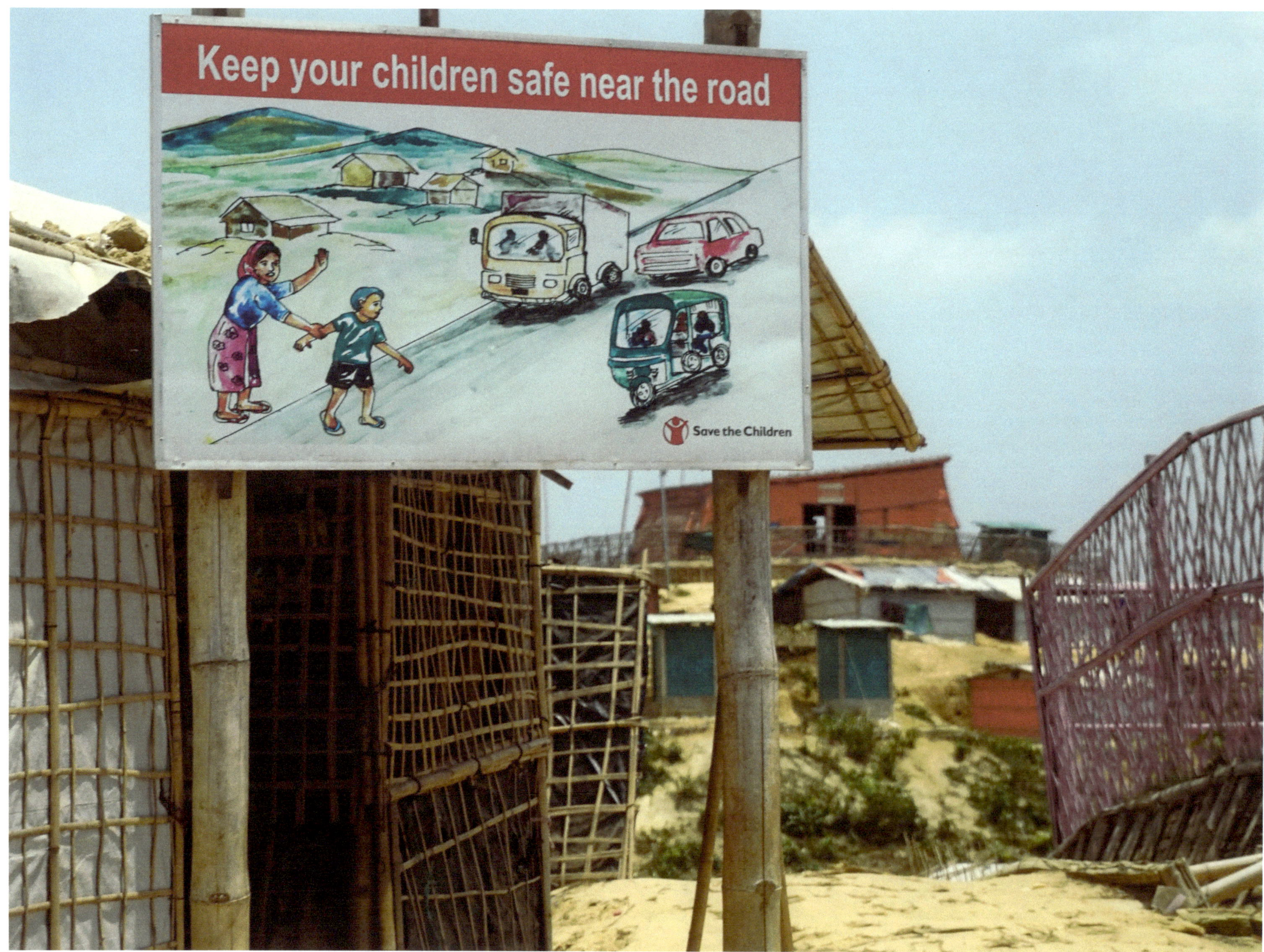
Keep your children safe near the road
Save the Children

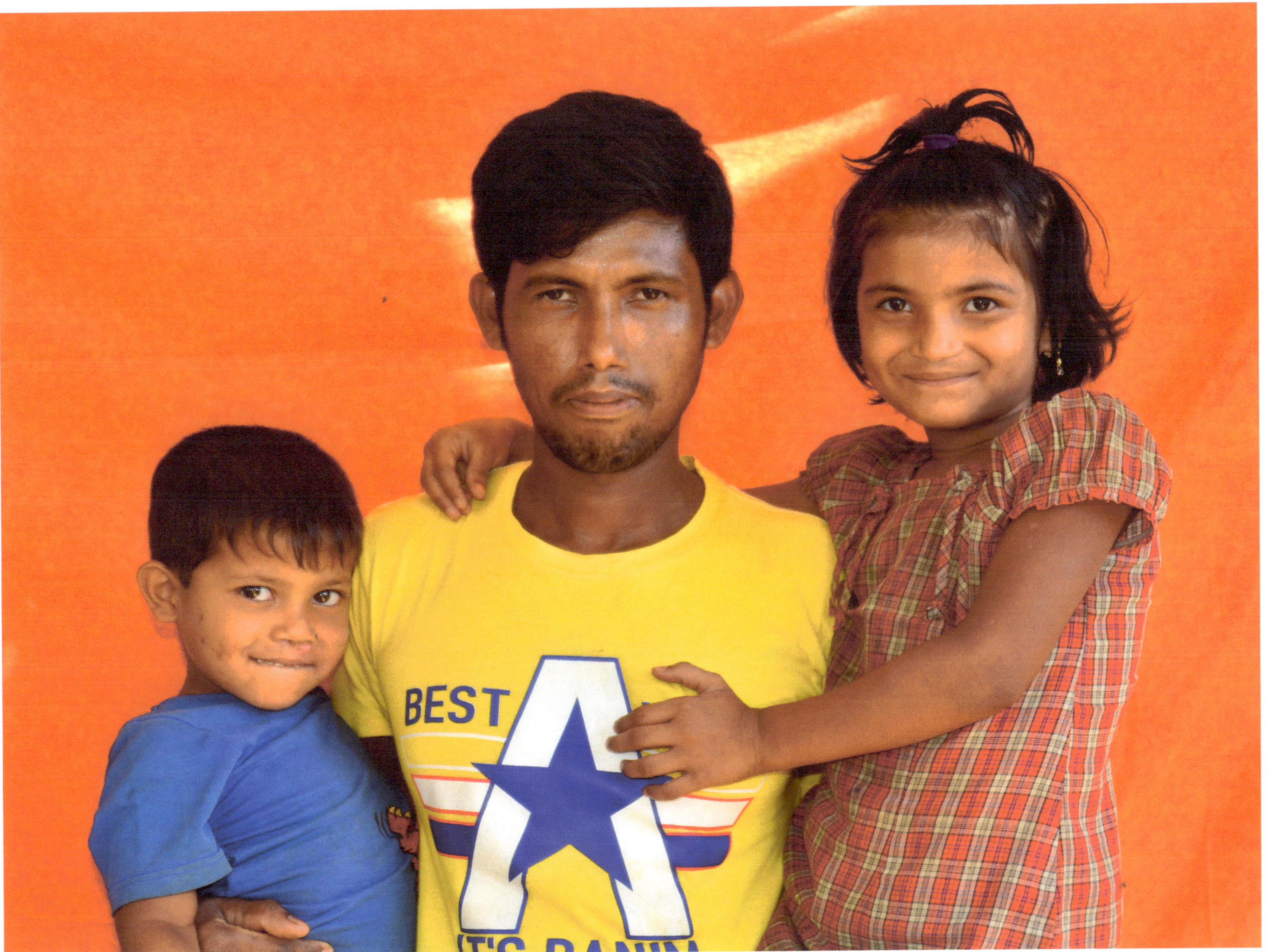

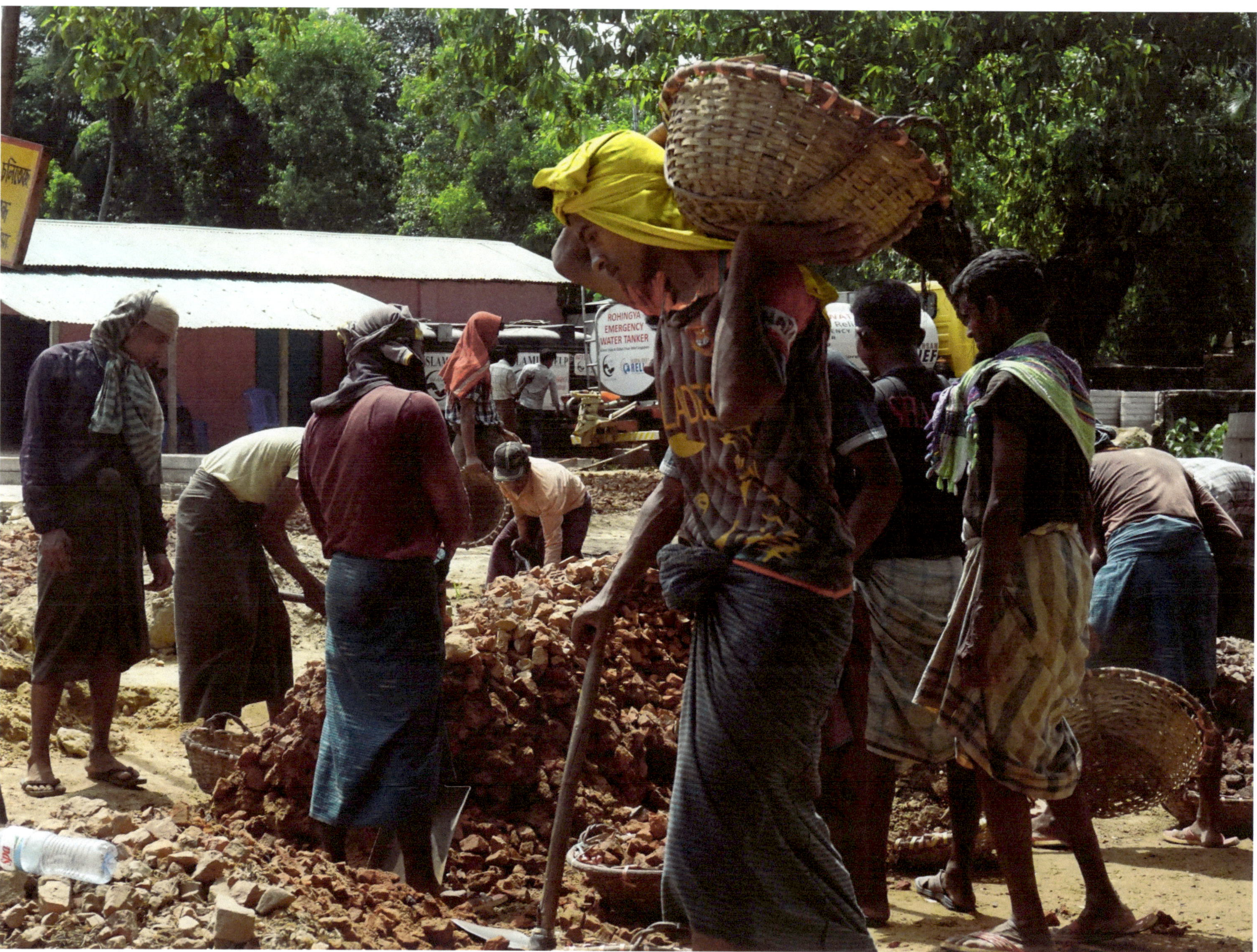

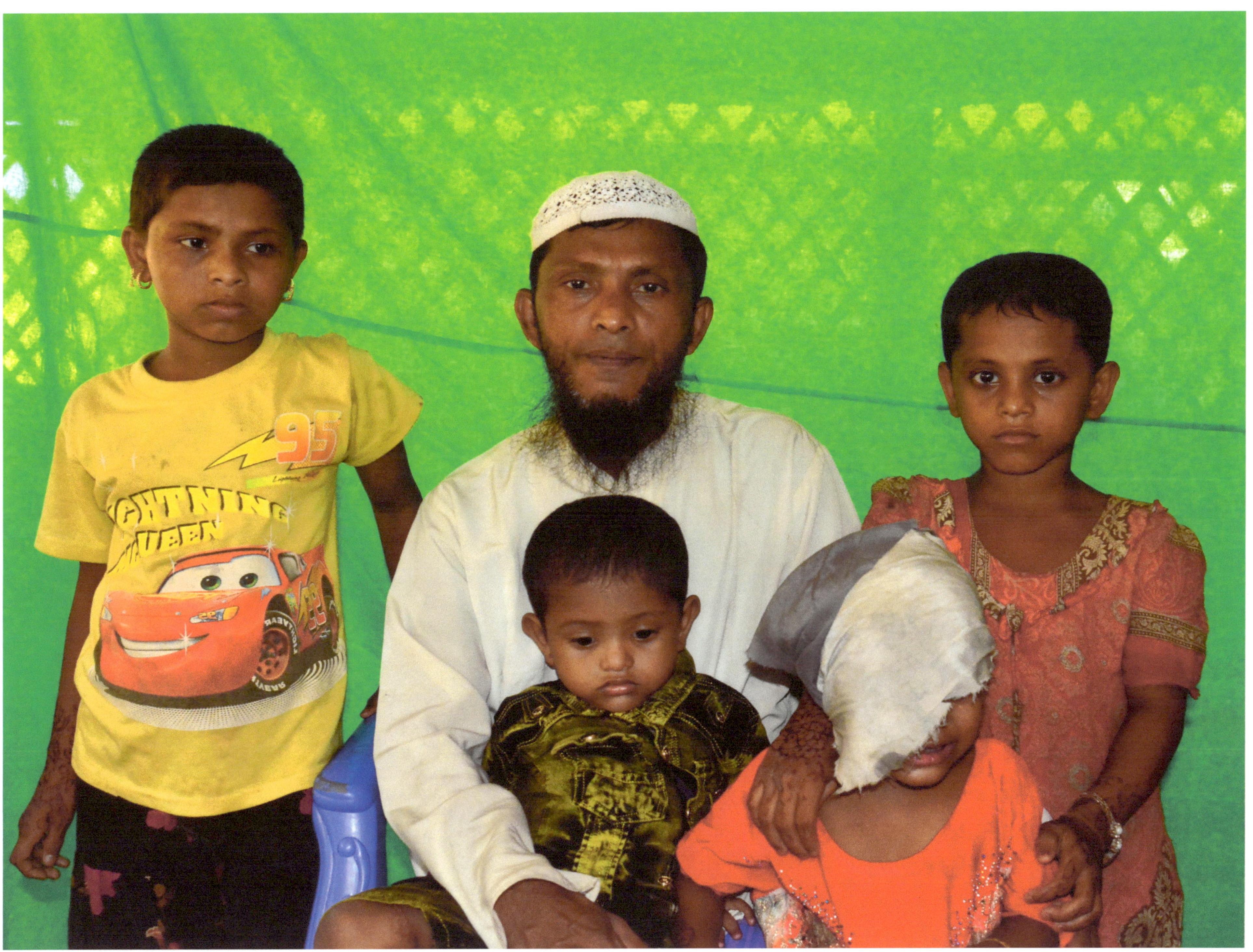

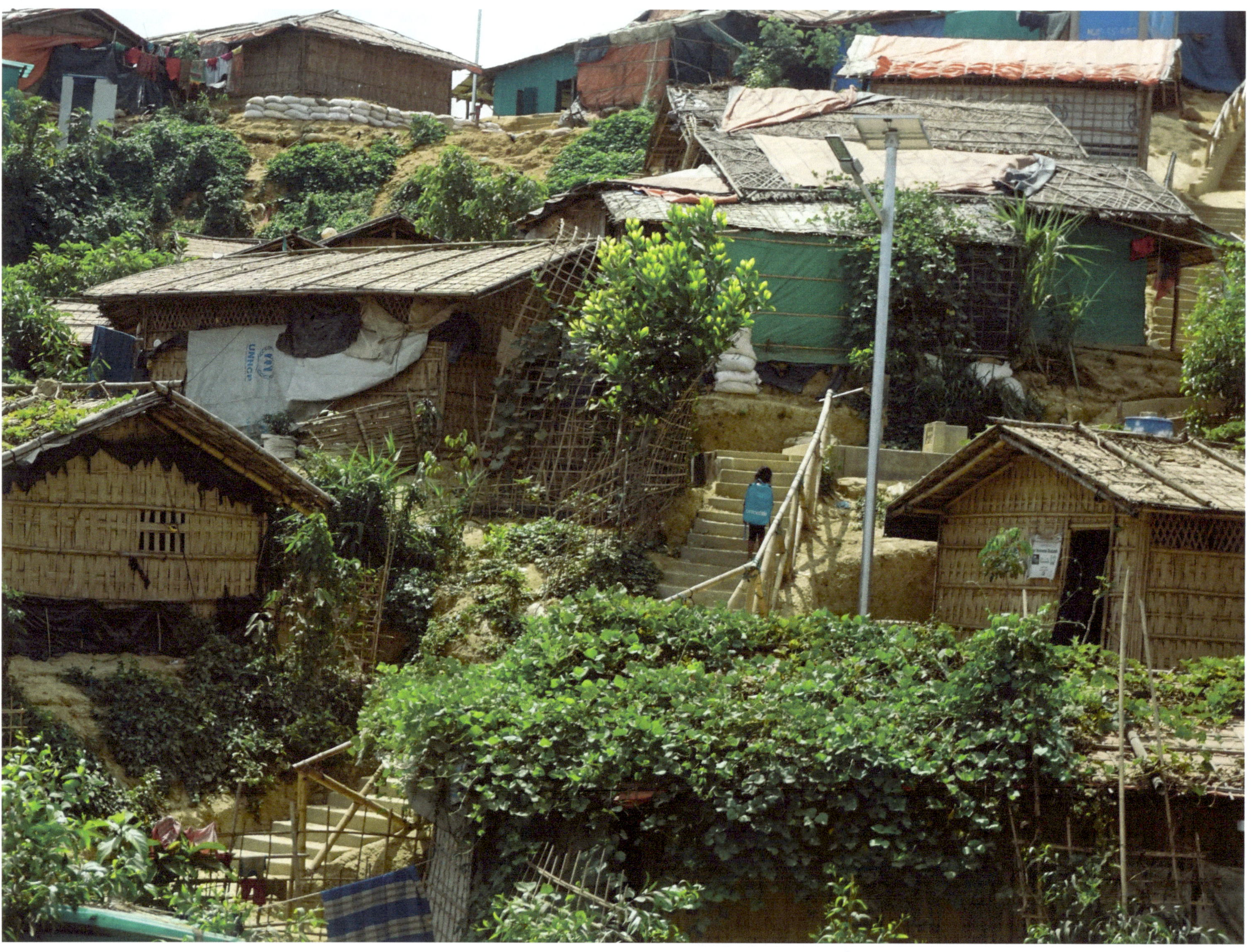

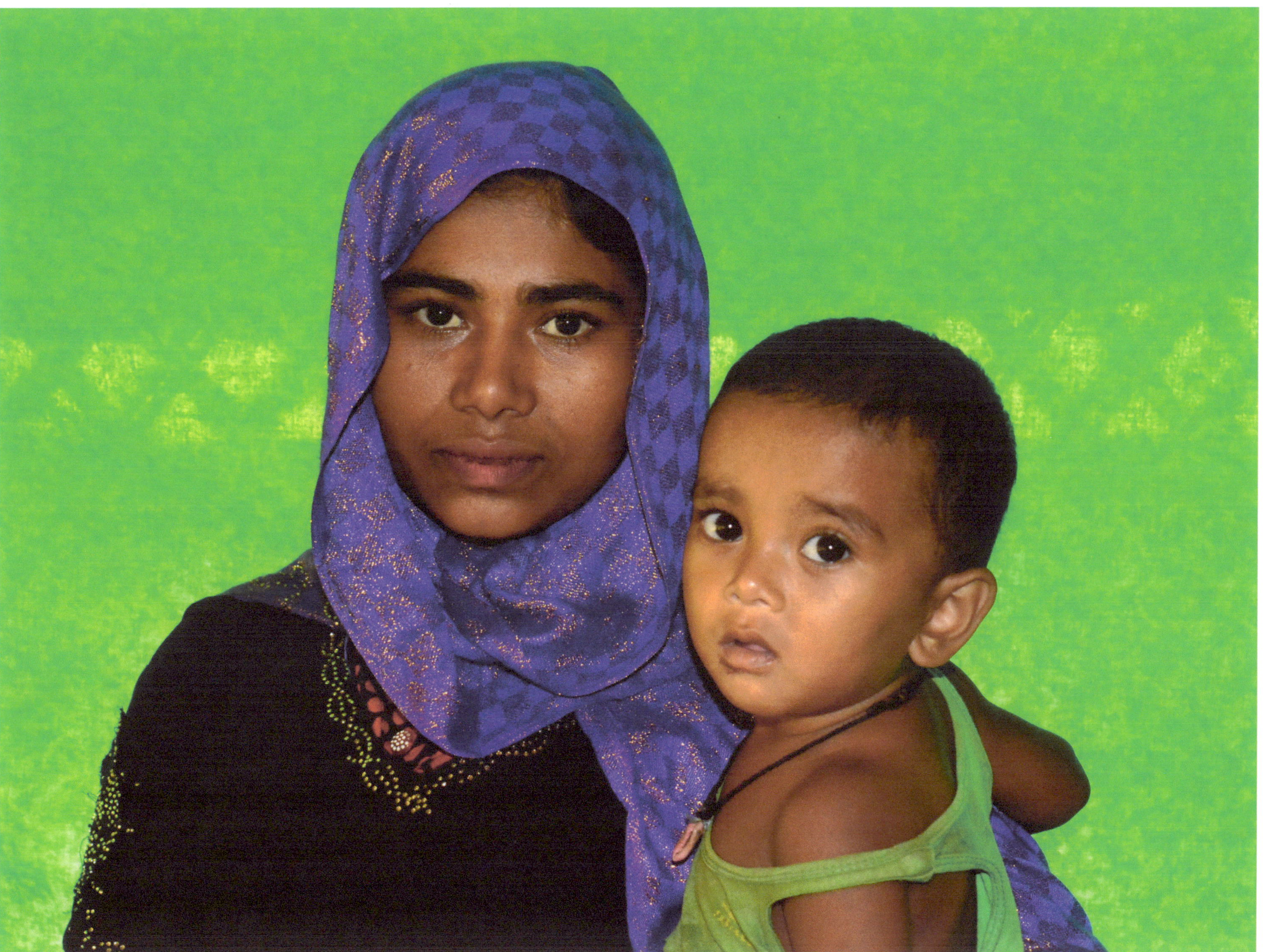

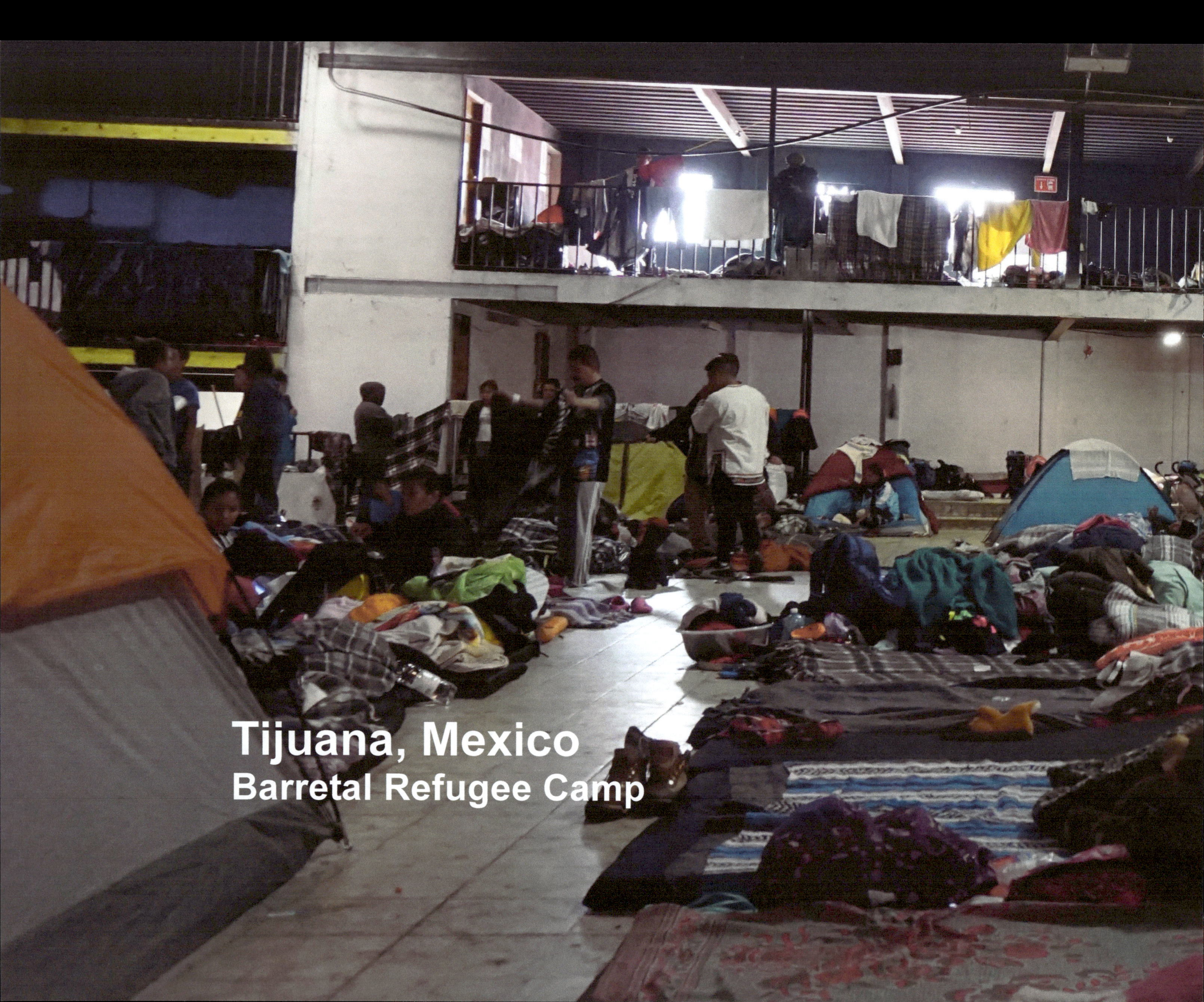
Tijuana, Mexico
Barretal Refugee Camp

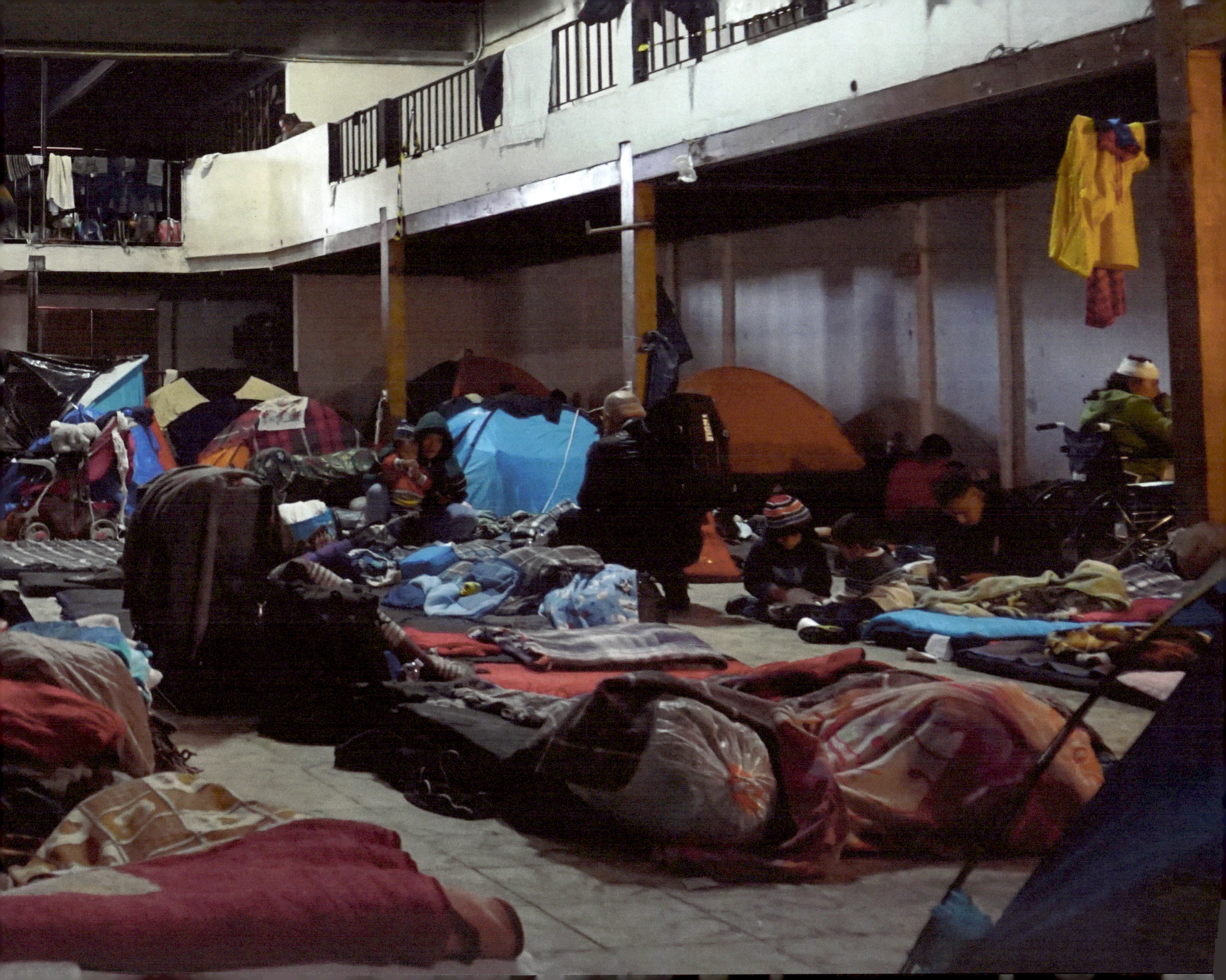

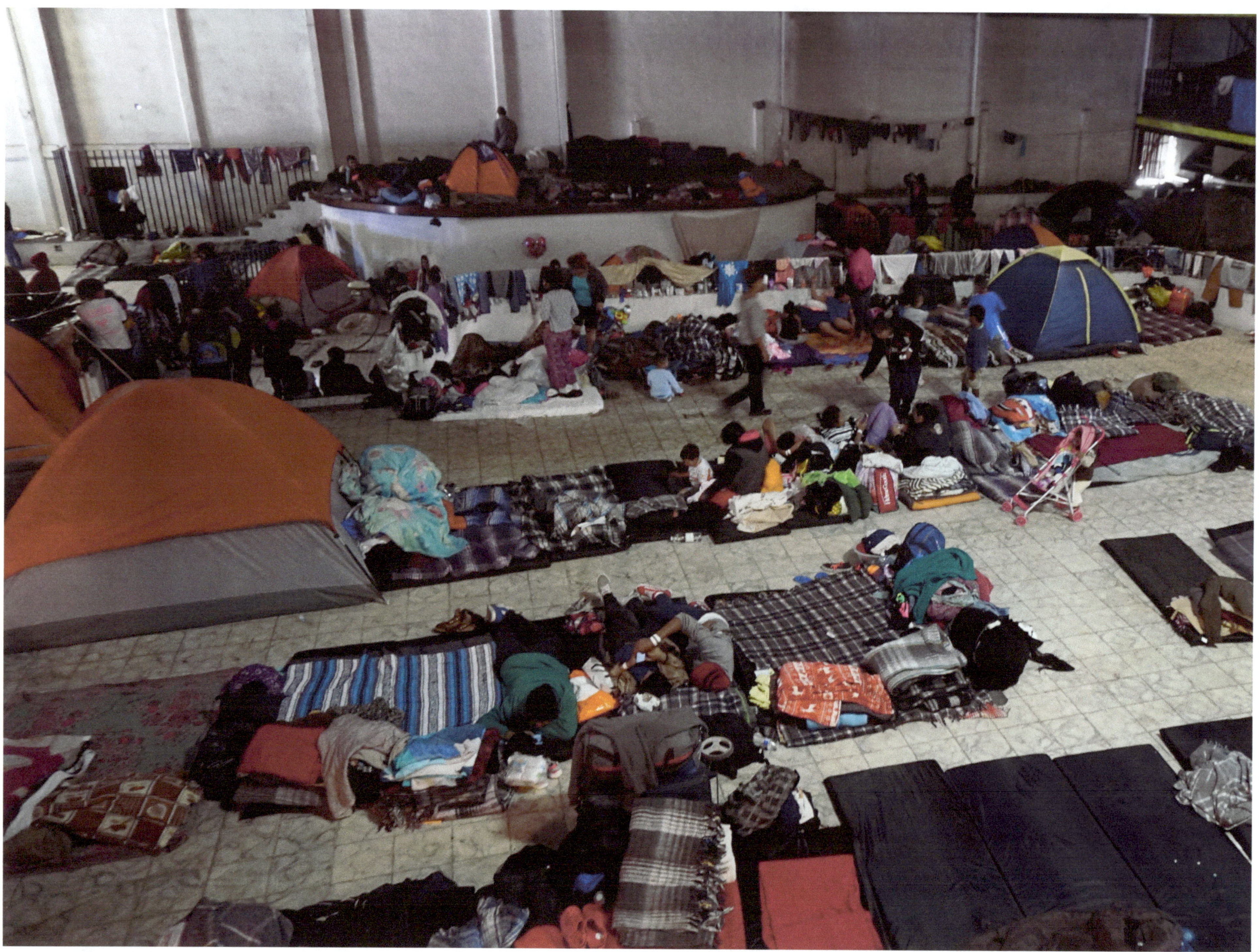

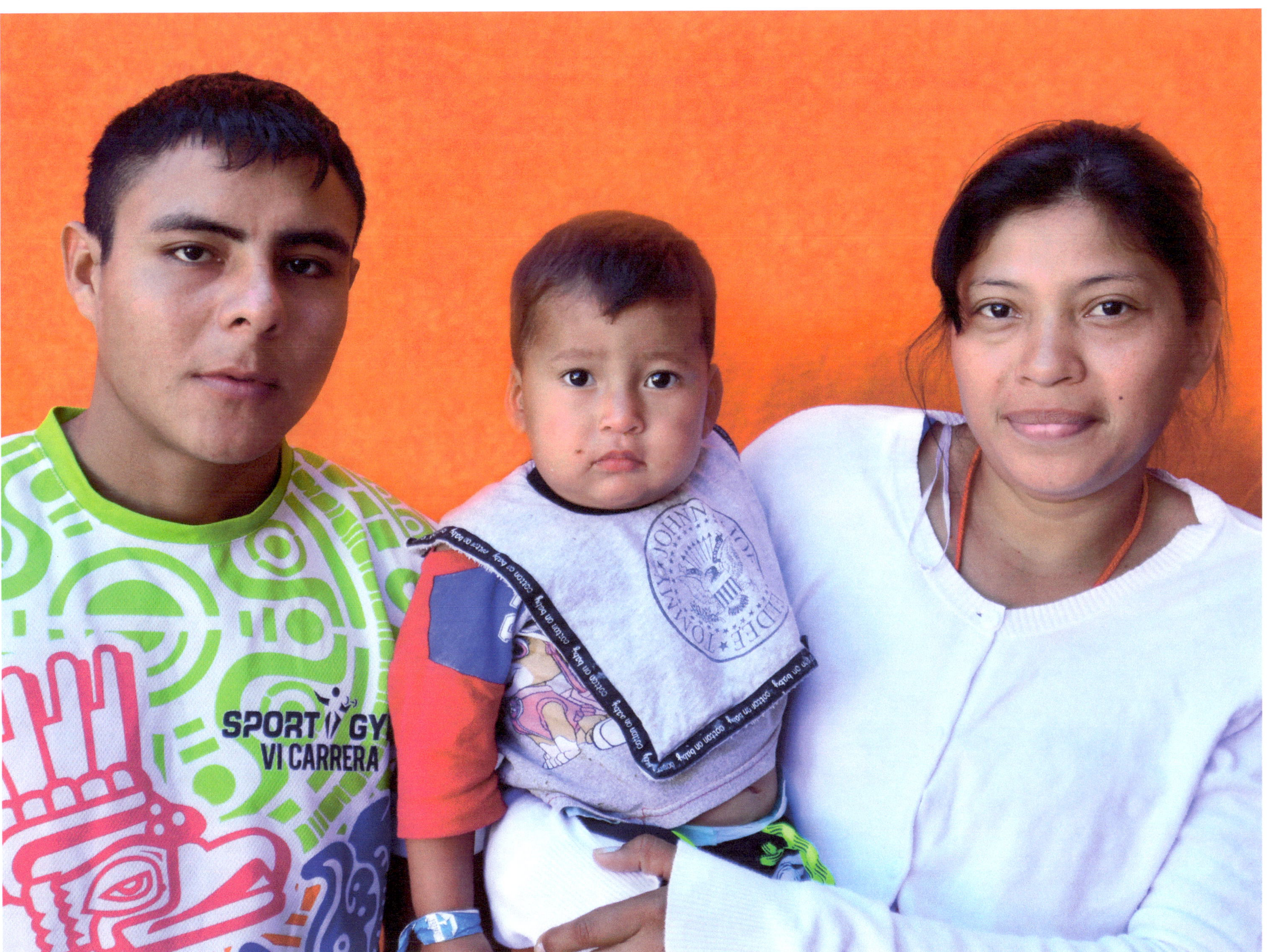

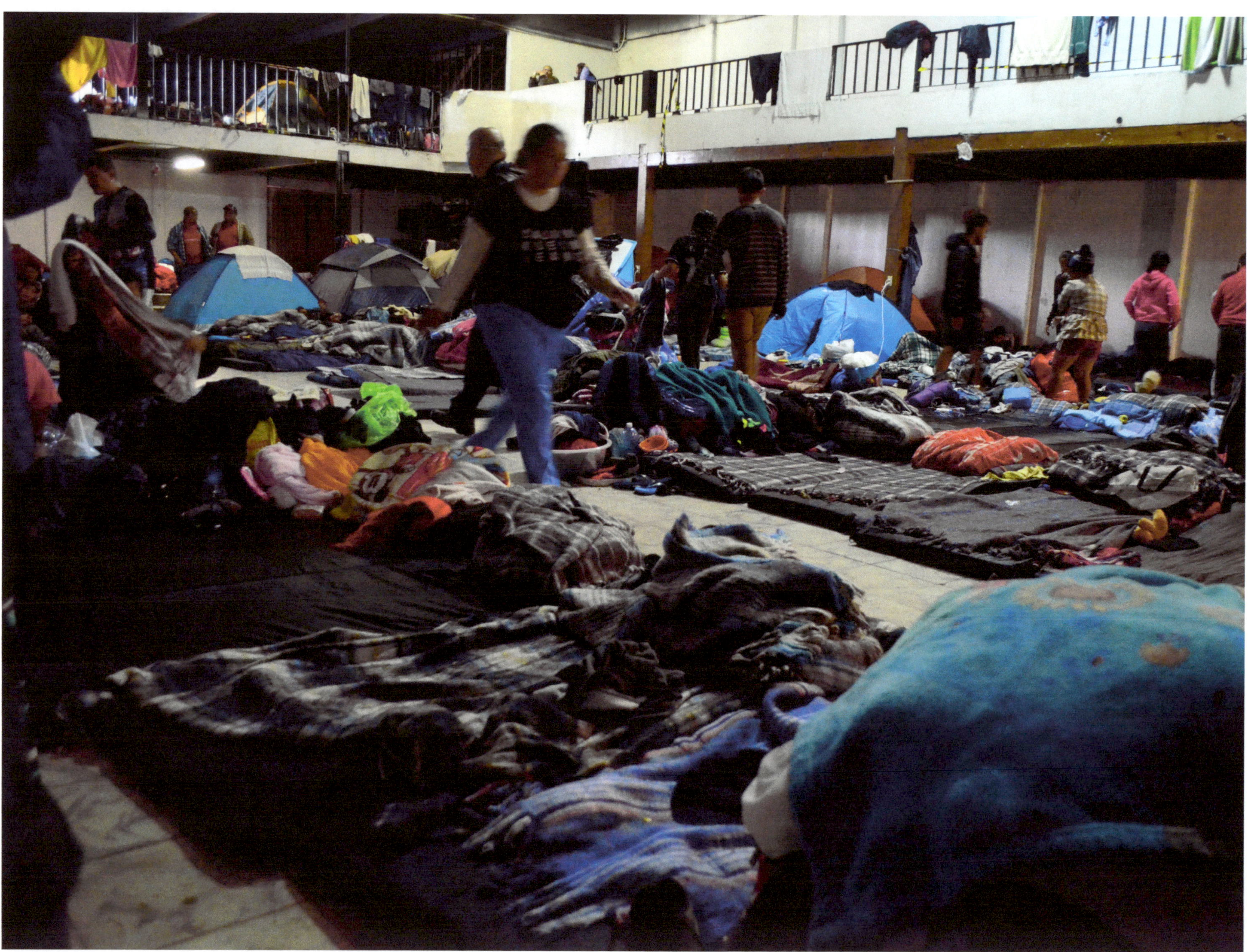

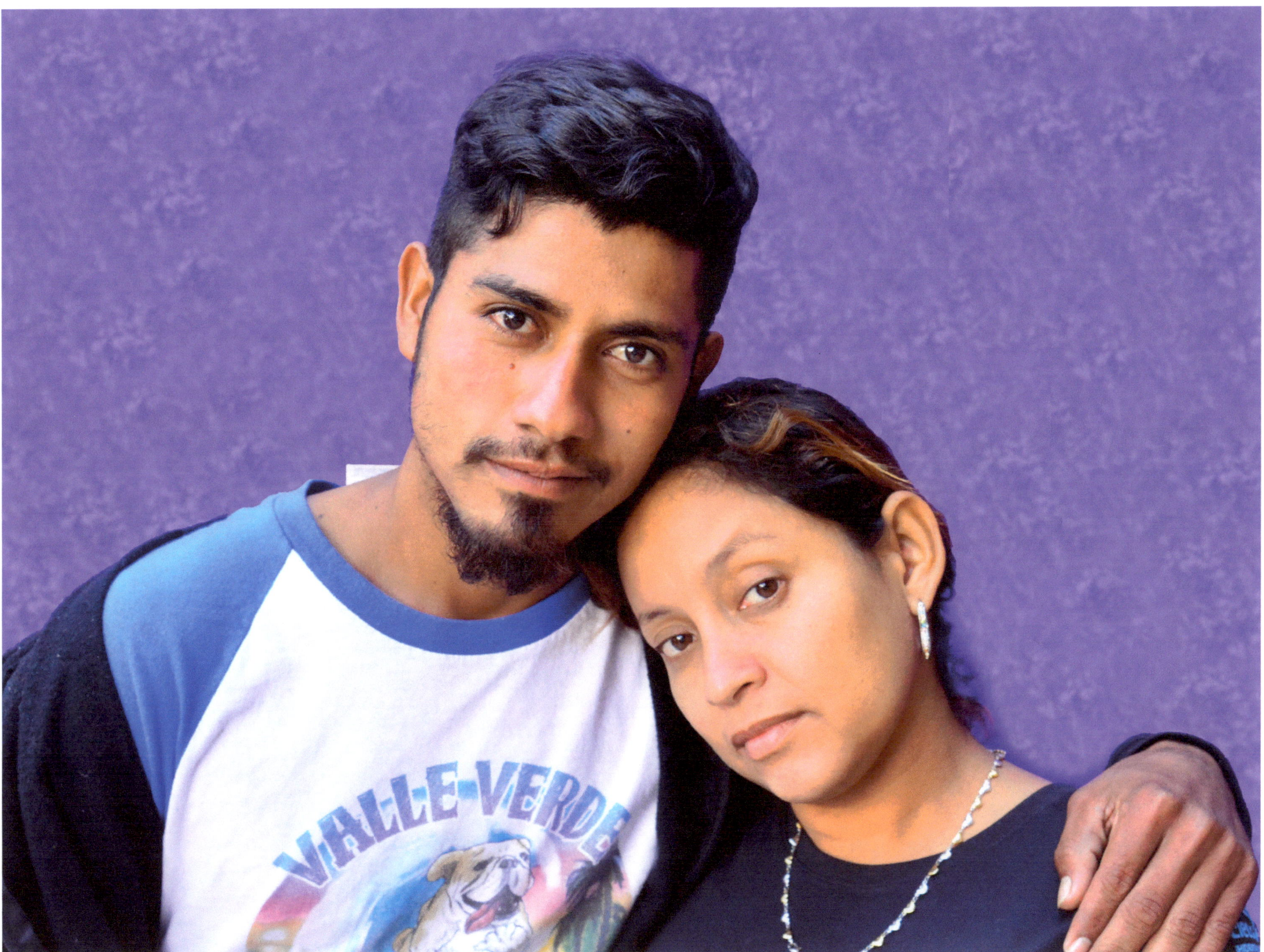

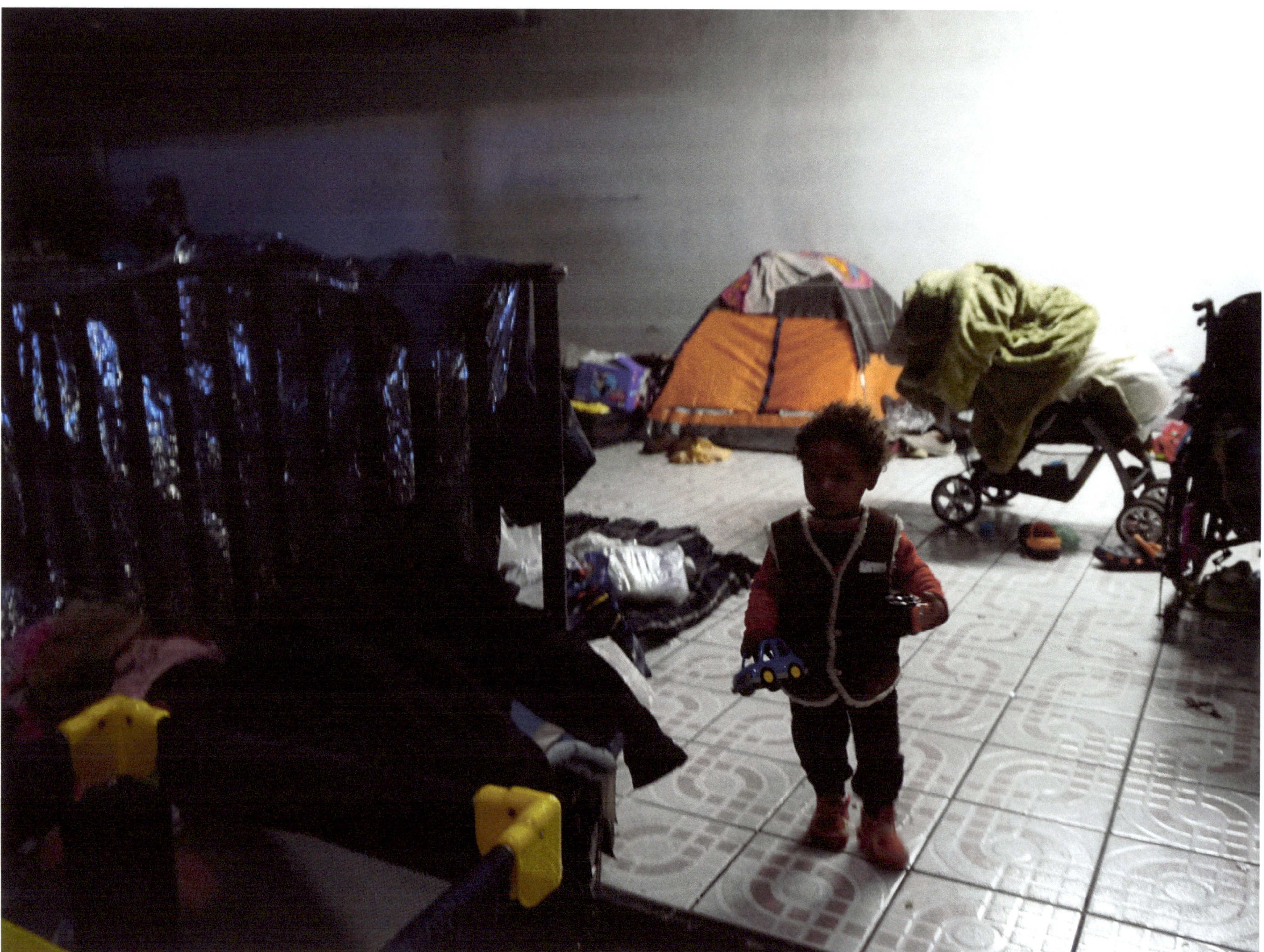

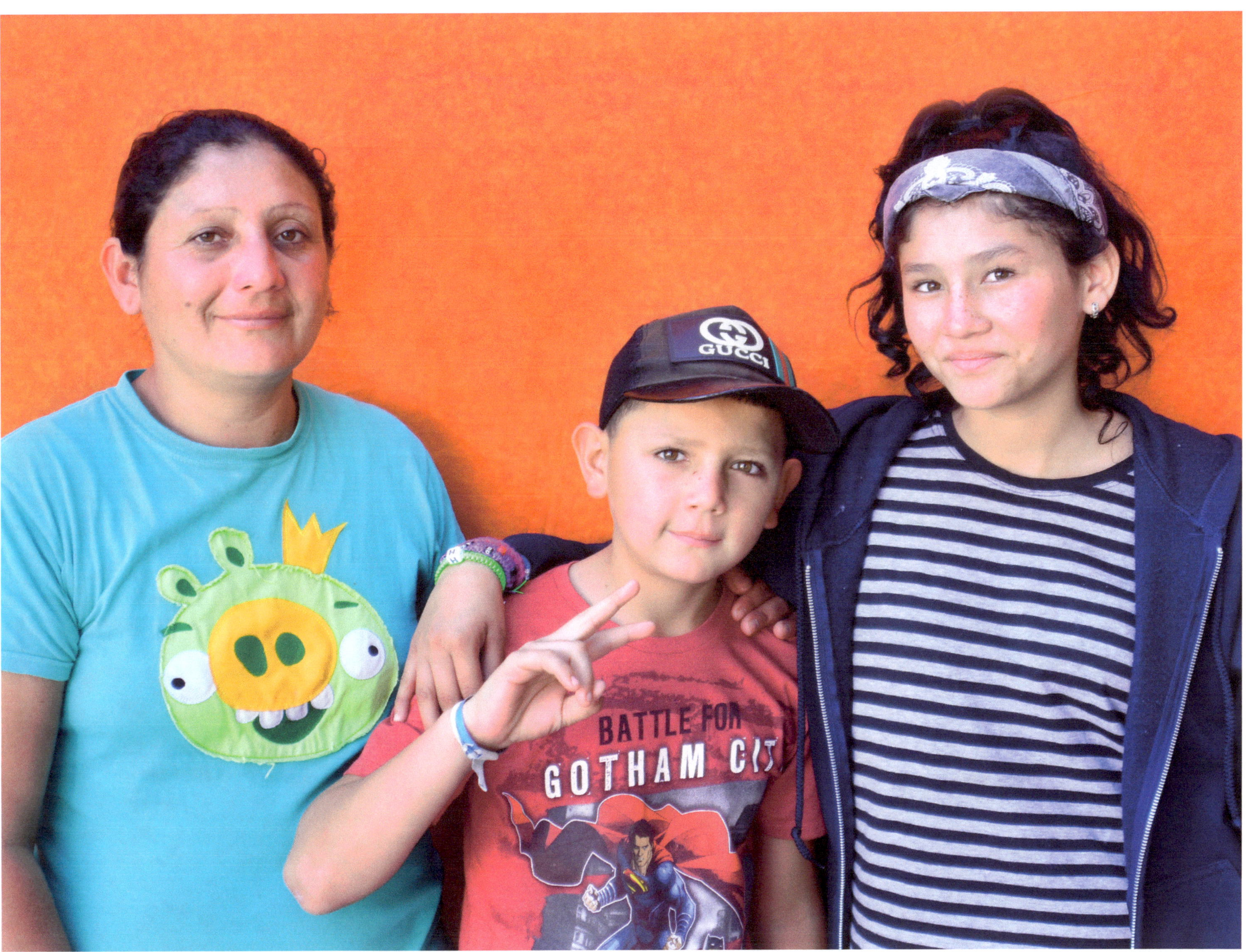

GUCCI
BATTLE FOR
GOTHAM CITY

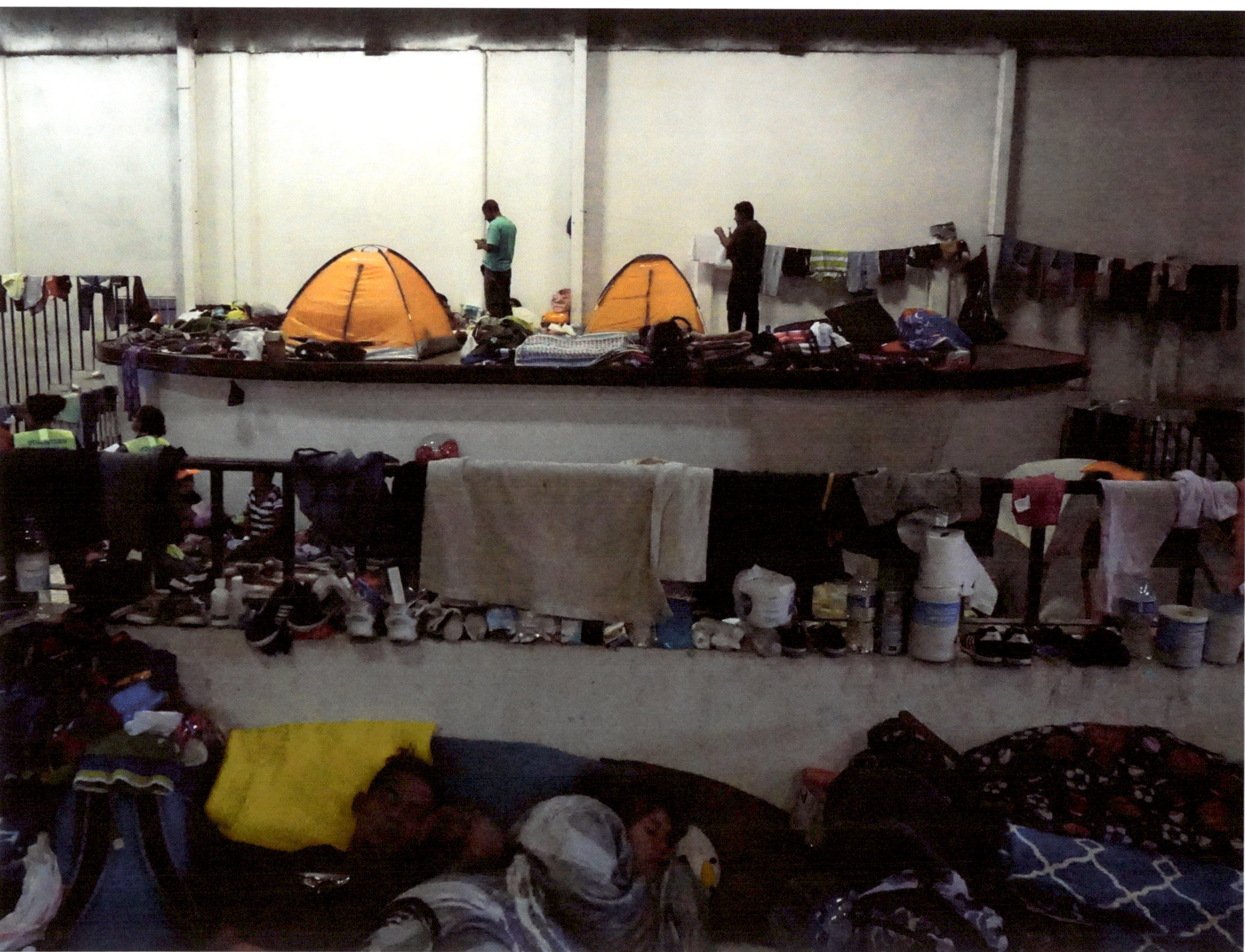

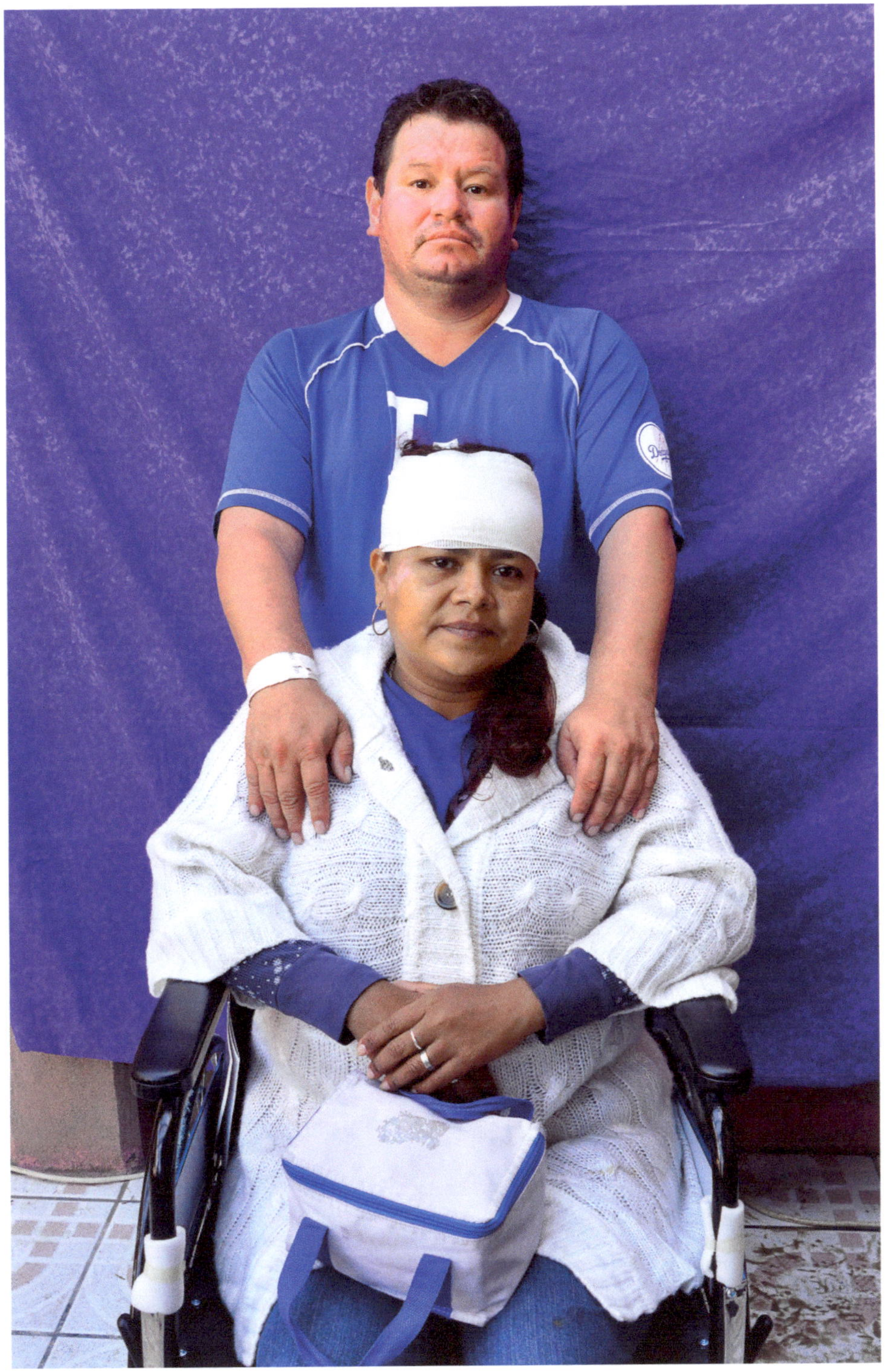

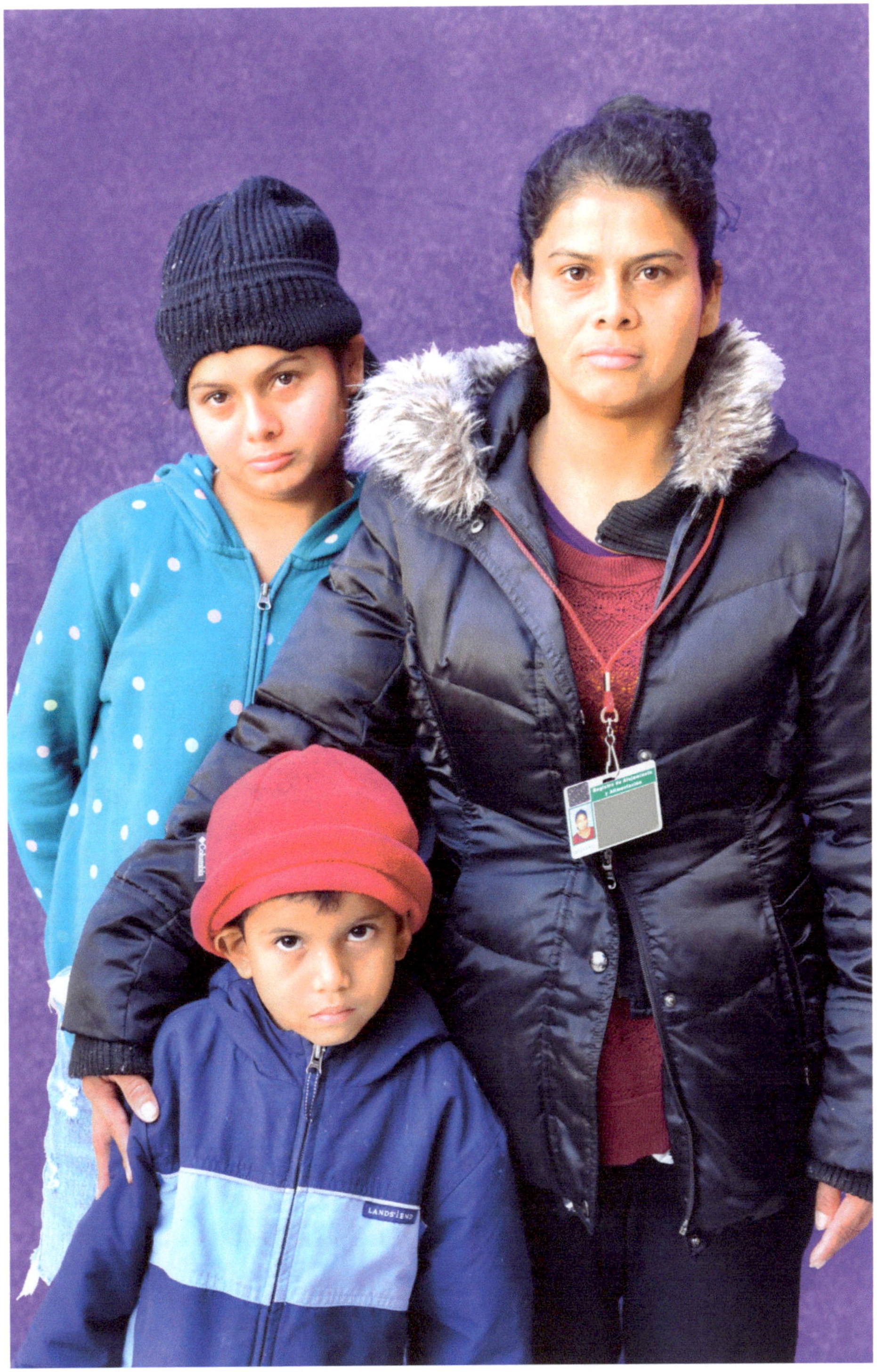

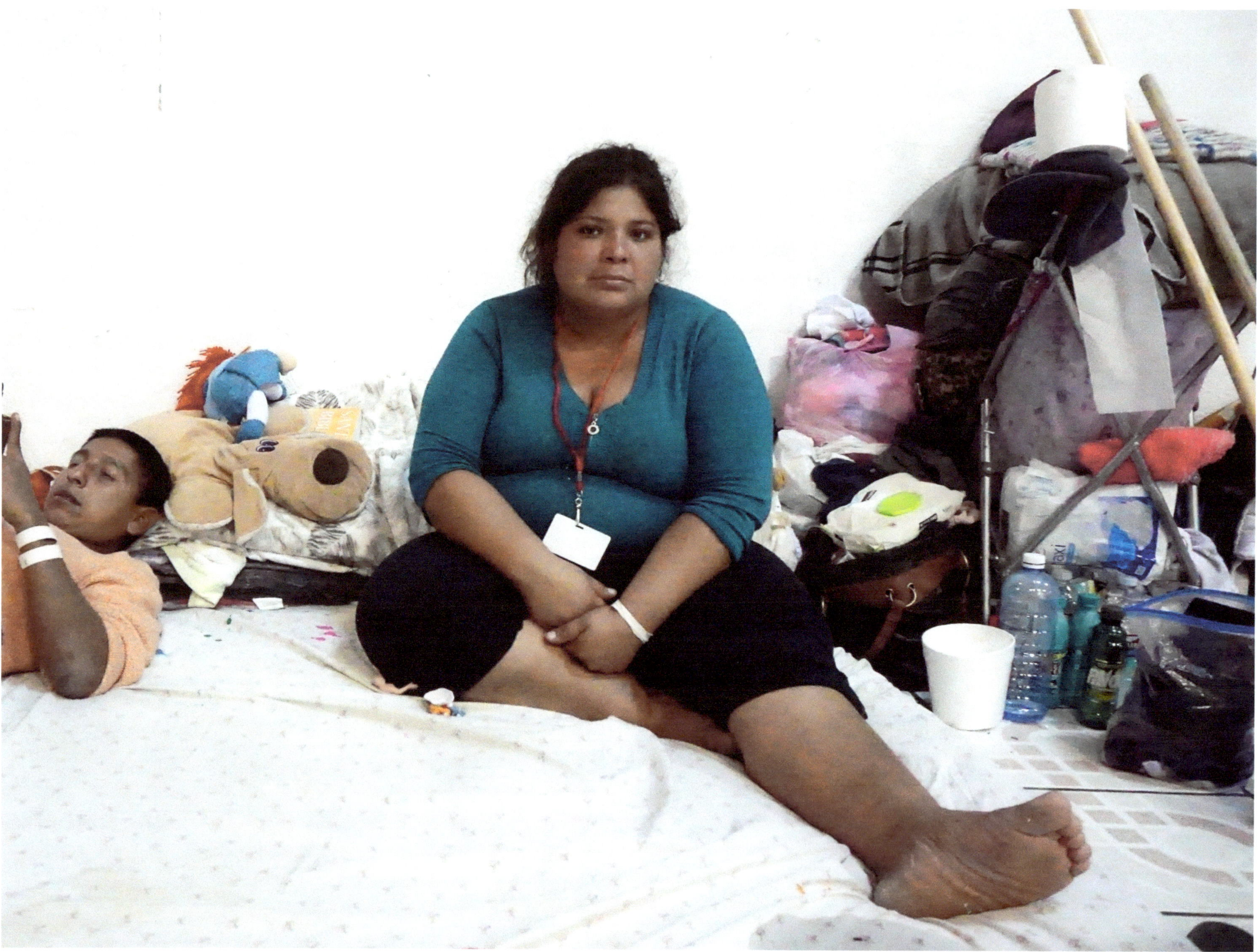

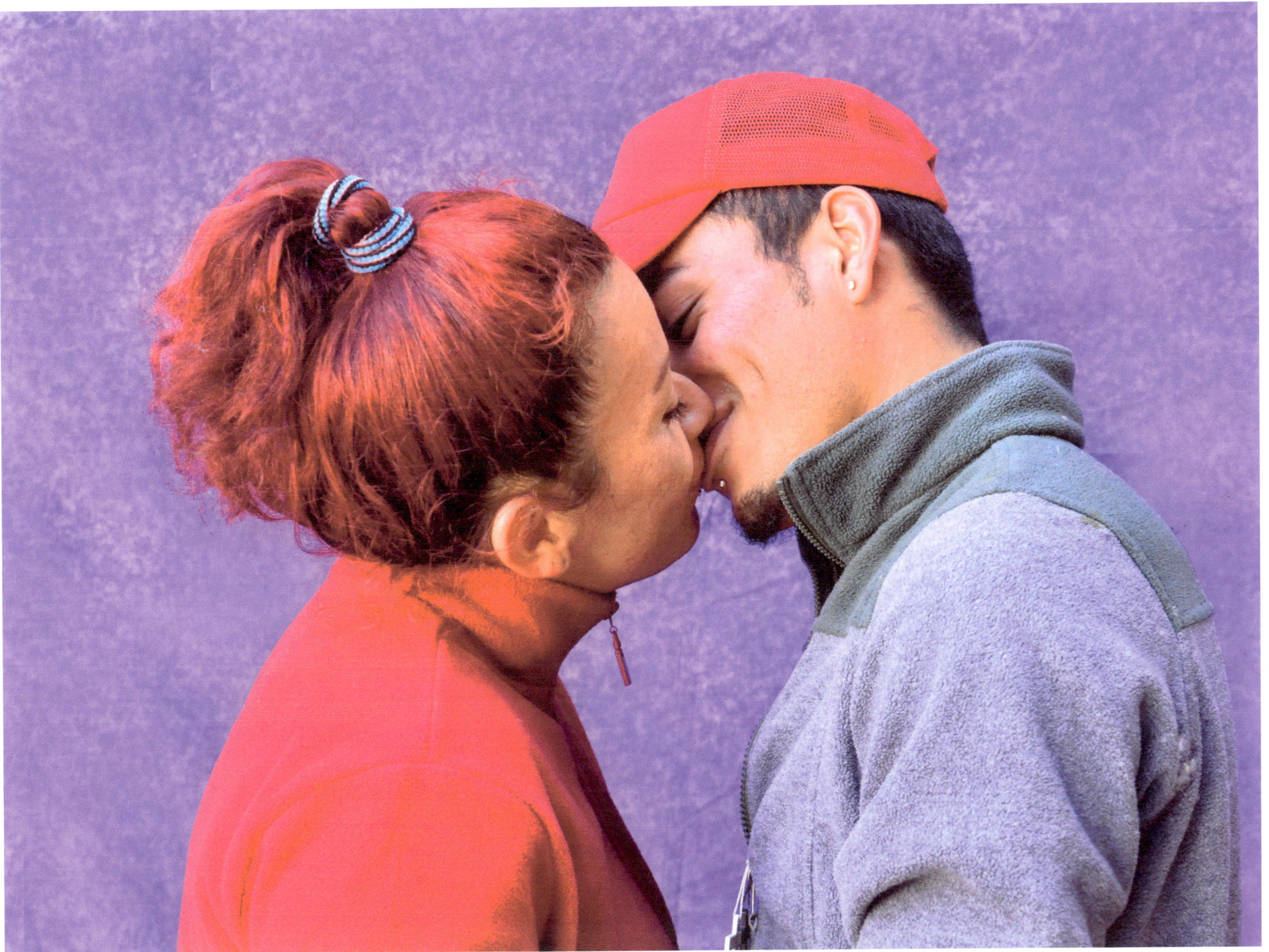

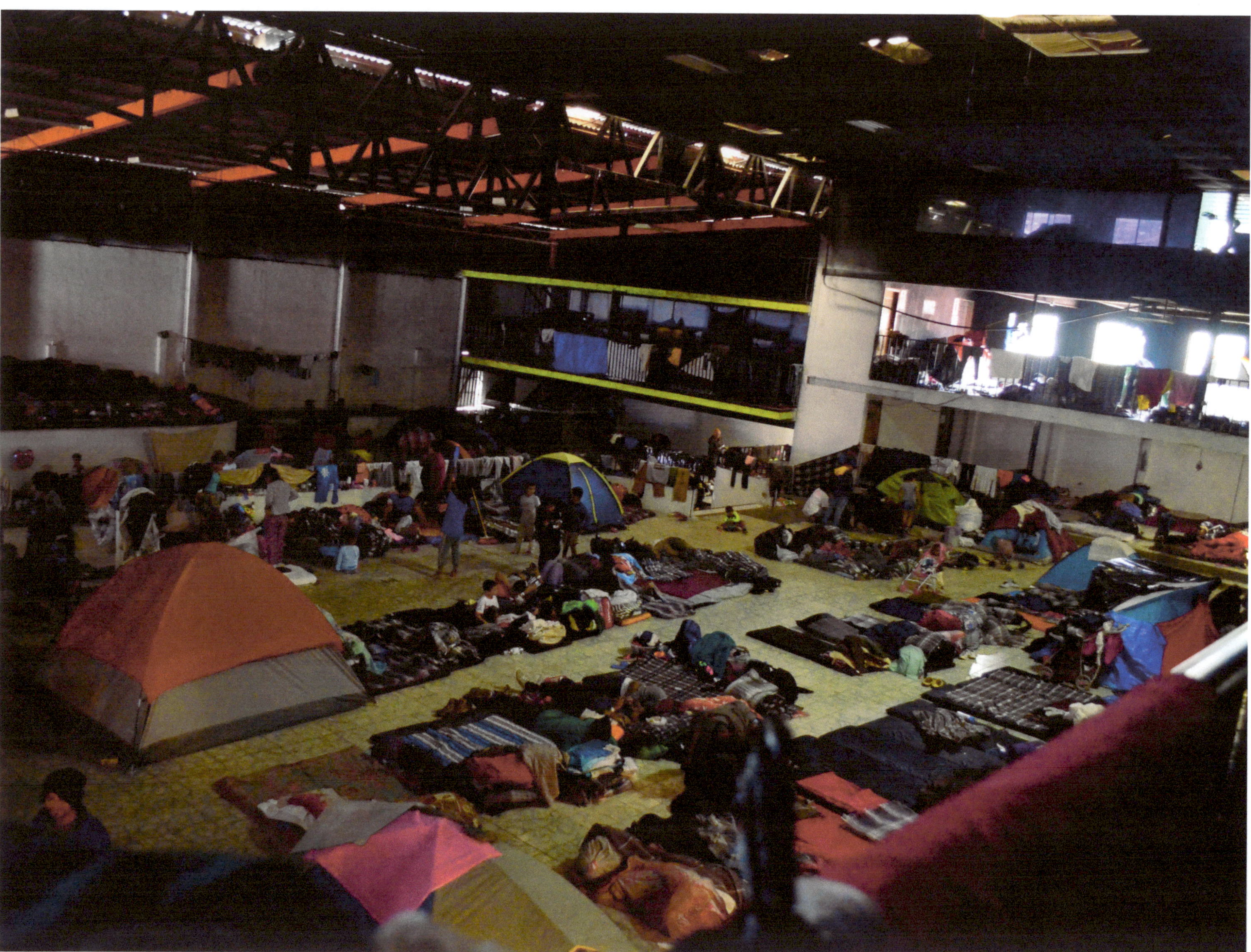

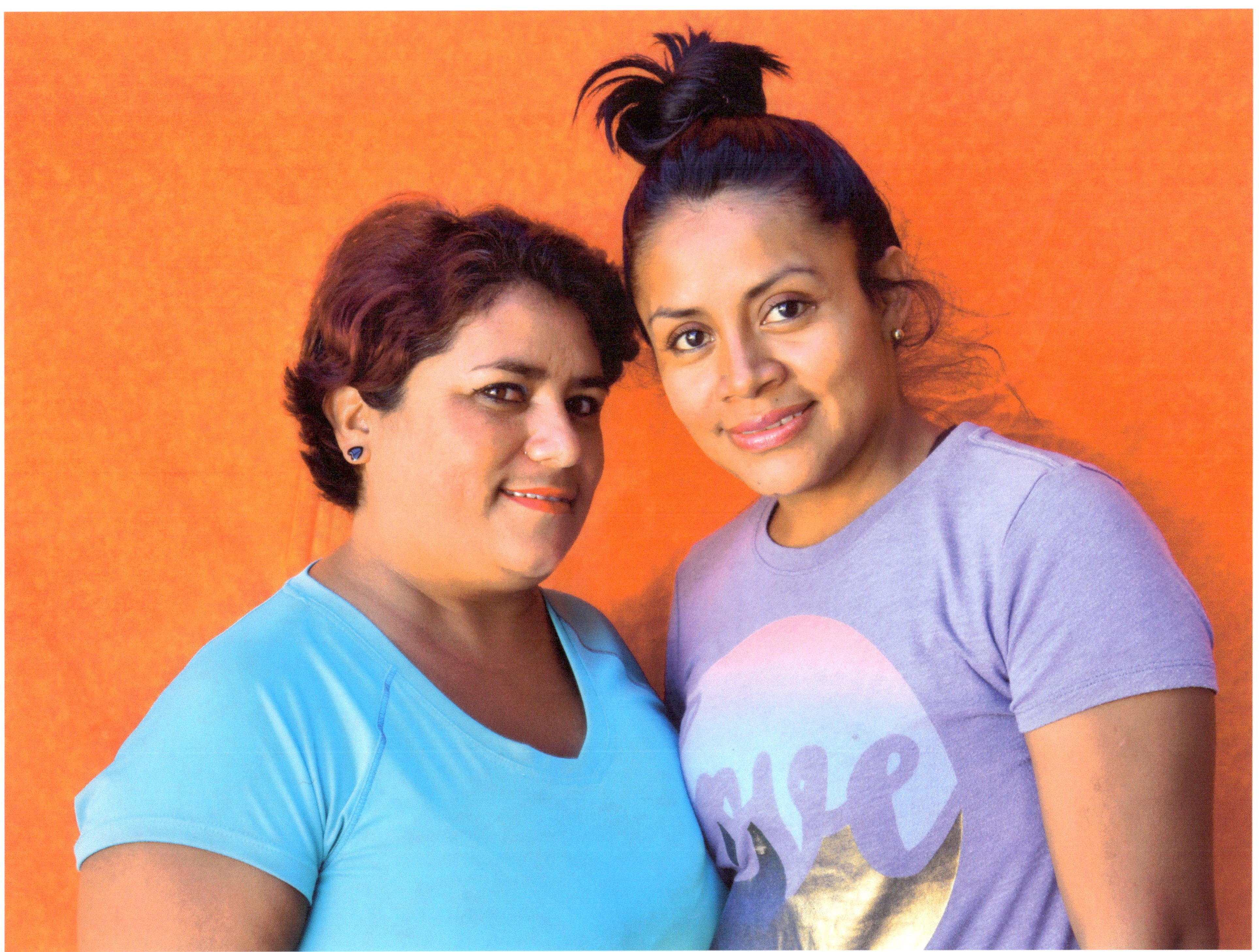

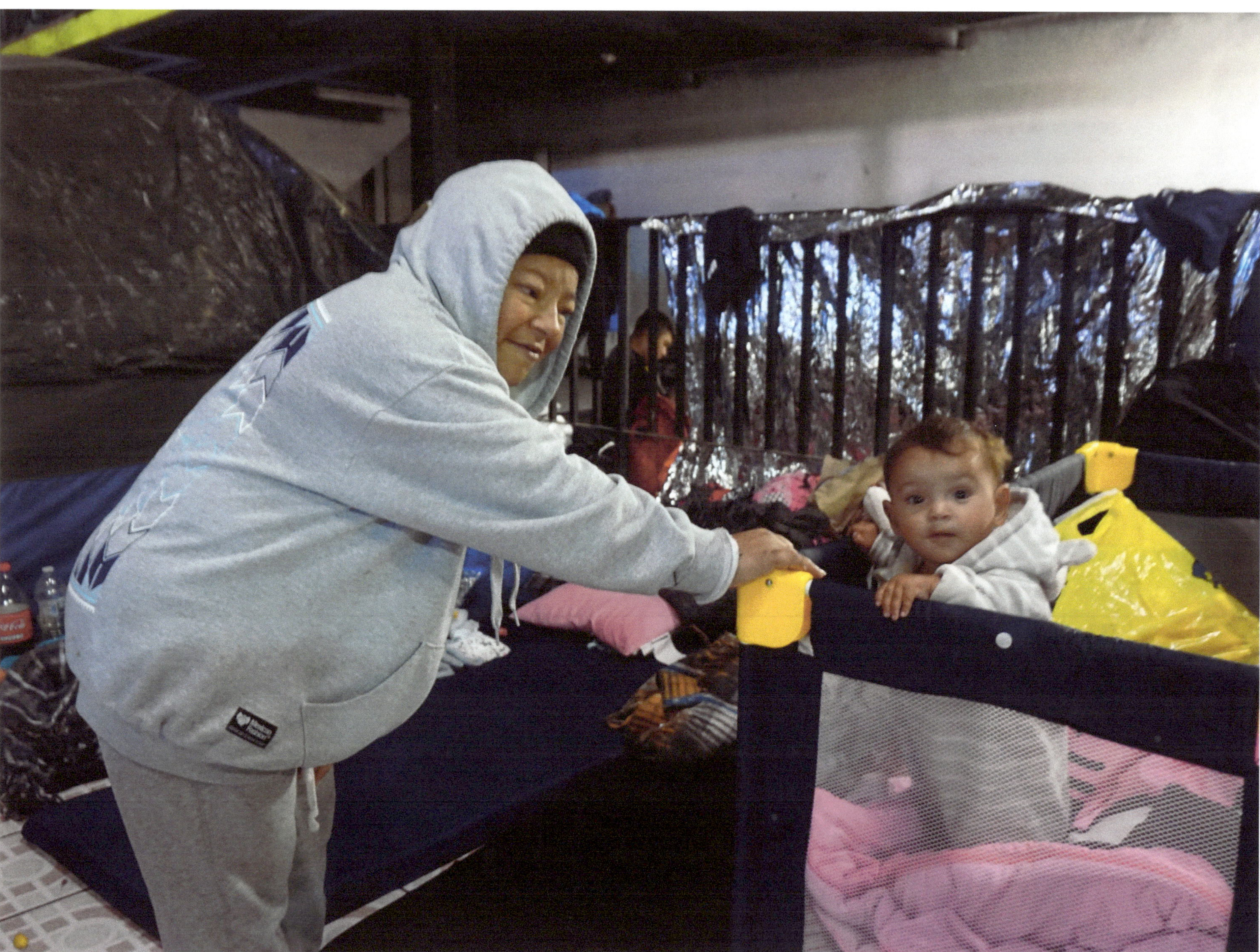

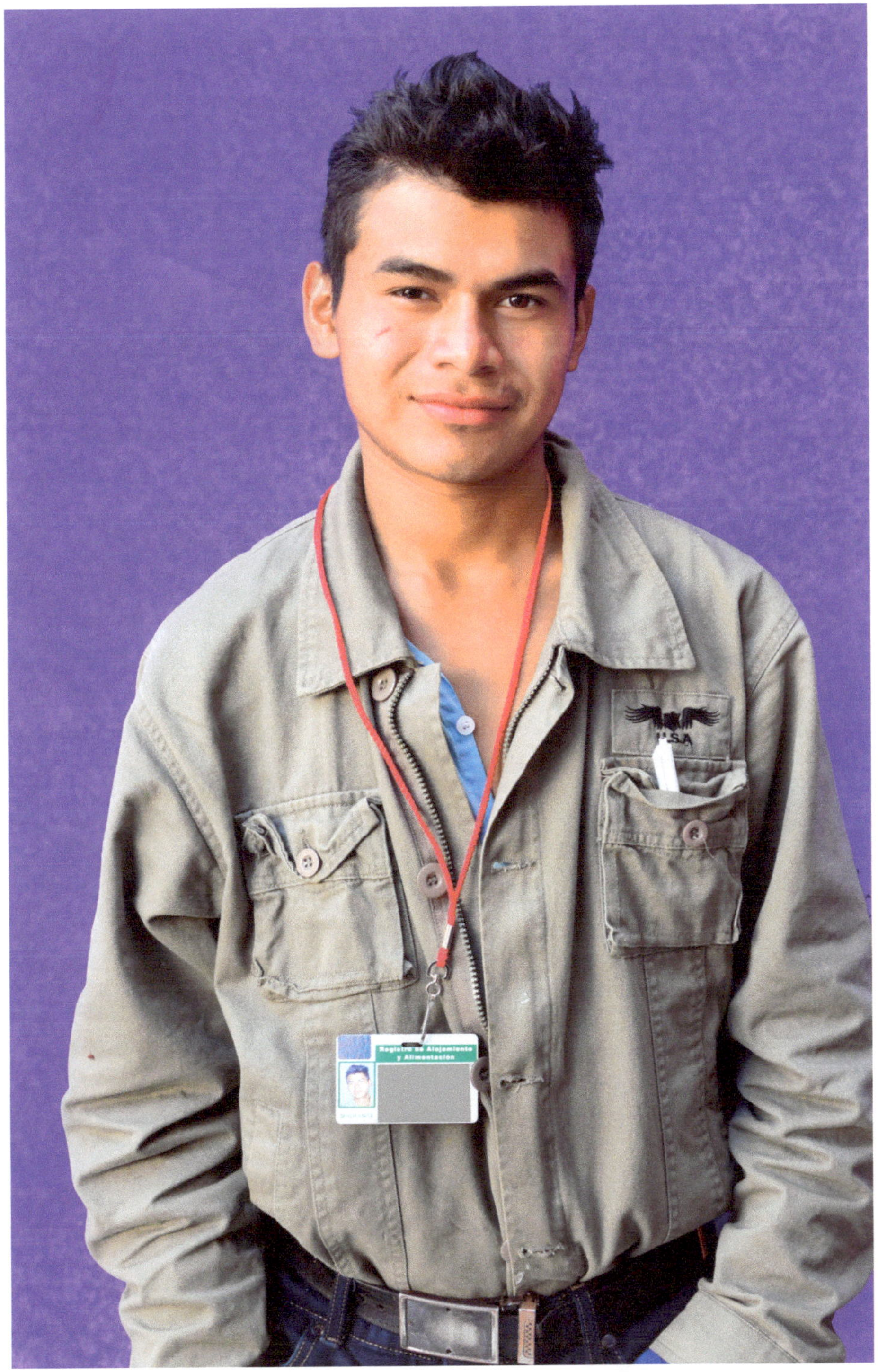

U.S.A
Registro de Alojamiento
y Alimentación

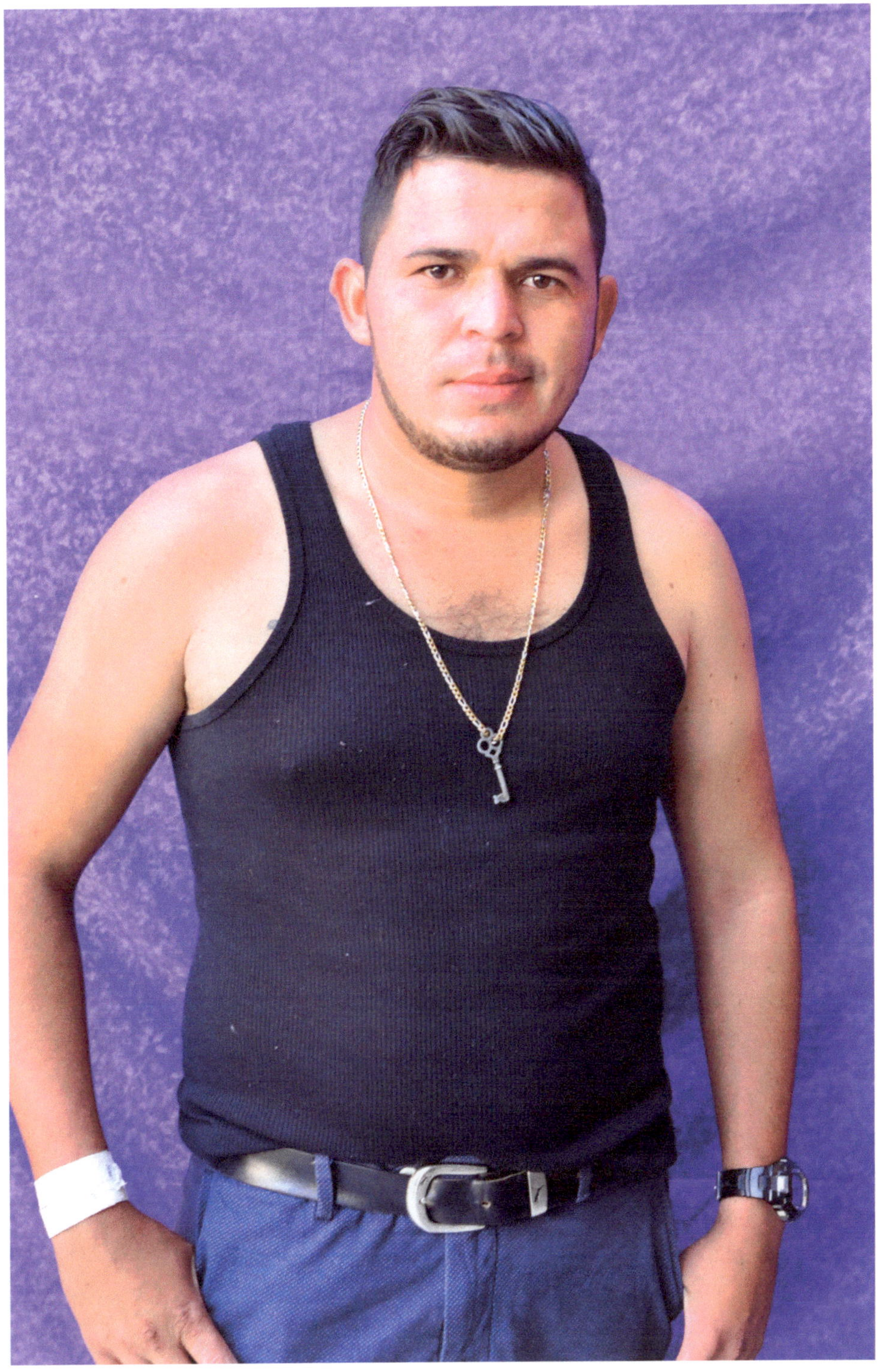

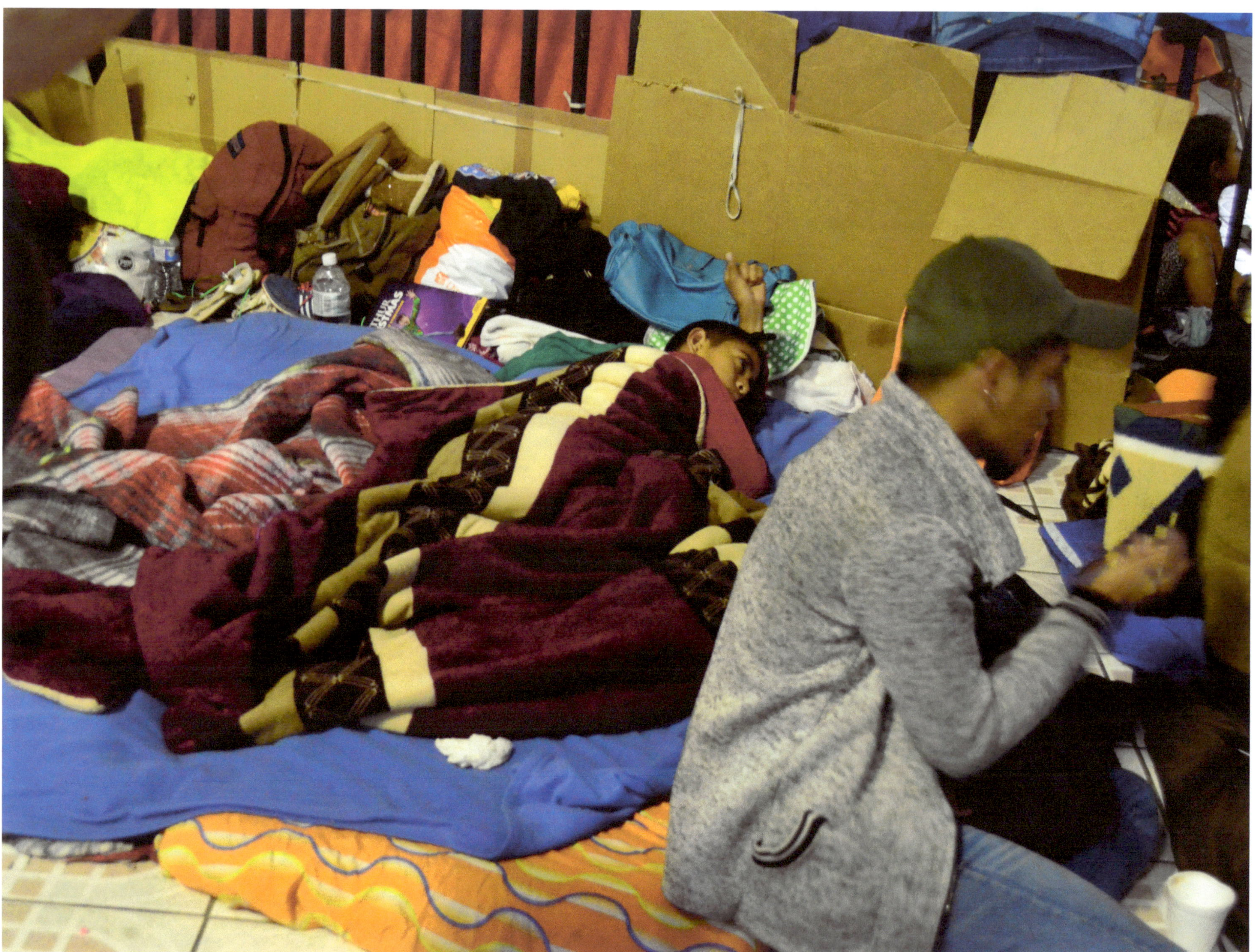

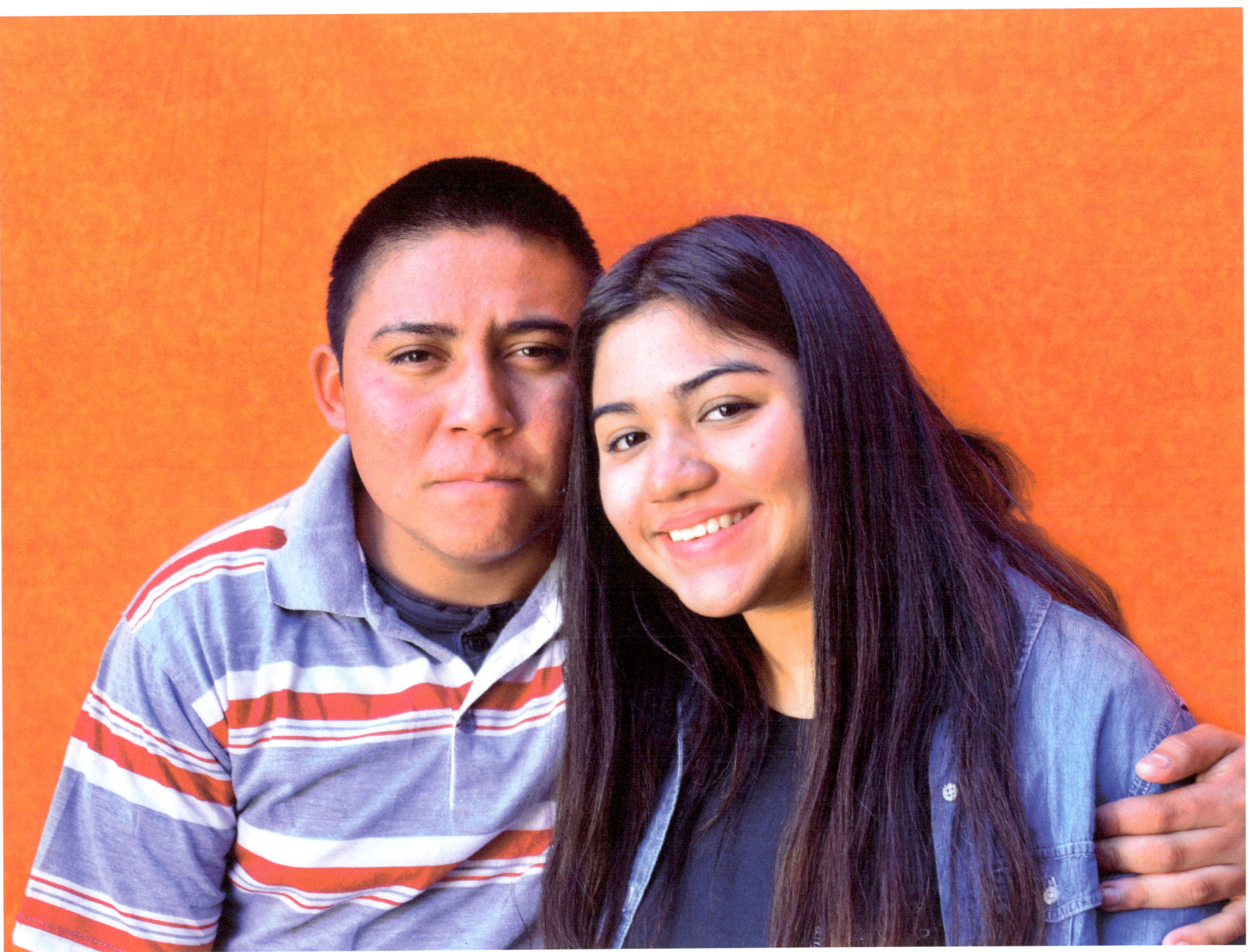

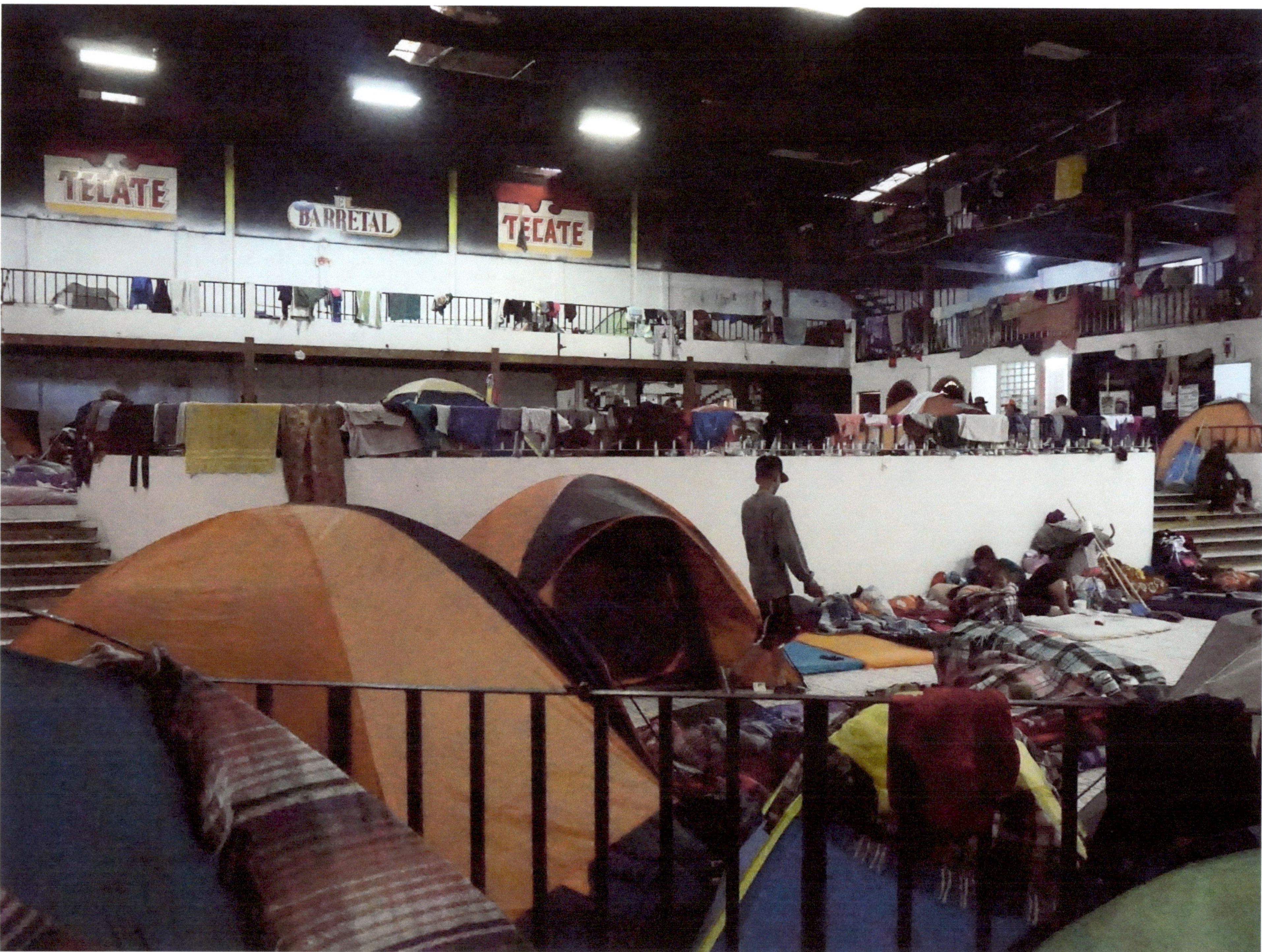
TECATE
EL BARRETAL
TECATE

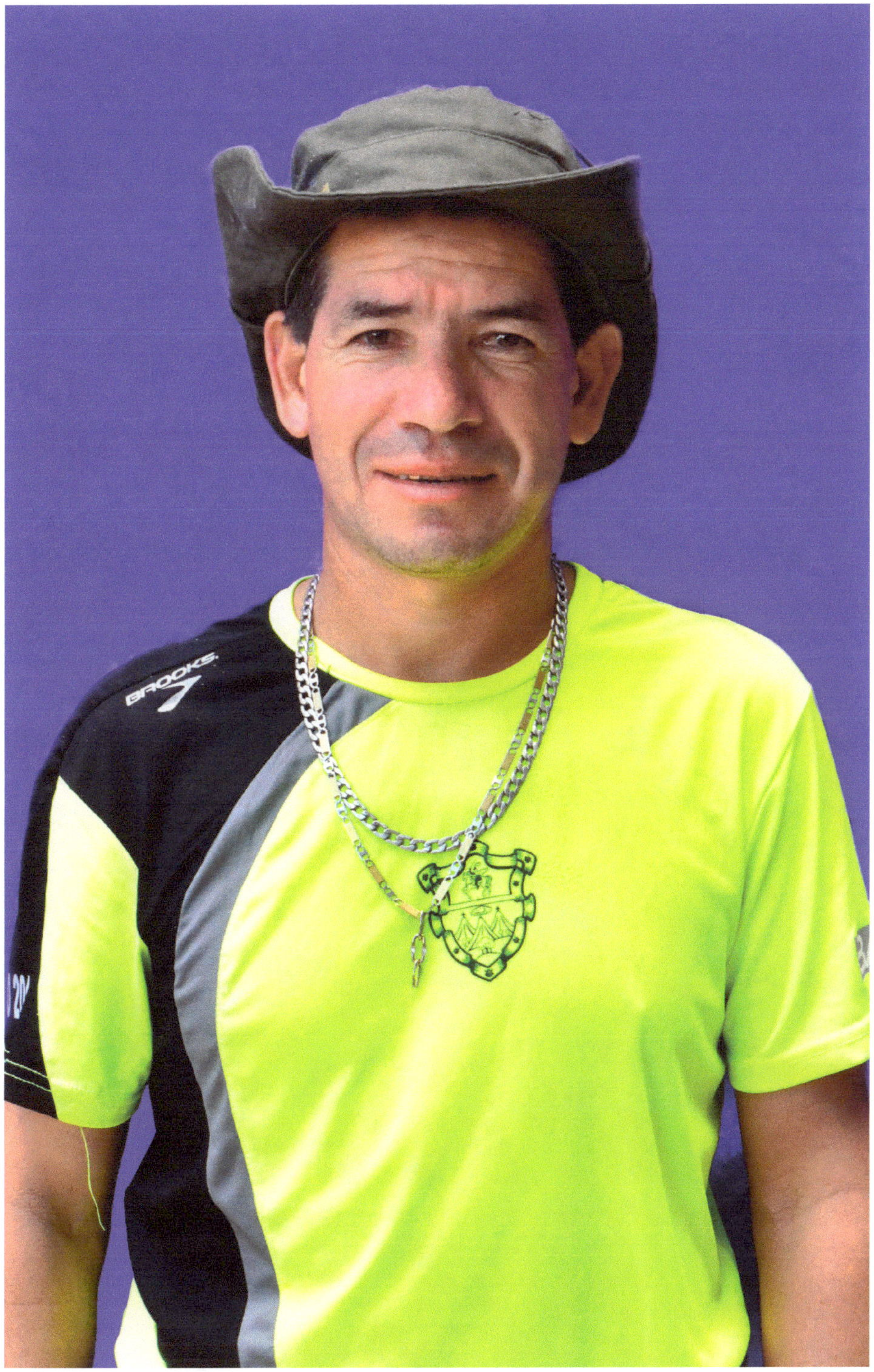

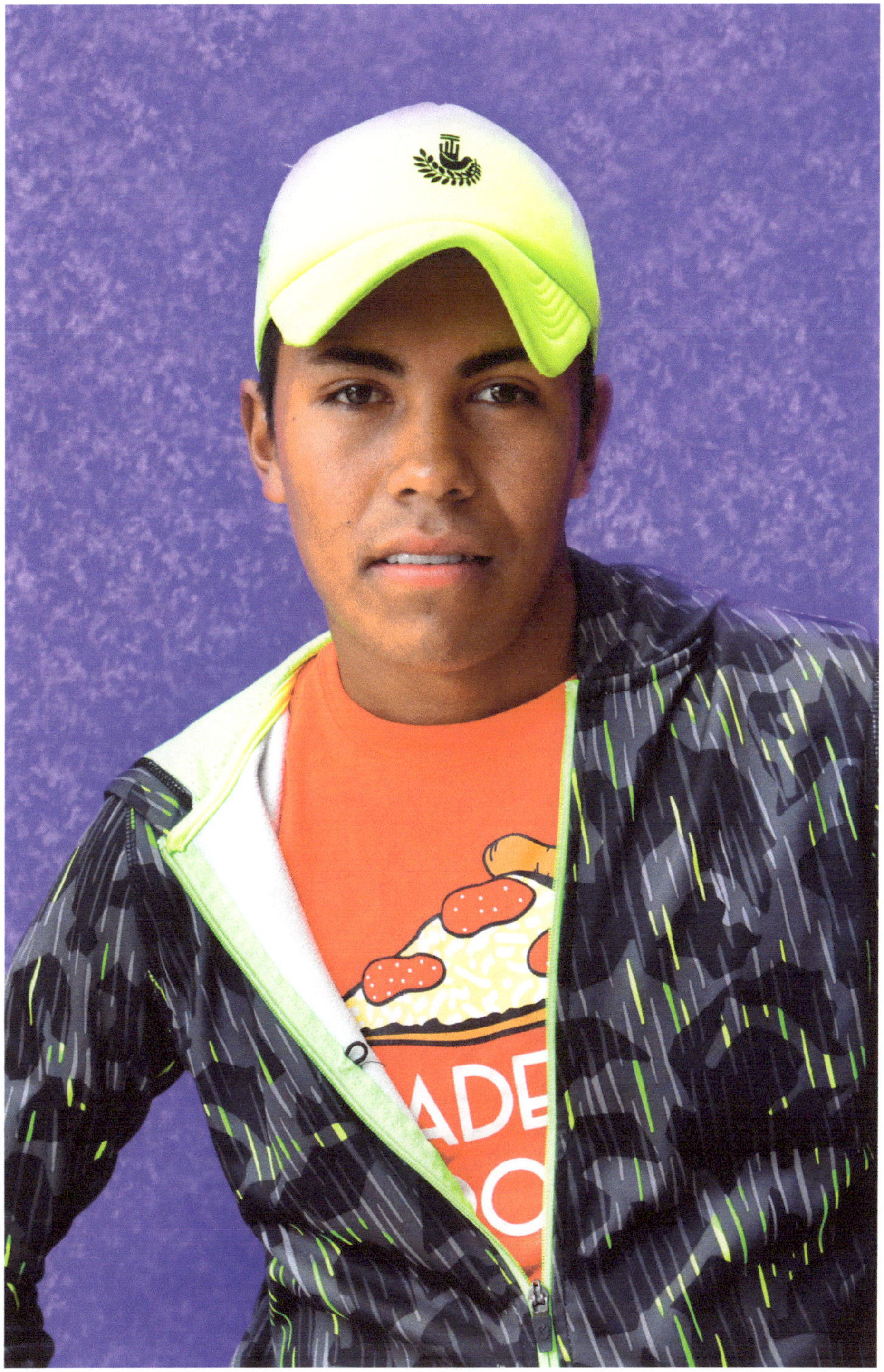

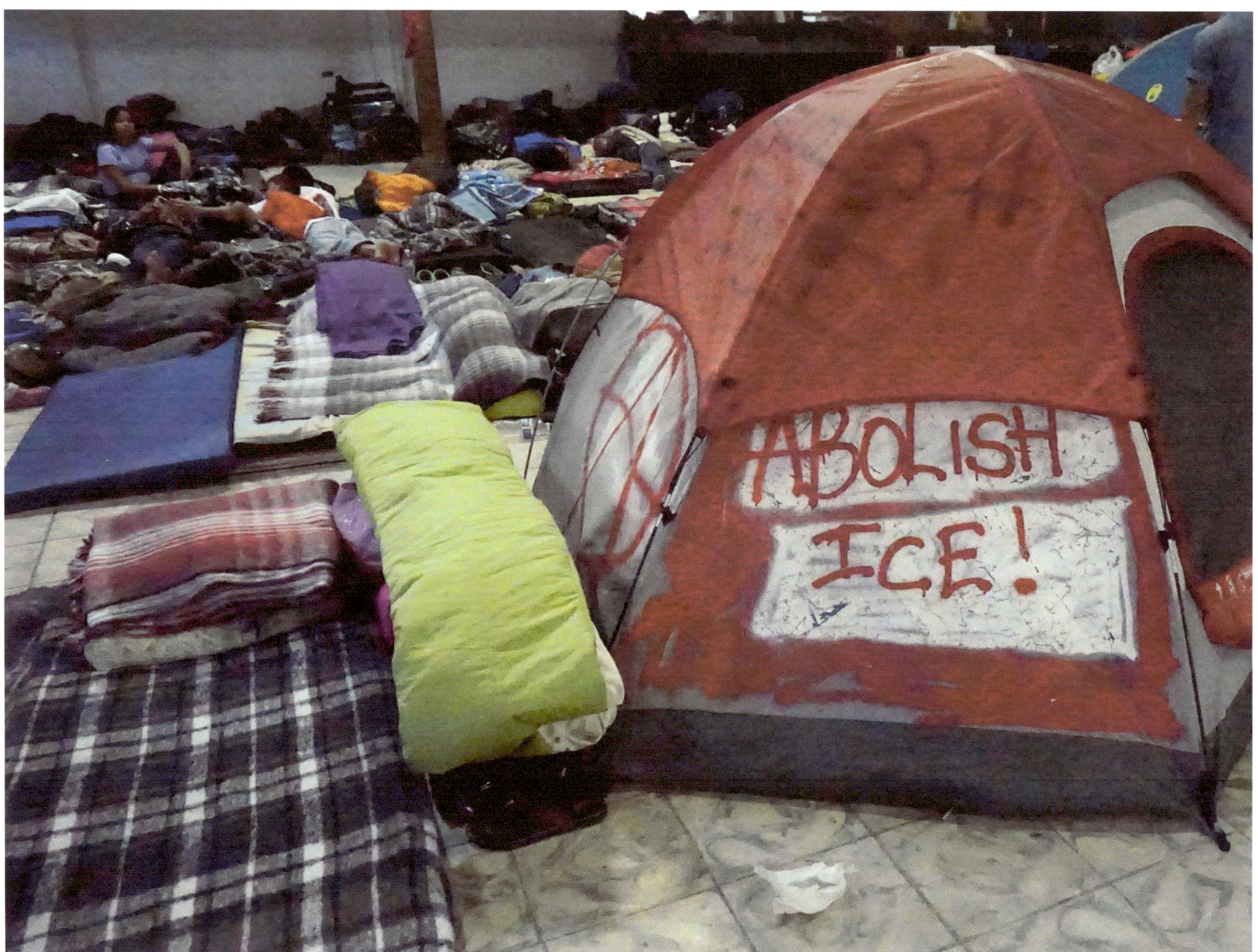
ABOLISH
ICE !

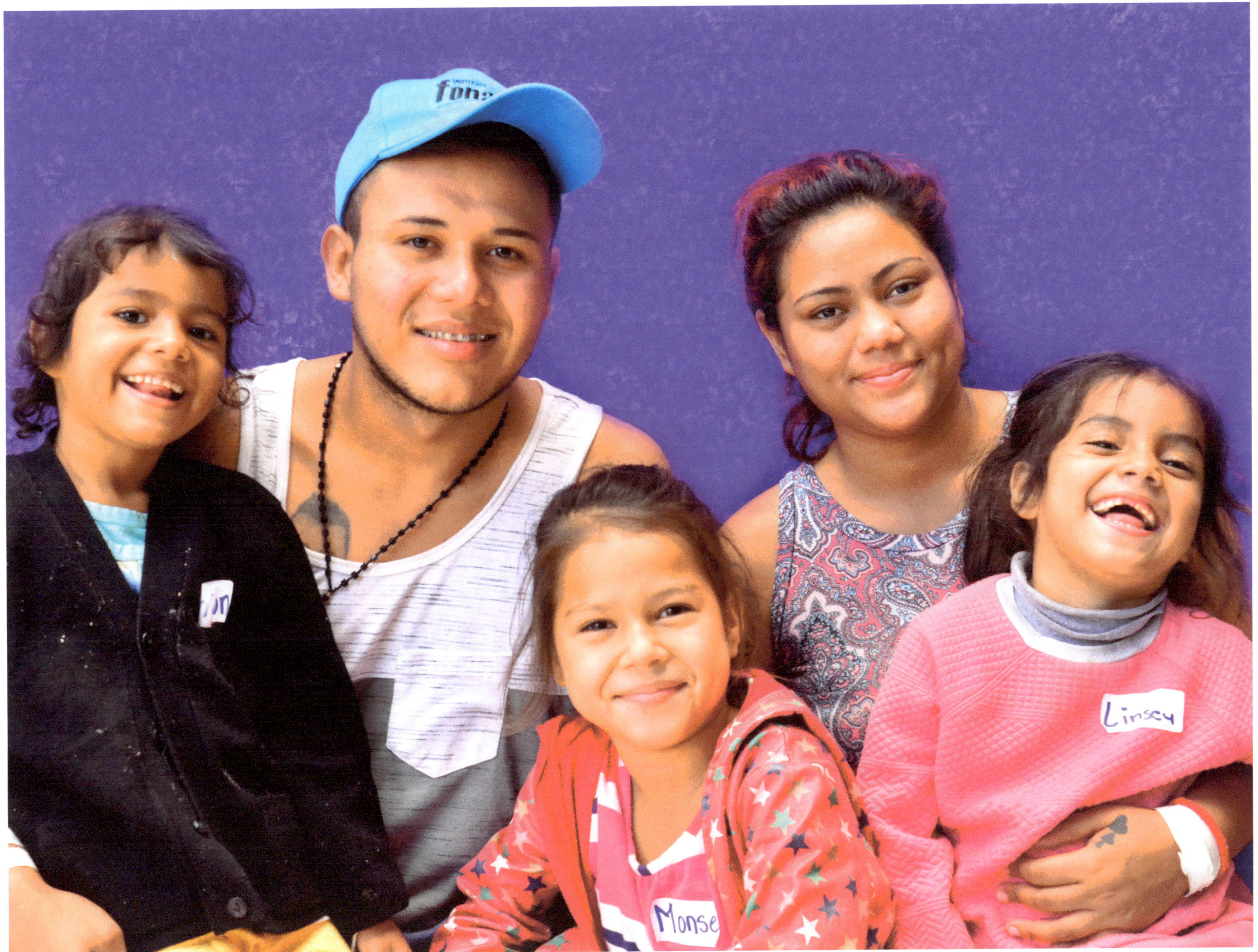

Monse
Linsey

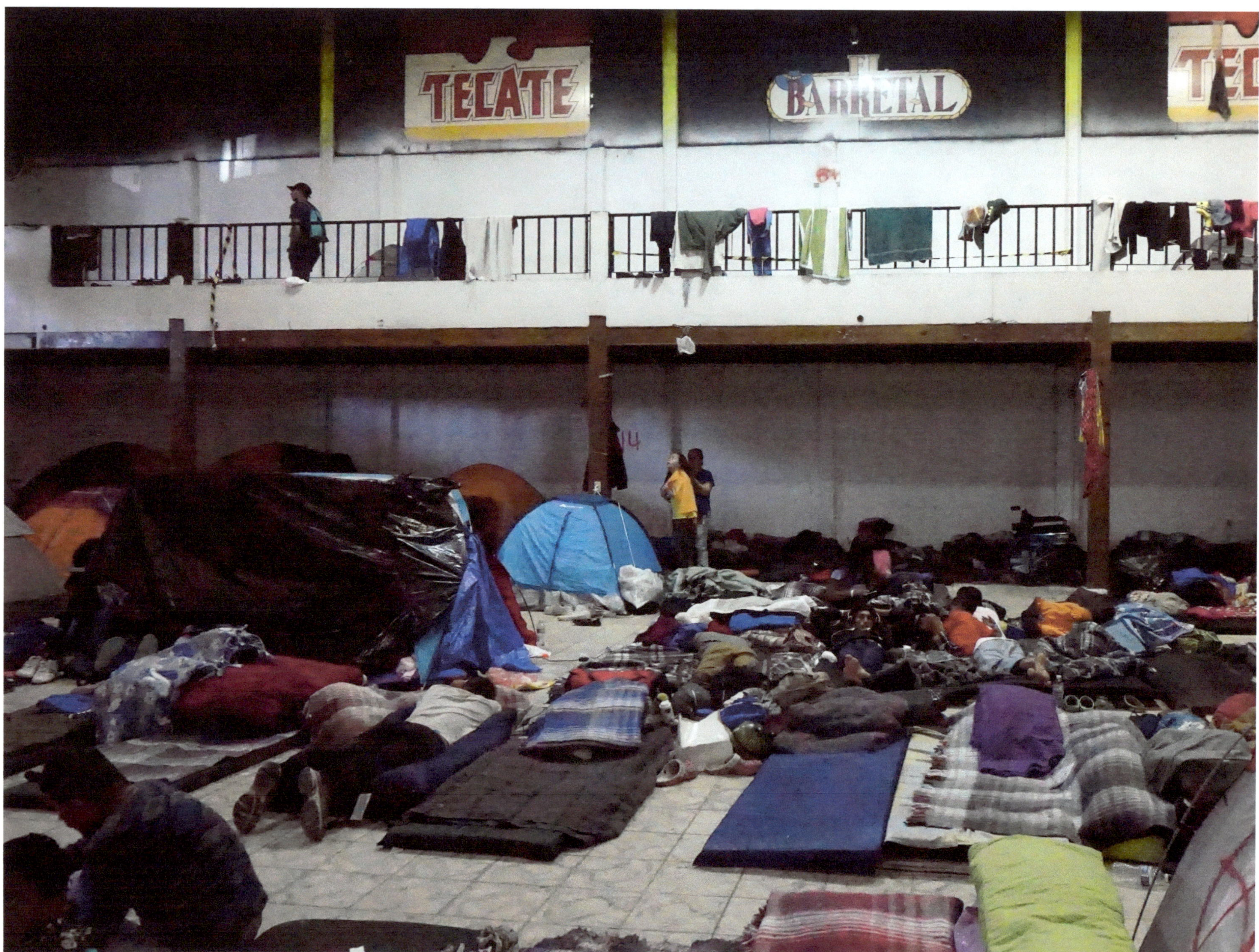

TECATE
BARRETAL
TEC

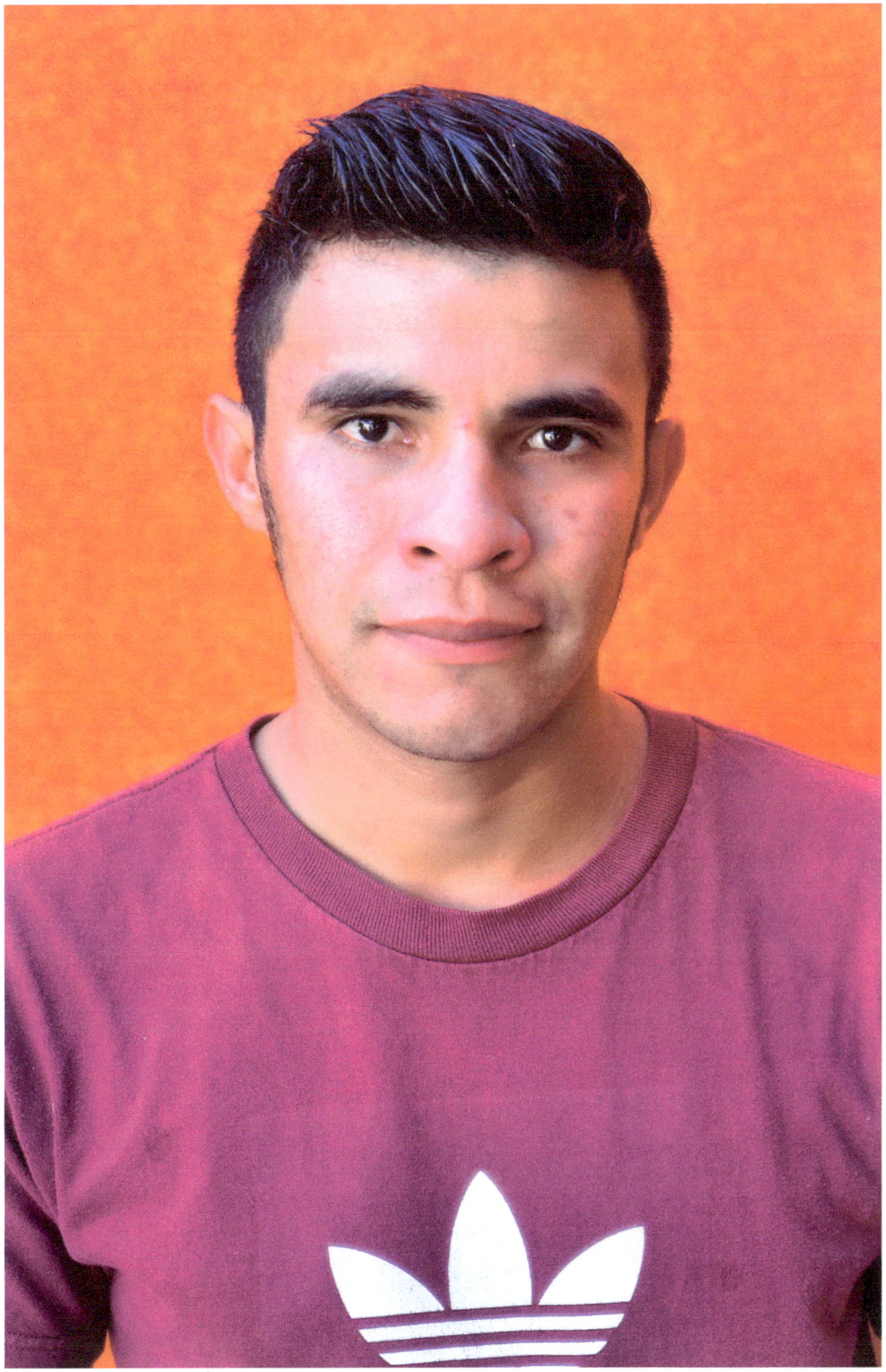

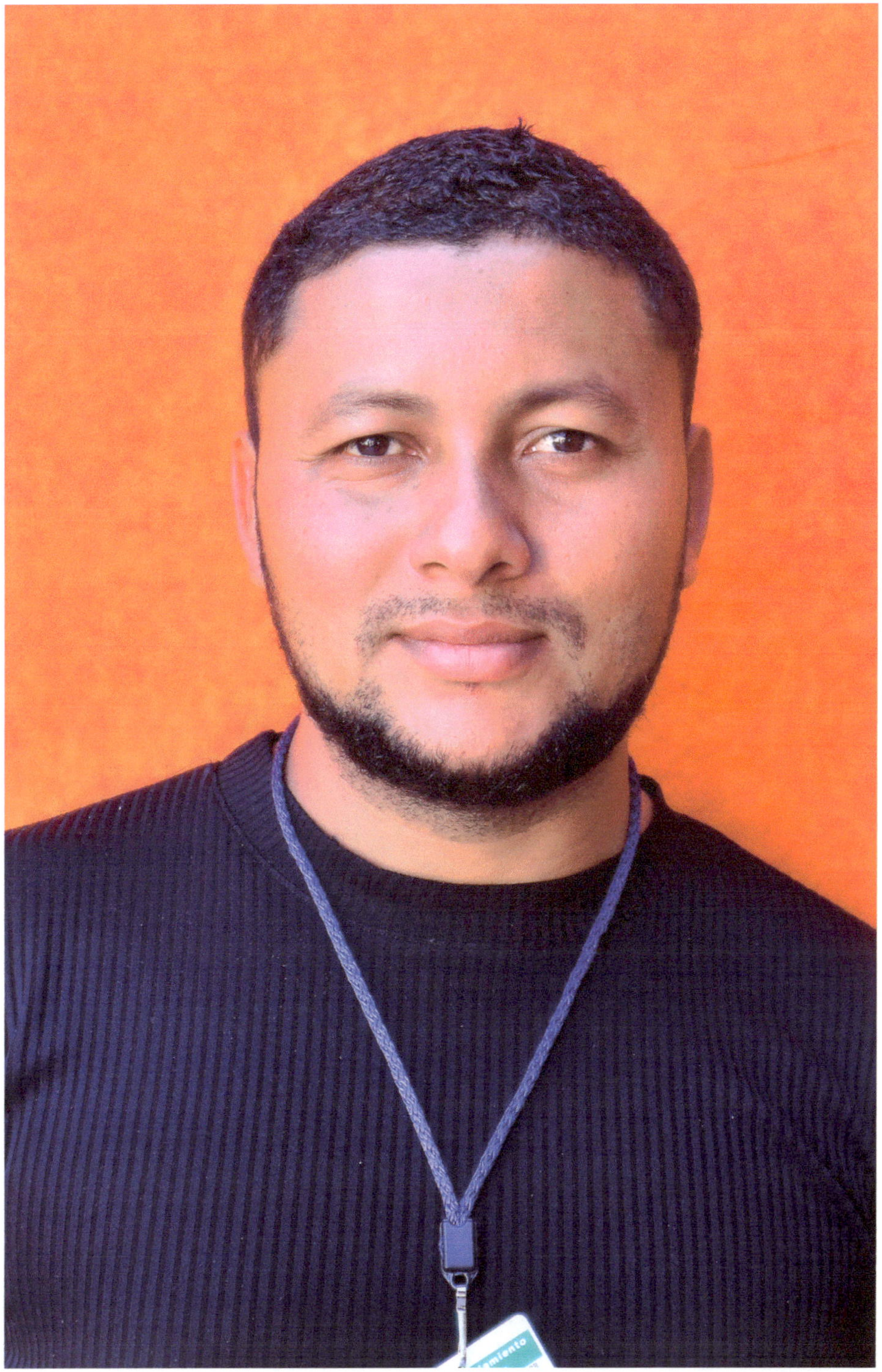

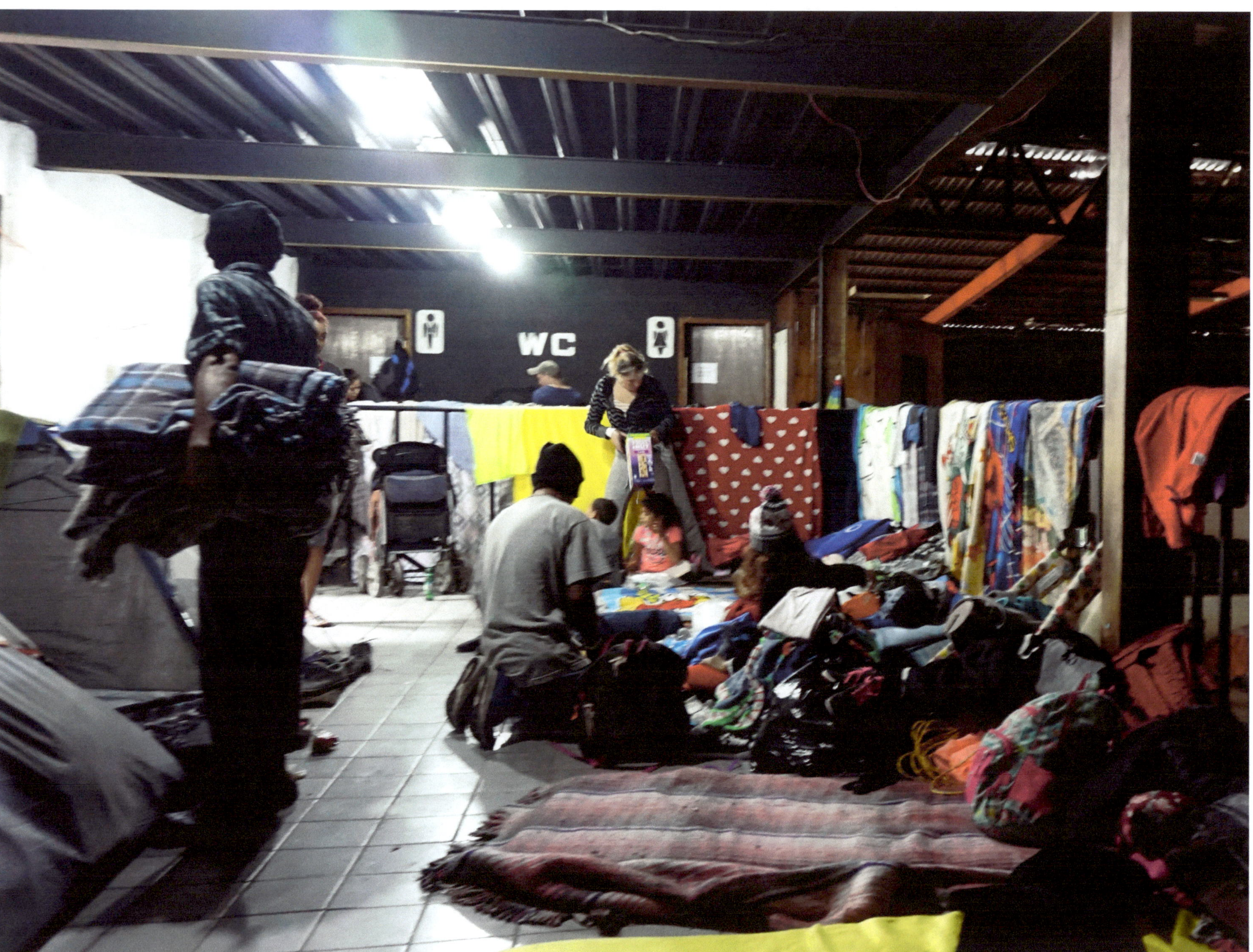
WC

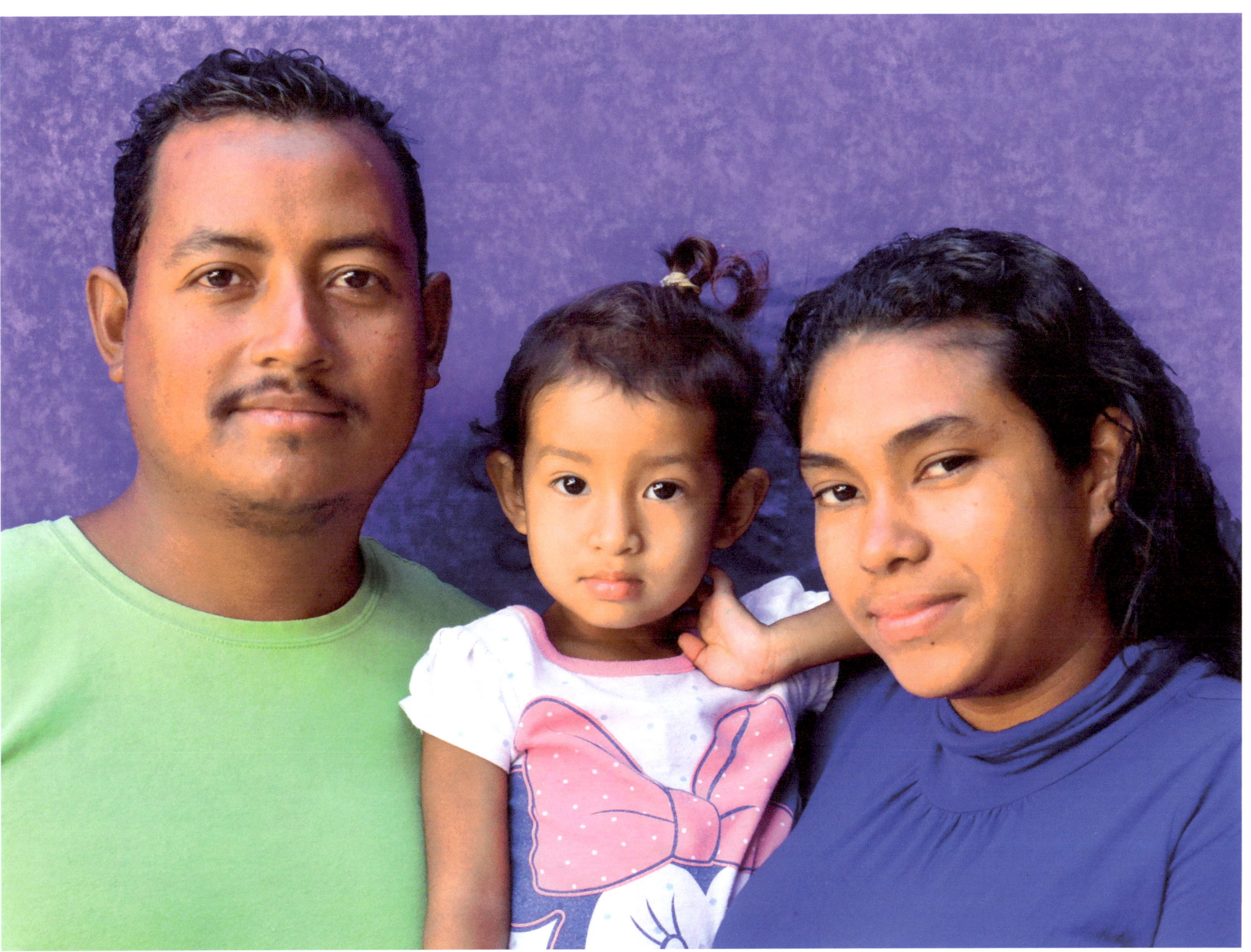

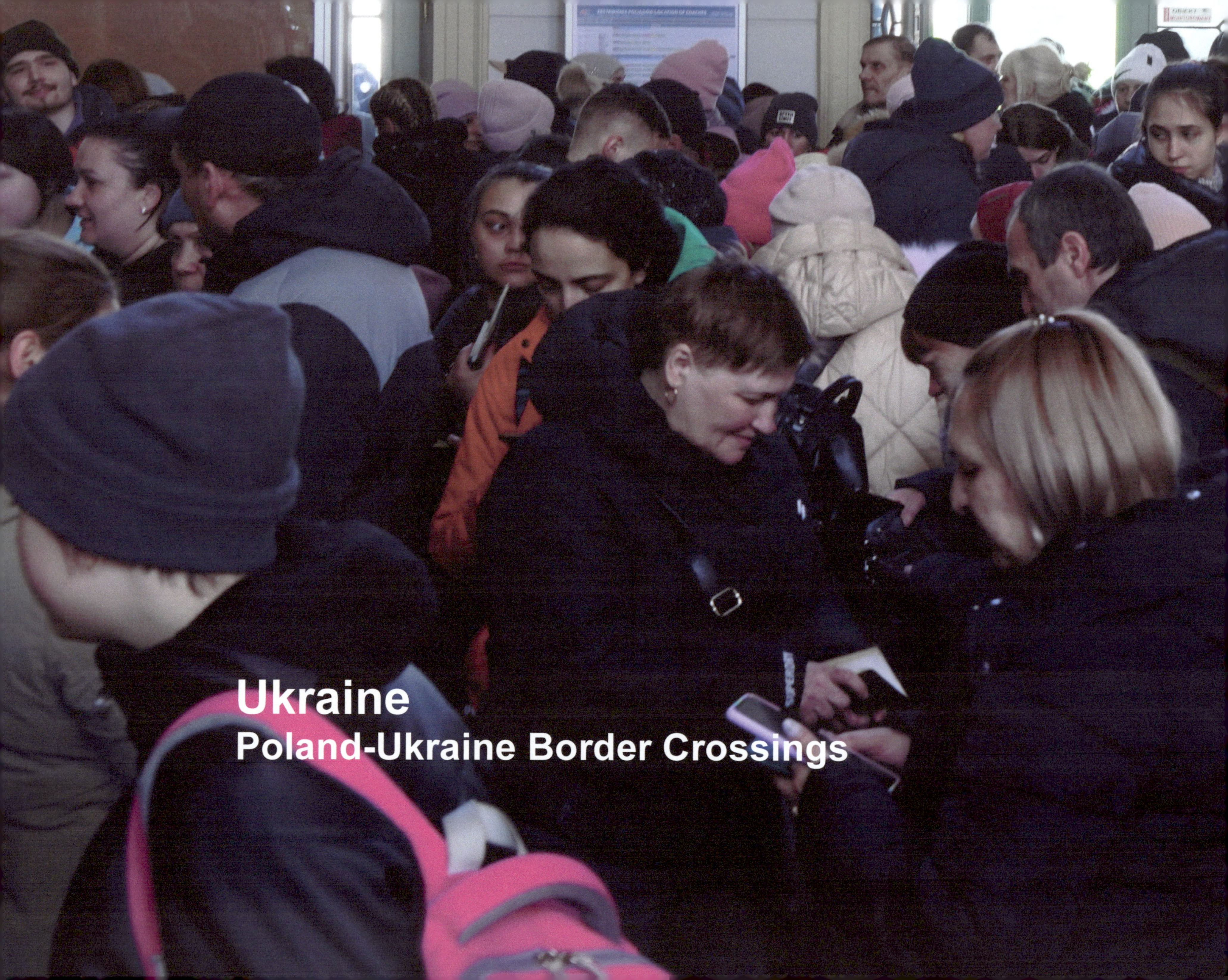

Ukraine
Poland-Ukraine Border Crossings

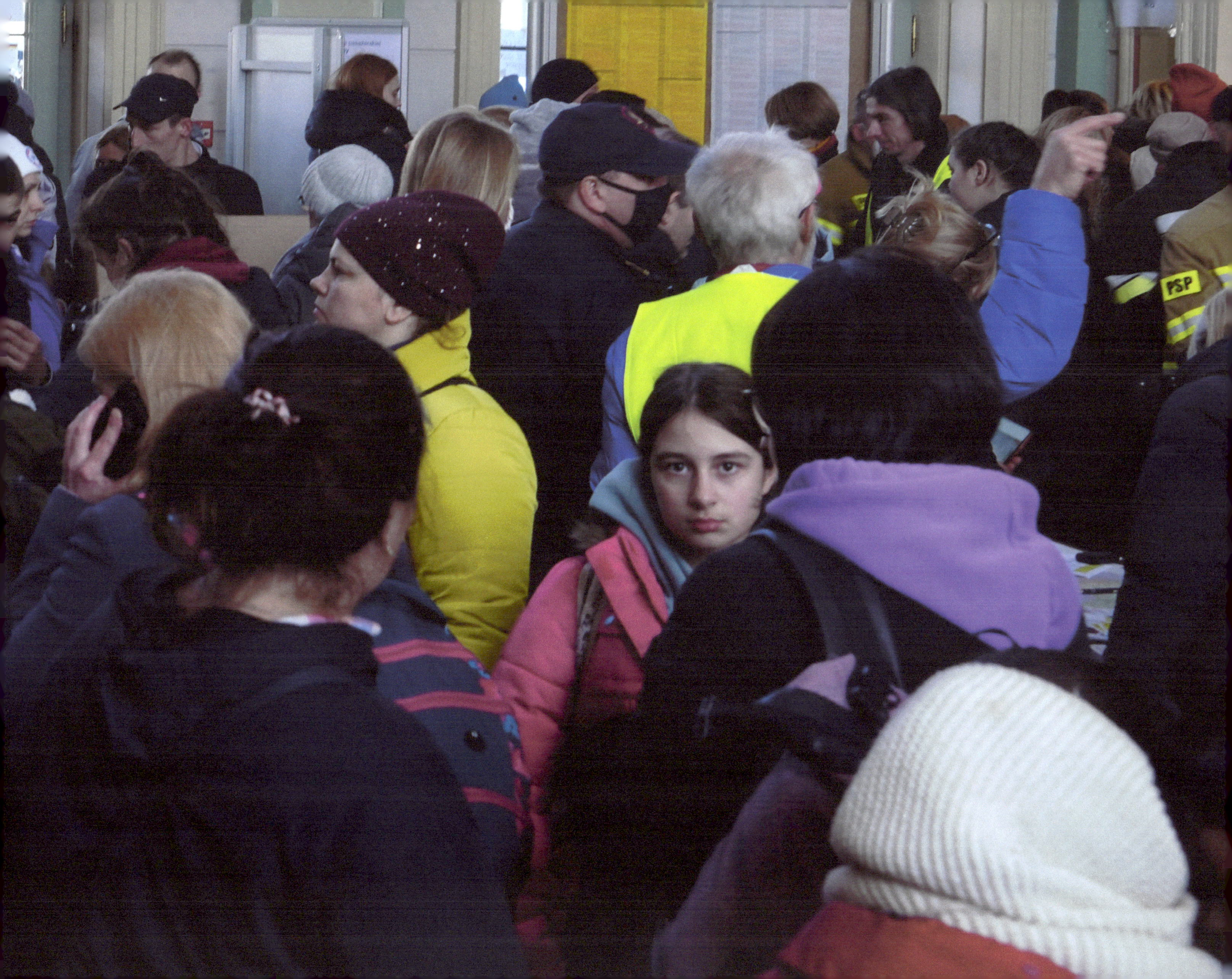

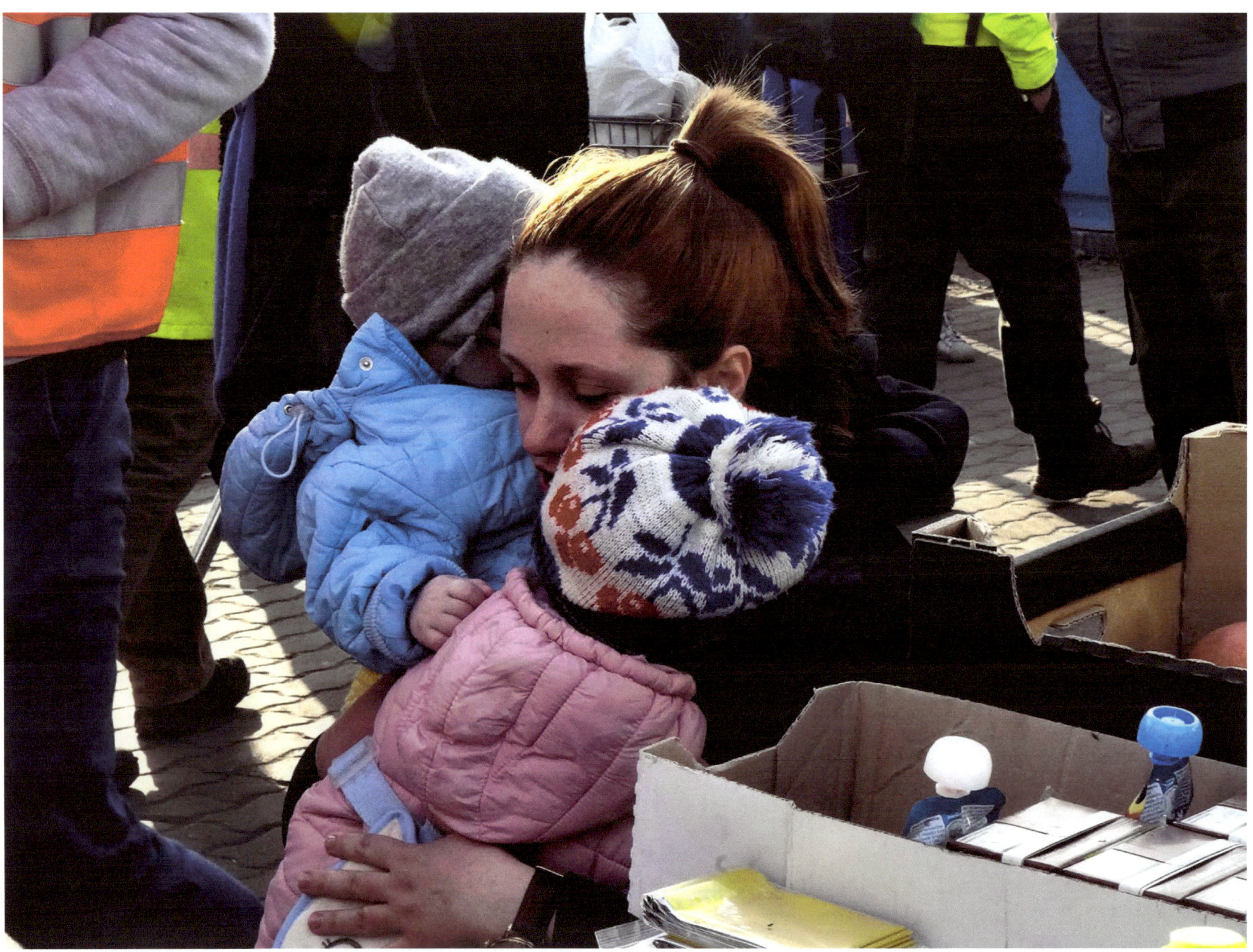

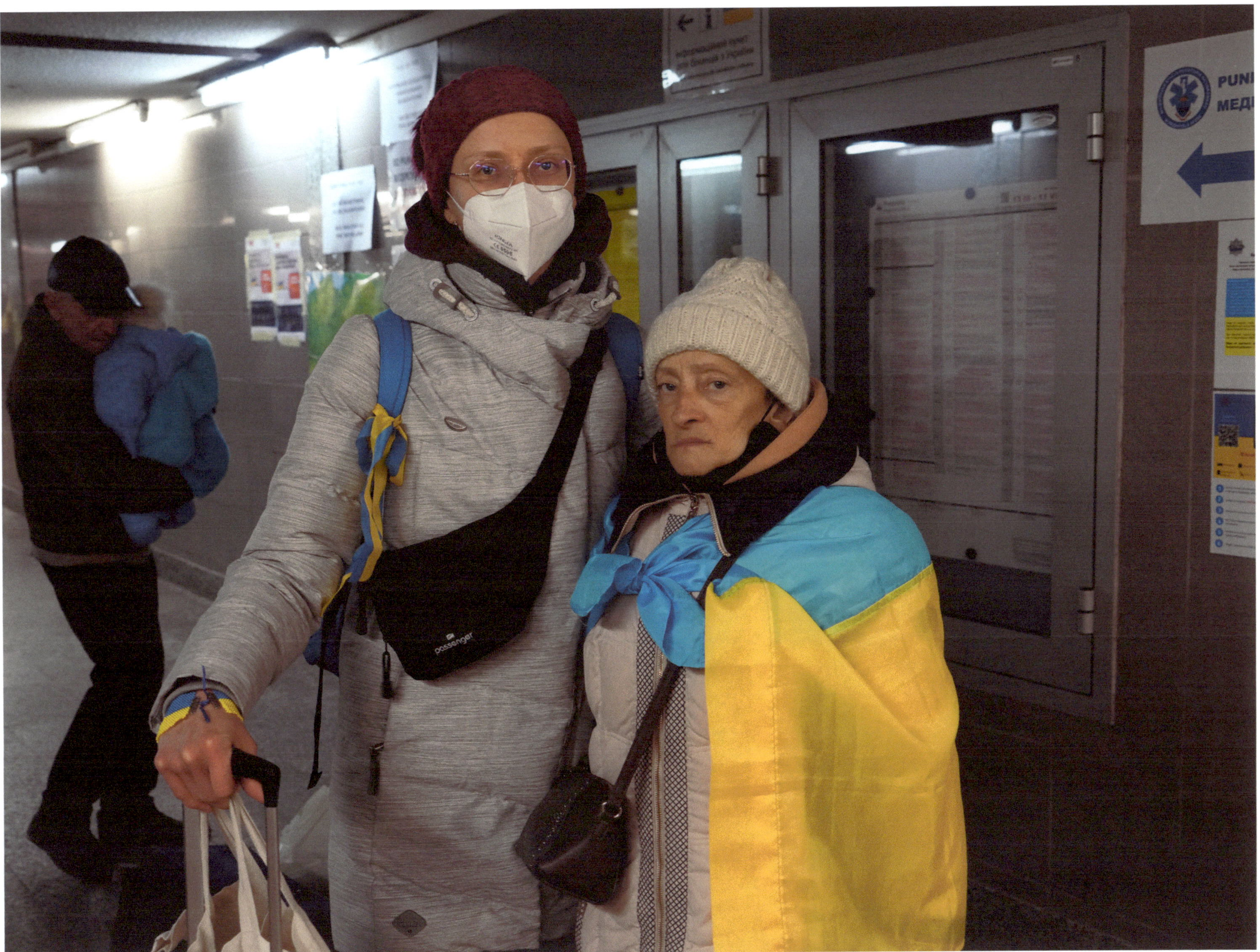

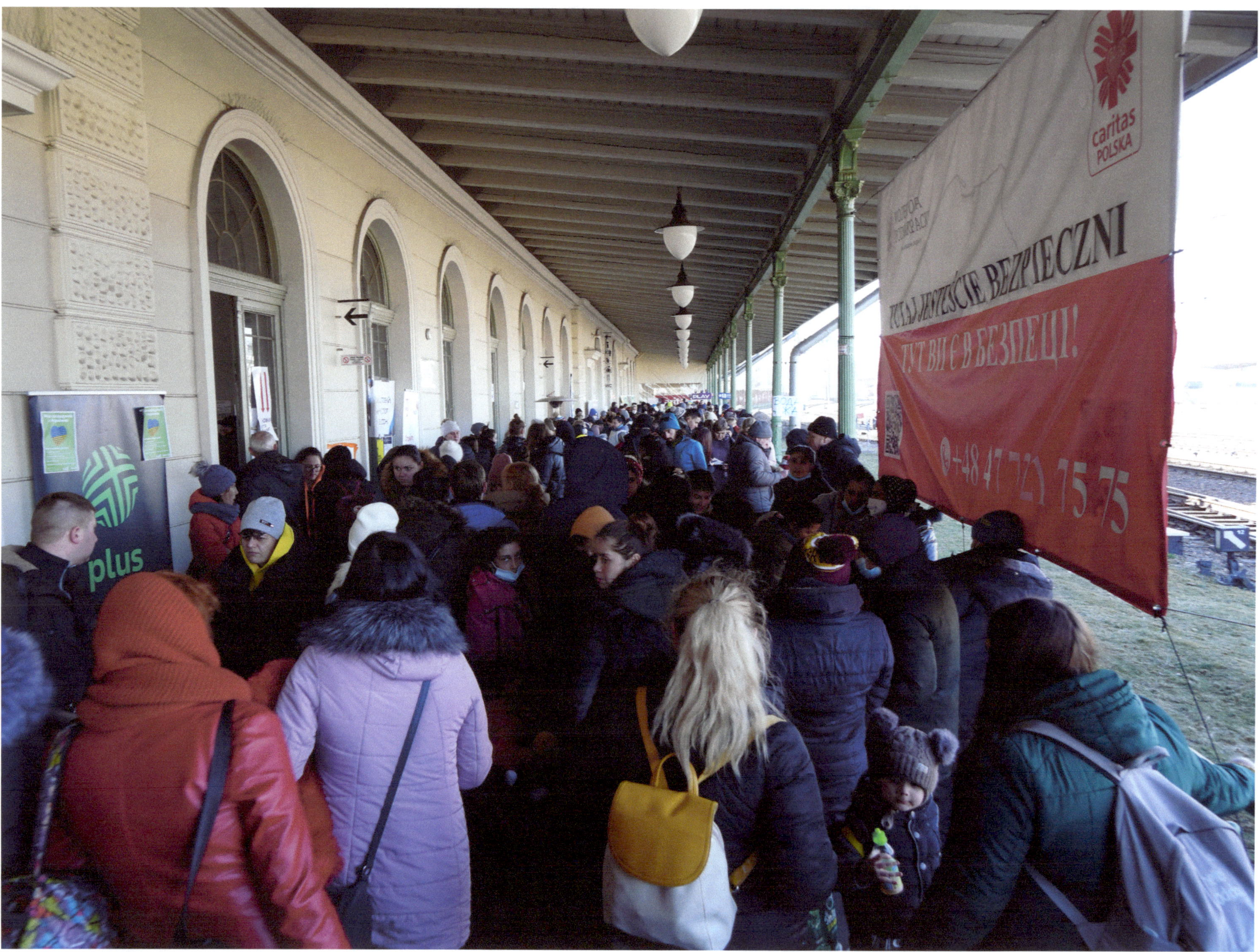

caritas
POLSKA
TUTAJ JESTEŚCIE BEZPIECZNI
ТУТ ВИ Є В БЕЗПЕЦІ!
+48 47 7ZY 75 75
plus

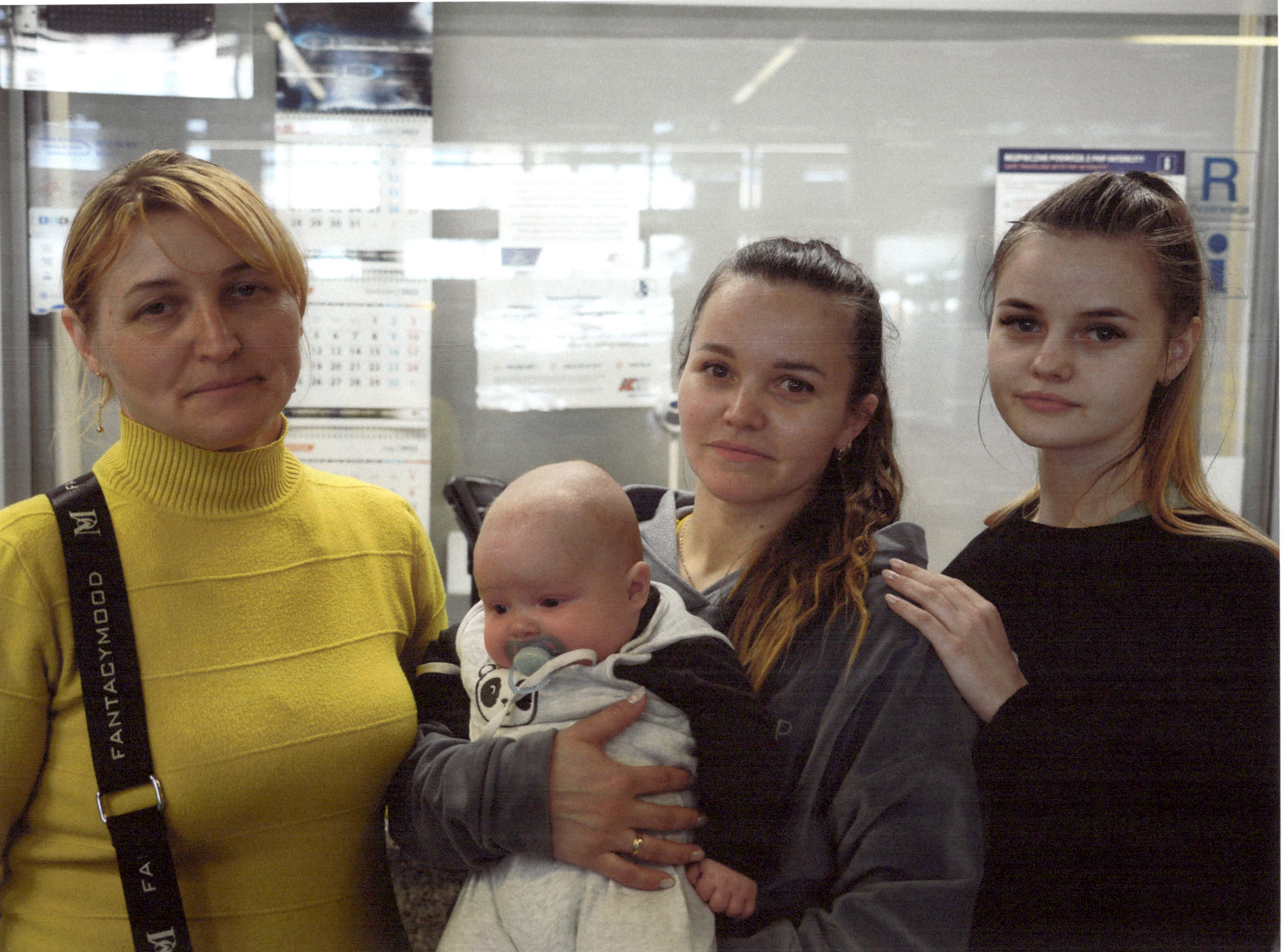

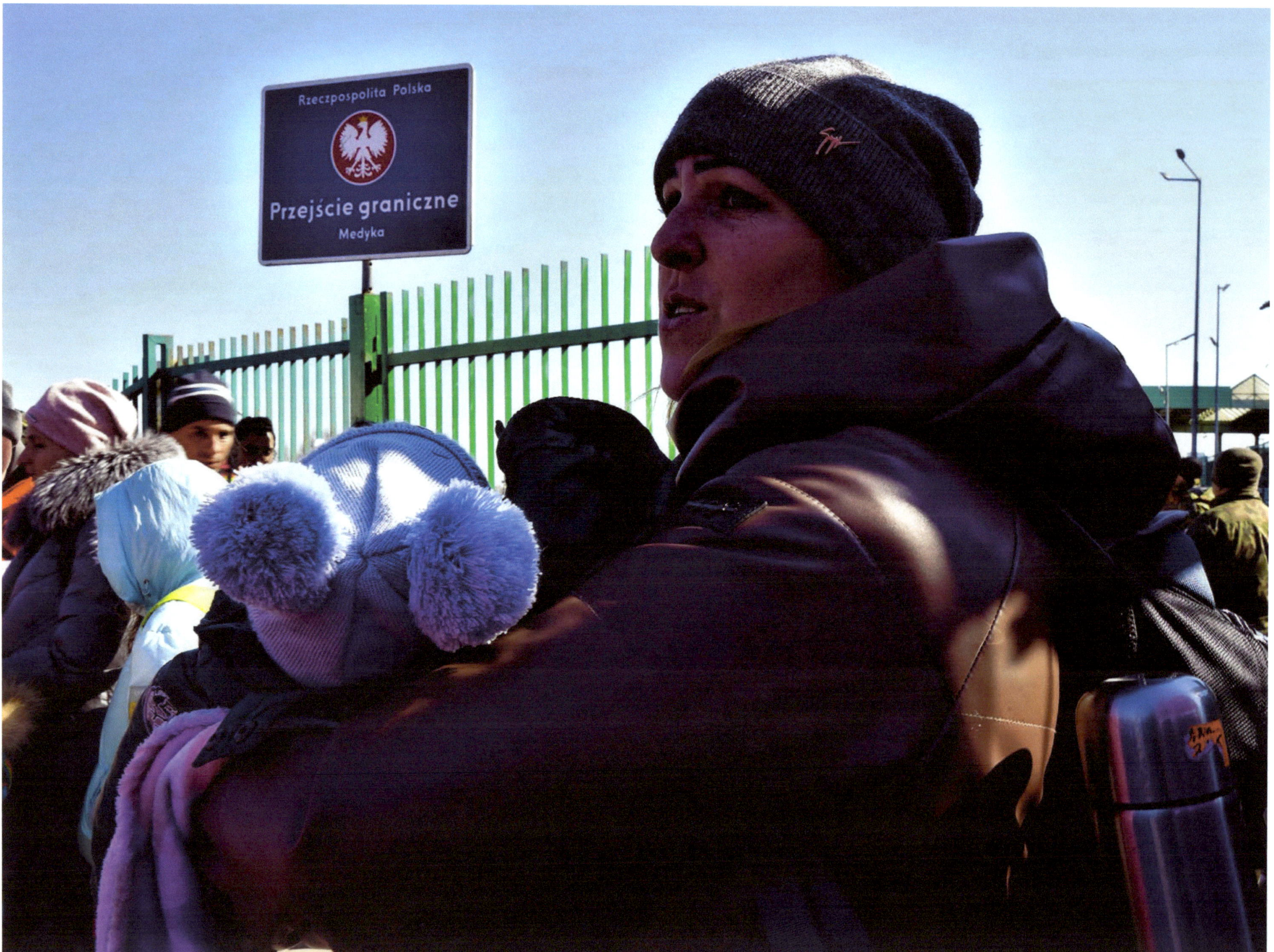
Rzeczpospolita Polska
Przejście graniczne
Medyka

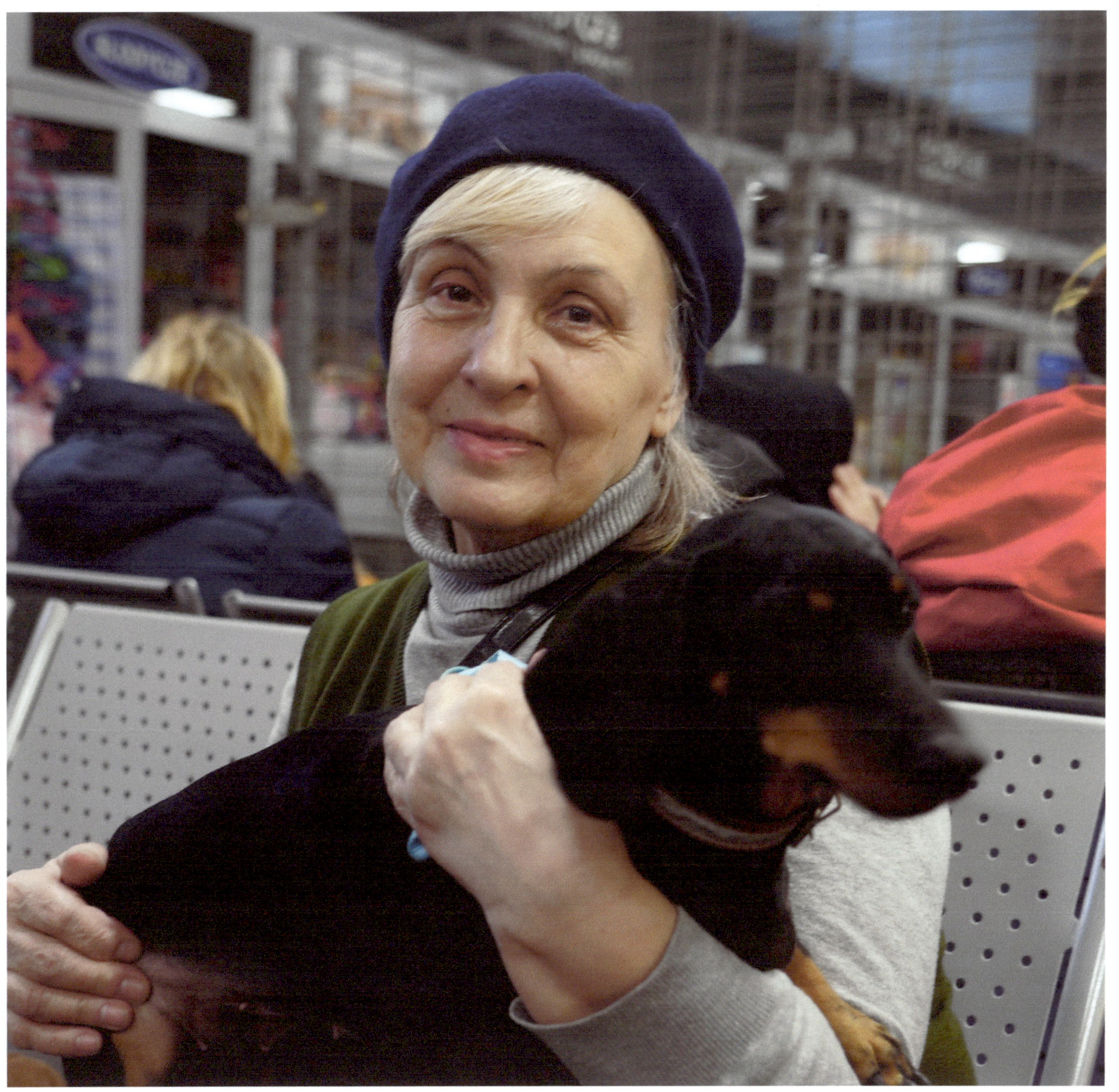

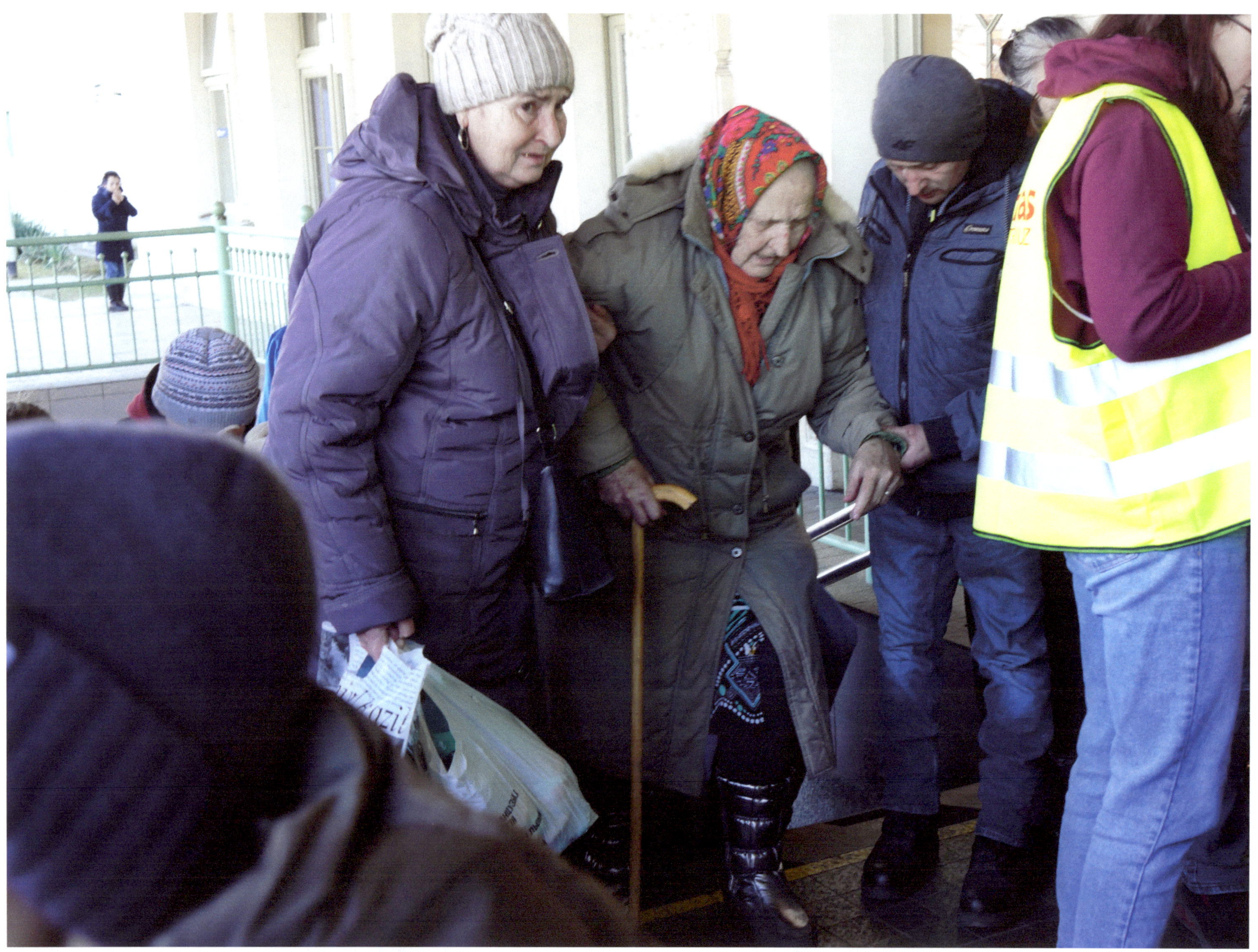

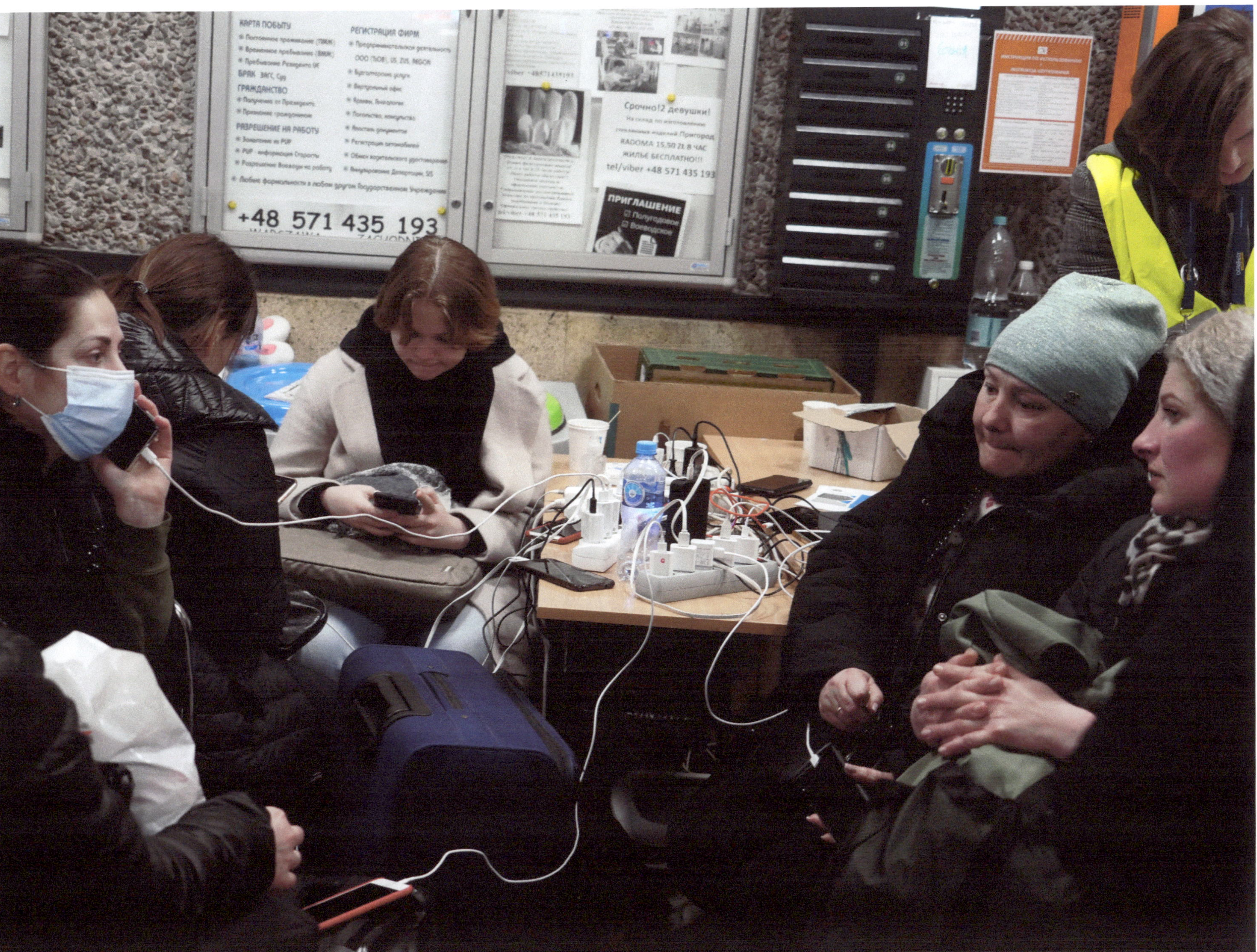
КАРТА ПОБЫТУ
РЕГИСТРАЦИЯ ФИРМ
ГРАЖДАНСТВО
РАЗРЕШЕНИЕ НА РАБОТУ
+48 571 435 193
Срочно!2 девушки!
ЖИЛЬЕ БЕСПЛАТНО!!!
tel/viber +48 571 435 193
ПРИГЛАШЕНИЕ

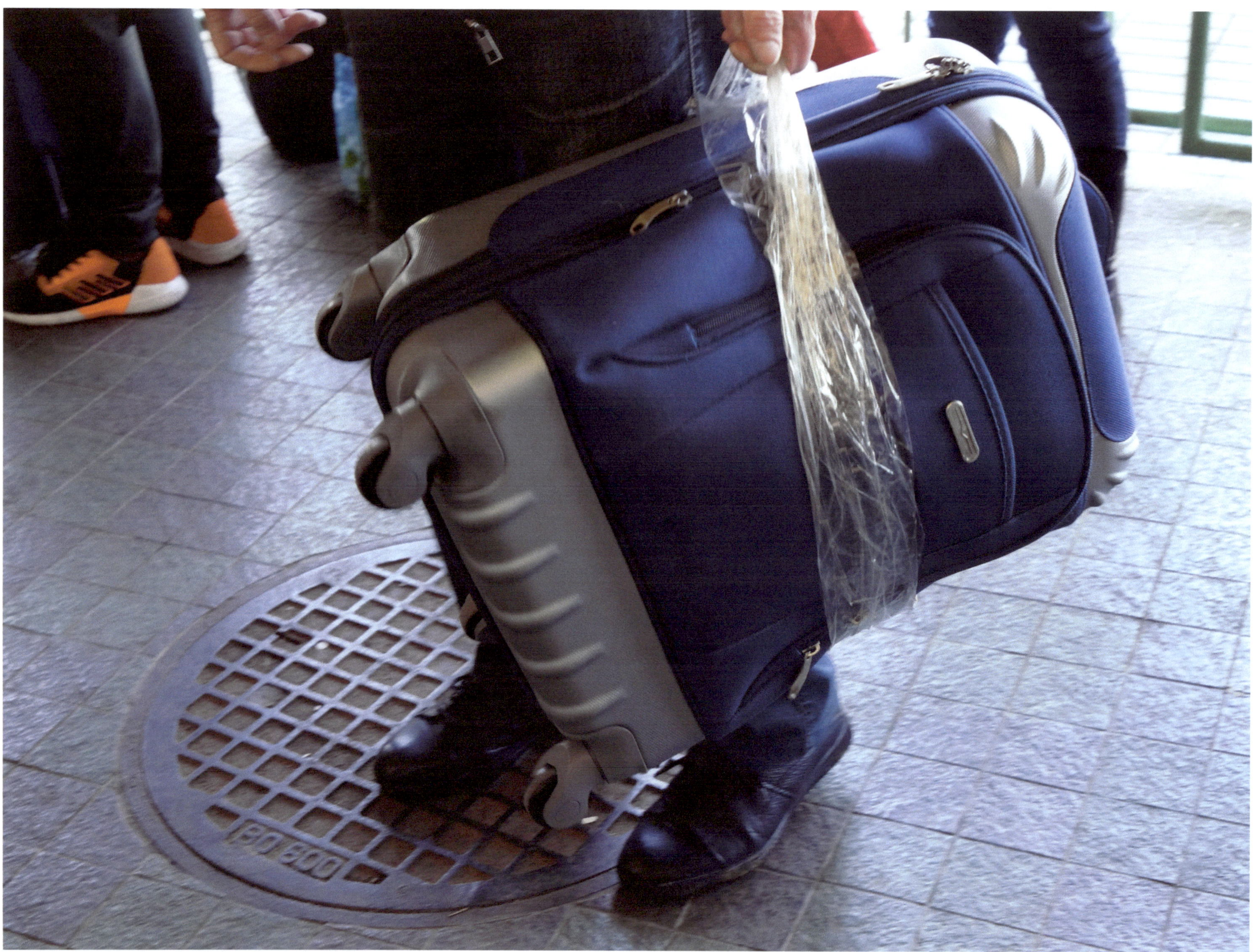

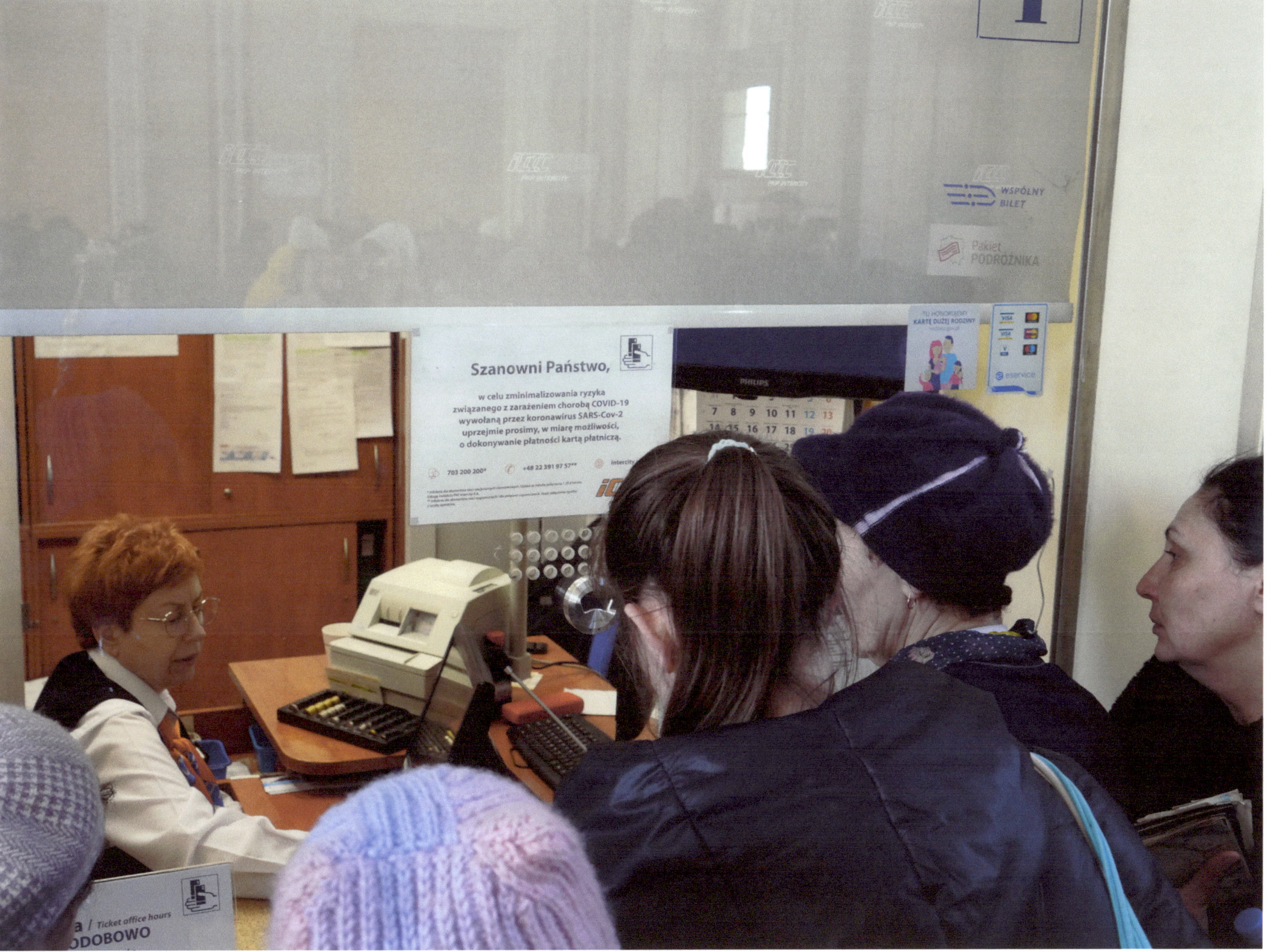

1
WSPÓLNY BILET
Pakiet PODRÓŻNIKA
Szanowni Państwo,
w celu zminimalizowania ryzyka
związanego z zarażeniem chorobą COVID-19
wywołaną przez koronawirus SARS-Cov-2
uprzejmie prosimy, w miarę możliwości,
o dokonywanie płatności kartą płatniczą.
703 200 200*
+48 22 391 97 57**
intercity
TU HONORUJEMY
KARTĘ DUŻEJ RODZINY
VISA
VISA
eservice
PHILIPS
7 8 9 10 11 12 13
14 15 16 17 18 19 20
a / Ticket office hours
ODOBOWO

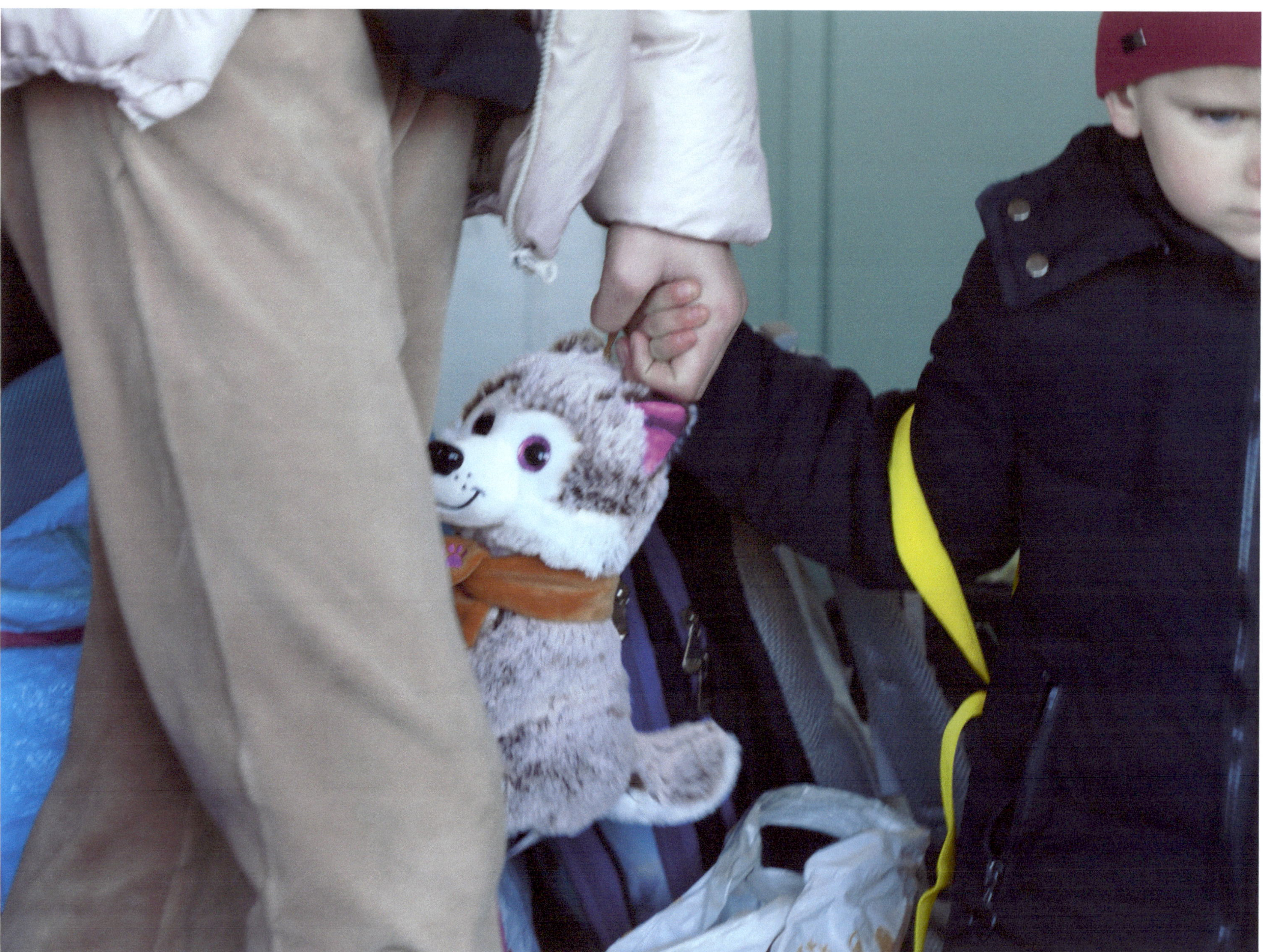

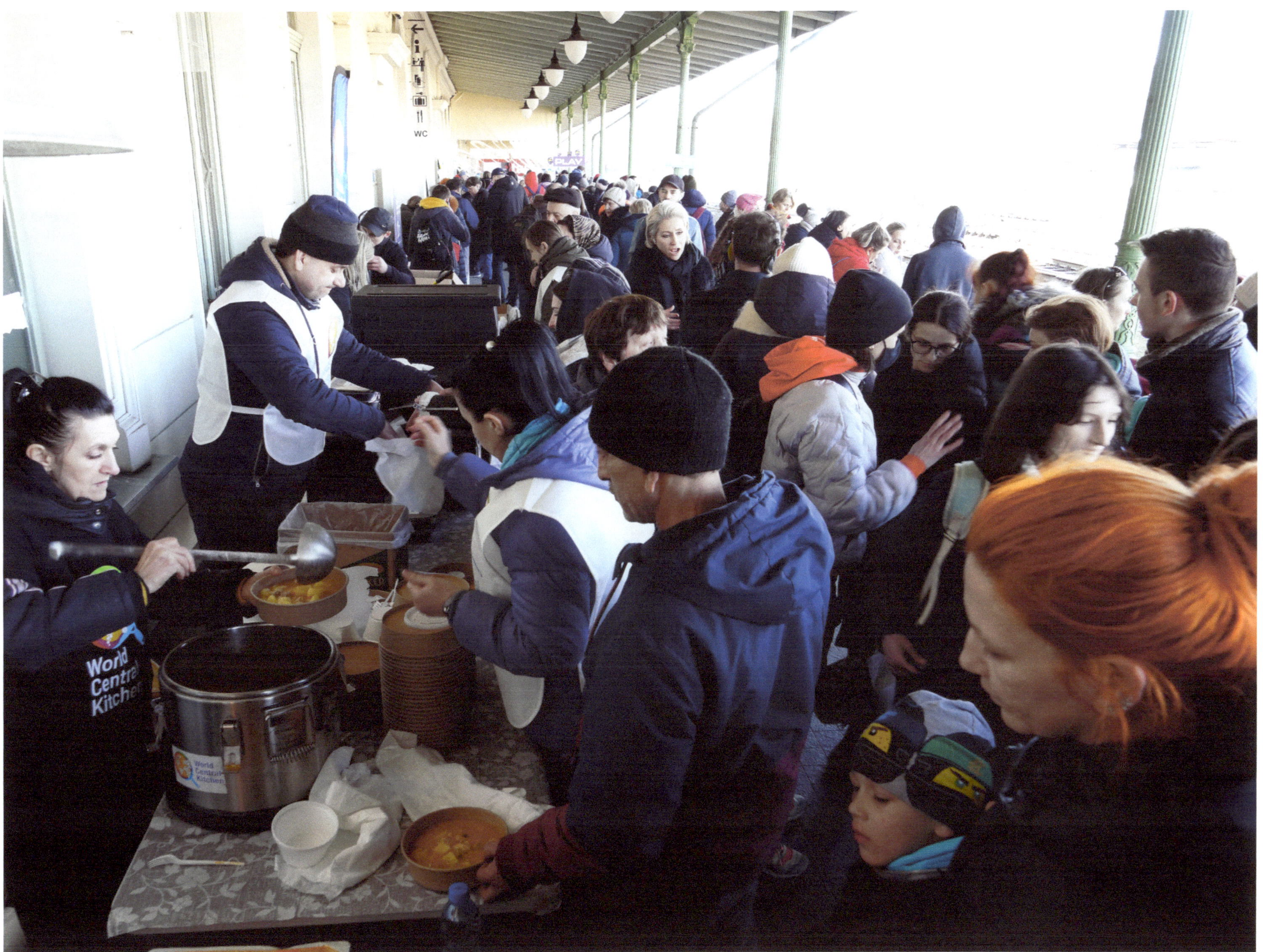

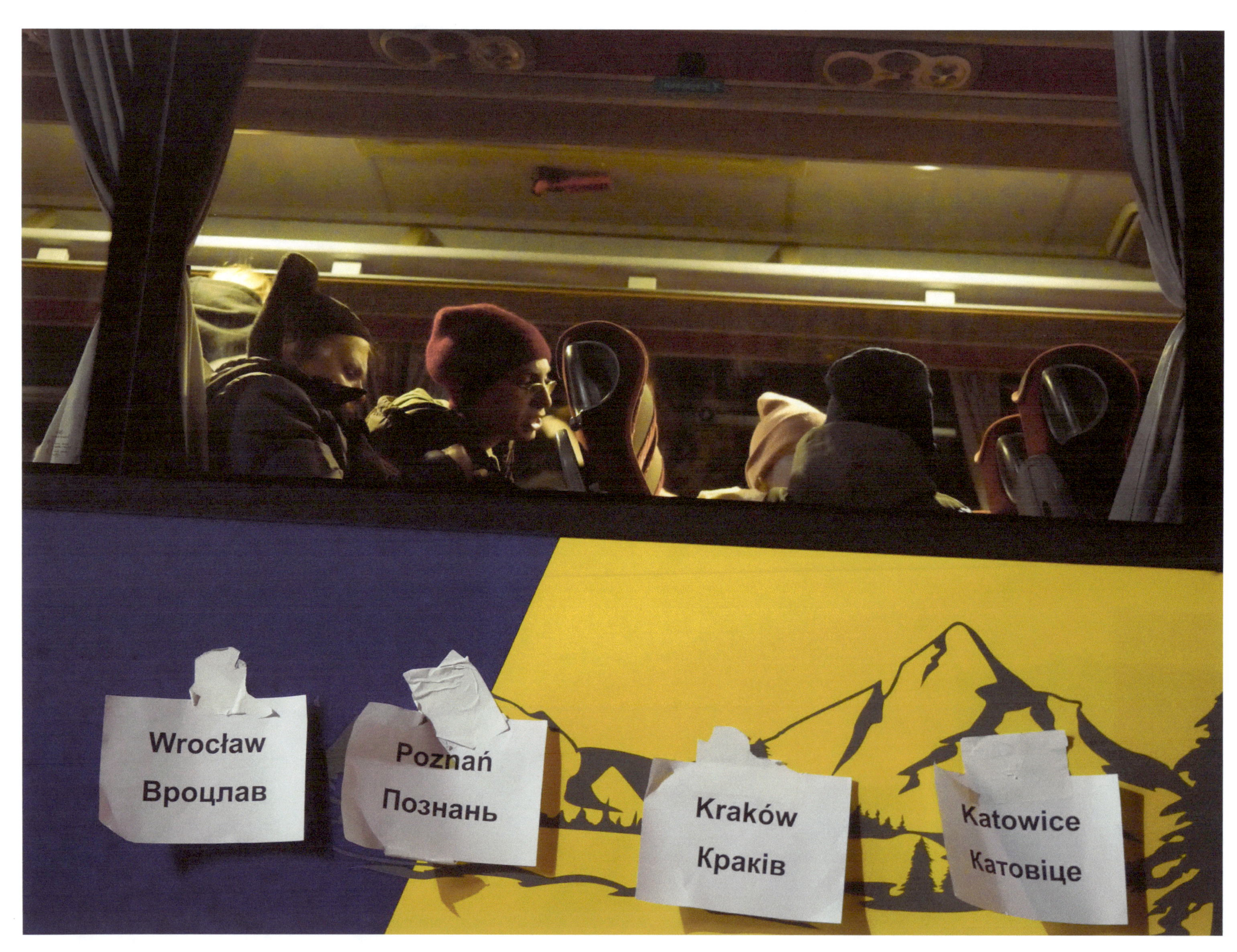

Wrocław
Вроцлав

Poznań
Познань

Kraków
Краків

Katowice
Катовіце

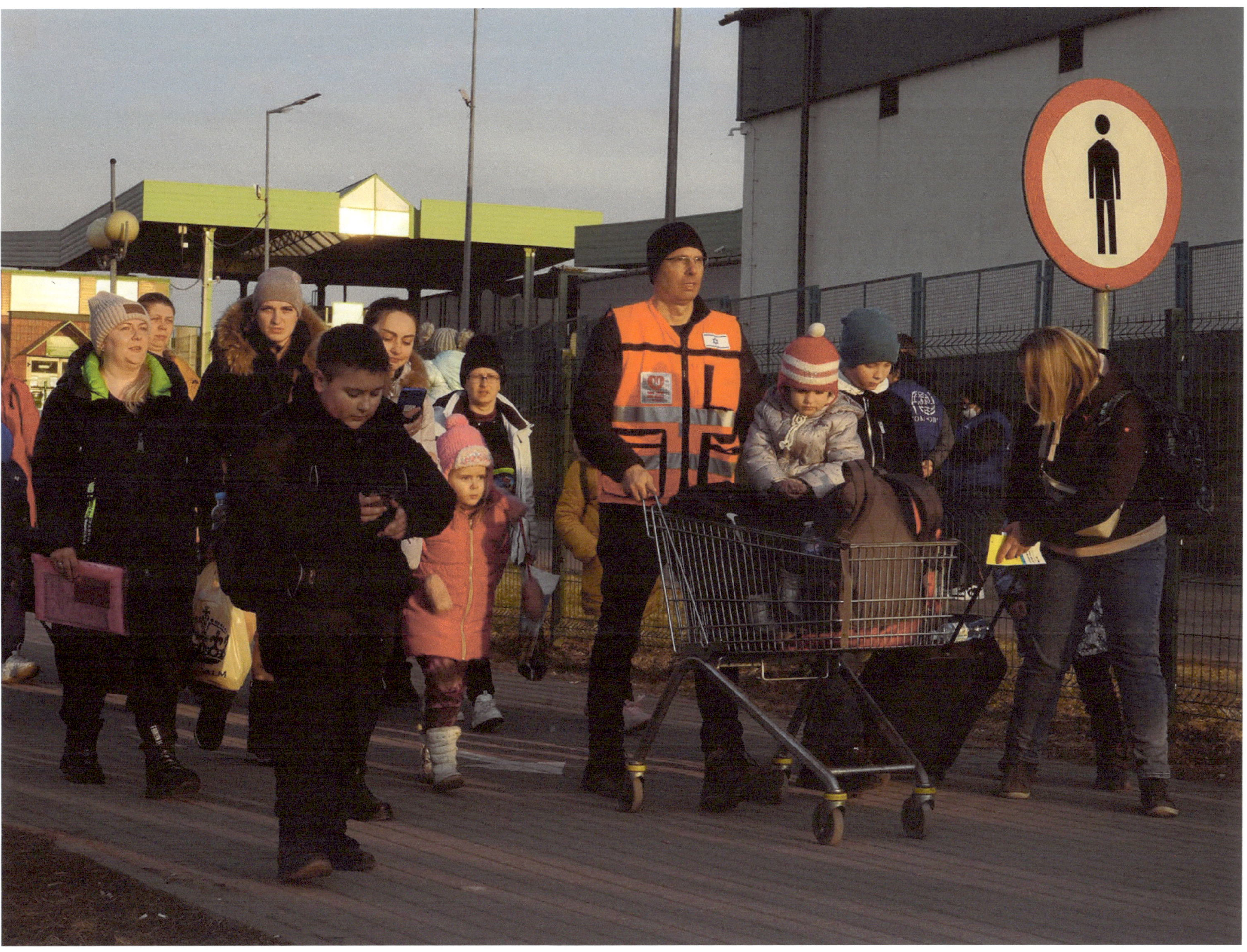